Banoo

Iranian Women and Their Stories

Banoo

Samaneh Khosravi

KERBER PHOTO

“Ask the mirror the name of your savior”

Forugh Farrokhzad (1934–1967)
A famous contemporary Iranian poet
From a poem titled “Window”

Author's Preface

When I returned to my native Iran in September 2023, after two years of absence, to work on my current research project, I expected to be greeted by the familiar image of my hometown, possibly with subtle changes. However, the Iran I experienced this time was no longer the same one I had left two years ago after my last visit. A palpable atmosphere of change now pervaded the capital Tehran, manifesting not only in a part of society but penetrating deeply into the hearts of most families, even those that are conservative or religiously influenced and from whom I would not have expected change two years ago.

For over a decade, as a photographer and visual researcher, I have dedicated myself to the themes of self- and external perception of women living in Iran. My motivation for this developed slowly and has roots in my own past. Until 2008, I was myself part of this Iranian society and, as a young twenty-four-year-old woman who was born and raised in Iran, experienced the situation firsthand. There were social restrictions, norms, and traditional female roles that I faced. There were moments of rebellion, at least within my family, but a deeper confrontation was absent. For me, these aspects belonged to the societal normality that I somehow had to accept.

Now, having lived in Germany for fifteen years, the external view of Iran has given a new dimension to the significance of my past experiences. The spatial distance from my homeland and the confrontation with the new culture led me to consciously reflect on the situation of Iranian women in Iran while I studied and worked in Germany. I found similarities and differences in terms of women's rights between both countries. Germany is ahead of many countries in this respect, but also has not yet fully achieved its goal. This change in perspective has sharpened my view on the issue of equality and equal rights in Iran, and I now view the challenges facing women in Iran with a more sensitive and differentiated eye.

Inspired by this new perspective, I focused on the self- and external perception of Iranian women during my photography studies in Germany. As a result, my first book *Among Women* was published in 2015 about Iranian women and their views on beauty ideals. From 2017 to 2019, I worked on the present book project, *Banoo*, which, like the previous one, is published by Kerber Verlag. It was this latest project that also motivated me to start my current doctoral studies. My research is dedicated to Generation Z women in Iran, who, in my opinion, have so far received insufficient attention from scholars.

While photographing and interviewing the women in this book, it became clear to me how Generation Z women have become what they are today. The women portrayed in this volume represent four different generations: the Baby Boomers and the Generations X, Y, and Z. It is fascinating to observe how they confidently take their place and raise their voices despite cultural restrictions, societal expectations, and legal regulations.

The change over decades is visible and will continue to evolve. Nevertheless, my last trip to Iran made a lasting impression on me. In September 2023, exactly two weeks before the first anniversary of Jina Mahsa Amini's death, I visited my home country again. The twenty-two-year-old young woman had been arrested by the morality police in Tehran a year ago, allegedly for not wearing her hijab correctly, and died mysteriously two days after her arrest. Her tragic death sparked the nationwide and now internationally known "Women, Life, Freedom" movement in the weeks and months that followed. Thousands of people, mainly young women—with Generation Z at the forefront—gathered on the streets to protest against human rights violations and for women's rights in Iran. There have been many protests in the past with little to no legal changes as a result, but each time they left traces and resonated within society. This time, however, the changes were no longer marginal observations but manifested as a broad mass phenomenon. During my stay in Tehran, I was able to experience situations that would have been unthinkable just a year ago. For example, public civil disobedience was displayed by women of different ages who stood up against the legal headscarf requirement by not wearing a headscarf. They encouraged and defended each other. One scene that I experienced myself in a subway station in Tehran was of a young Iranian woman, not wearing a headscarf, protecting and defending schoolgirls, who were also not wearing one, from other passengers who were upset about the behavior of the headscarf-less schoolgirls. But men also protected the schoolgirls. Whether in shopping malls, restaurants, or on public streets—everywhere you could see women taking off their headscarves. This happened despite strict penalties, such as the threat of sanctions for driving without a headscarf or the denial of public services. It marks the first time in the over forty-year history of the Islamic Republic of Iran that so many women in Tehran publicly appear without a headscarf, making a statement.

In my opinion, this does not yet indicate an actual change. However, within traditional and religious families, motivated by public debates and protests, young family members are now igniting discussions about gender discrimination. They are expressing their opinions by protesting against such discrimination and engaging their parents and other family members in conversations. At gatherings of family and friends, they are consciously choosing not to wear a headscarf, which they once wore out of respect for their parents and elders.

Seeing these scenes, my first thoughts were that this generation has achieved something that ours and the generations before us had achieved little or not at all. The young women of this generation are rebels. They fight for their visibility and autonomy in a traditionally patriarchal society. They courageously raise their voices to stand up for their rights and bring about change. But looking deeper at my own experiences, my findings from previous research projects, and the history of the women's movement in Iran, I have come to the conclusion that each of us has taken both small and large steps against traditional structures and sexism in our own way.

The memory of my first major resistance to the traditional structure of my family relates to the moment when I found the courage at age fifteen to protest against a form of the hijab, the chador—a full-body veil that was common within my family at the time. Even though my parents did not speak to me for a few days, and it was very difficult for me at that age, since then, I have not been forced, and if I wore it somewhere, it was my own decision. In retrospect, I would not have thought at the time that my individual resistance, which back then seemed small to me, might result in my younger sister and the next generation of girls in our family no longer being forced to wear the chador. The progress is also evident in the fact that my parents and many family members are now more tolerant and make an effort to understand us.

Opinions and beliefs can be culturally deeply rooted, and it takes time for change to occur. These actions, even if they seem small, should not go unnoticed, as they have also paved the way for the women after us.

These changes are particularly evident in the current situation in Iran and in Generation Z. Their pronounced sense of justice and equality differs from that of my Generation Y and those before. However, we should not overlook the fact that members of this young generation are also the children of my or the previous generation. A tolerant home environment will have contributed to this difference as much as the more natural access to social media and the Internet. Cultures change and are passed on from generation to generation, even if it is a long process until consciousness changes.

The first records of the struggle of Iranian women for equality date back more than 100 years, to the time of the Constitutional Revolution of 1906, although there were earlier cases of activism. The first major successes were finally recorded twenty years later.

During the Pahlavi era in Iran, which began in 1925 and ended in 1979, reforms were carried out to modernize Iranian society. This also included changes in the area of women's rights. Significant achievements were made during this period, including compulsory schooling for girls and boys, women's suffrage in 1963, the right to hold public office, and a comprehensive family protection law enacted in 1975. The latter raised the minimum age for the marriage of girls to eighteen, stipulated that divorce was no longer the exclusive right of men, and took mothers into account in child custody situations. All of this strengthened the self-confidence of many Iranian women.

The strengthened sociopolitical awareness of women was also evident during the Islamic Revolution of 1979. Many women hoped to gain further rights from the new government by participating in demonstrations and protest actions. However, after the revolution, women's demands were suppressed, and some of the improvements achieved during the Pahlavi era were even reversed. In view of the development to the detriment of women, they protested again on International Women's Day on March 8, 1979, against the announced hijab requirement and the supposed regression of women's rights in the Islamic Republic.

Although the women's demonstrations delayed the mandatory hijab law and the adoption of some discriminatory laws in the Islamic Republic, they did not prove to be successful in the long term. Finally, in the first years after the revolution, the family protection law gradually returned to its origins before the White Revolution of 1963, and the hijab became mandatory in 1983. Since then, the laws have been slightly modified again and again. Looking back, it is recognized that the development of society in the Islamic Republic with regard to the acceptance of women's equality has not come to a standstill.

Women have now also earned respect outside of their own four walls. They work in typical male domains and form the student majority at Iranian universities. Their high academic qualifications and success in the working world leave their mark on a male-dominated society. Nevertheless, they still face discriminatory laws and guidelines in their daily lives.

With this volume, I have tried to capture the achievements of Iranian women. Although these images were taken before the events of the "Women, Life, Freedom" movement, I see in them the actual reasons for the pronounced sense of justice and equality of Generation Z. The volume presents women from various social strata and regions of Iran, whom I was allowed to accompany in their daily life as part of my observations. In doing so, I not only gained insights into their realities of life but was also able to learn about their views, beliefs, professional challenges, and future plans.

Against this background, I dedicate my photobook *Banoo* to these women, who are making a significant contribution to Iranian society. They pave the way for future generations and thus shape the future of their country.

Bānu (بانو) is a Persian term that literally translates to "lady" or "woman." It is often used as a respectful address for women and expresses politeness and appreciation.

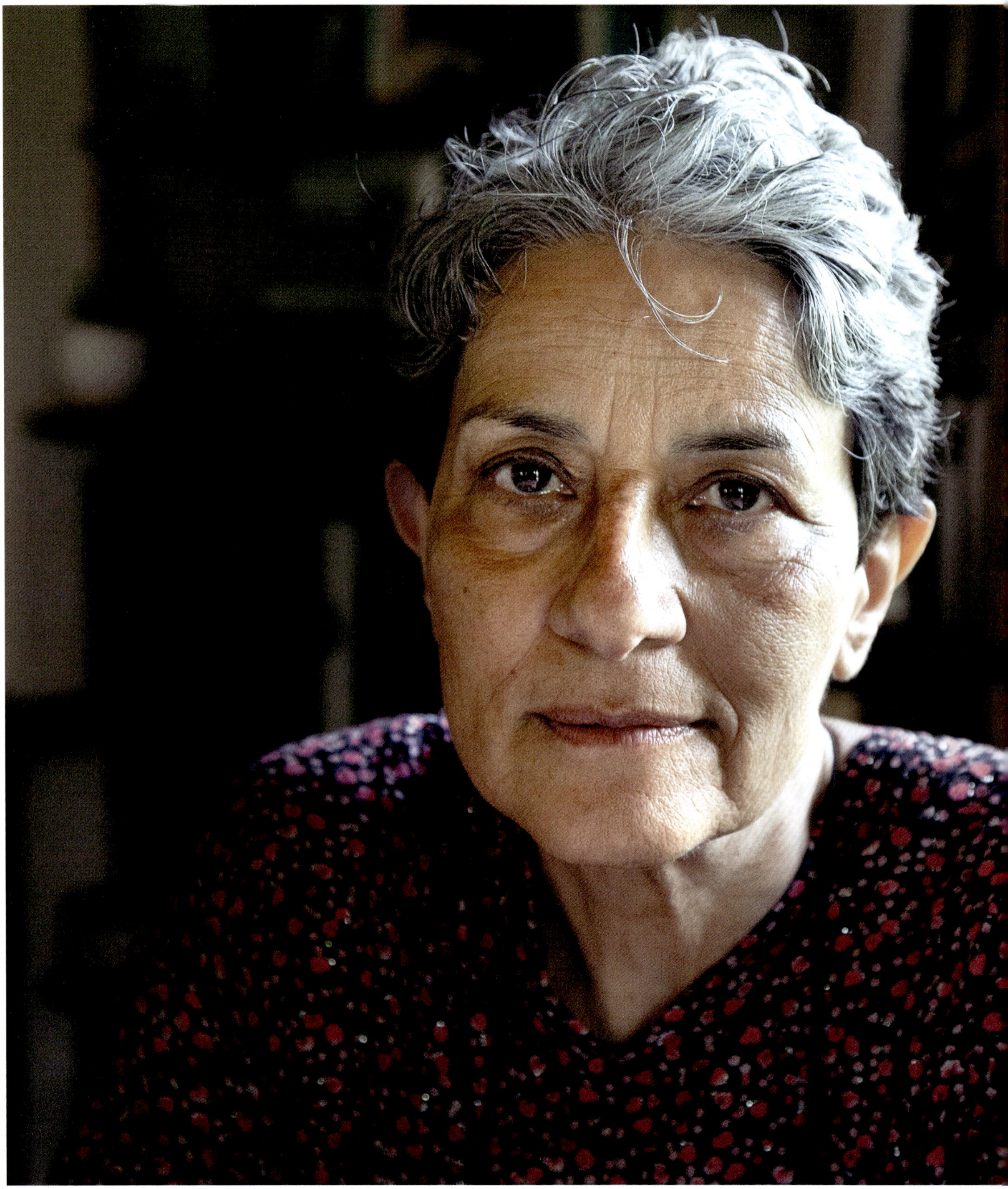

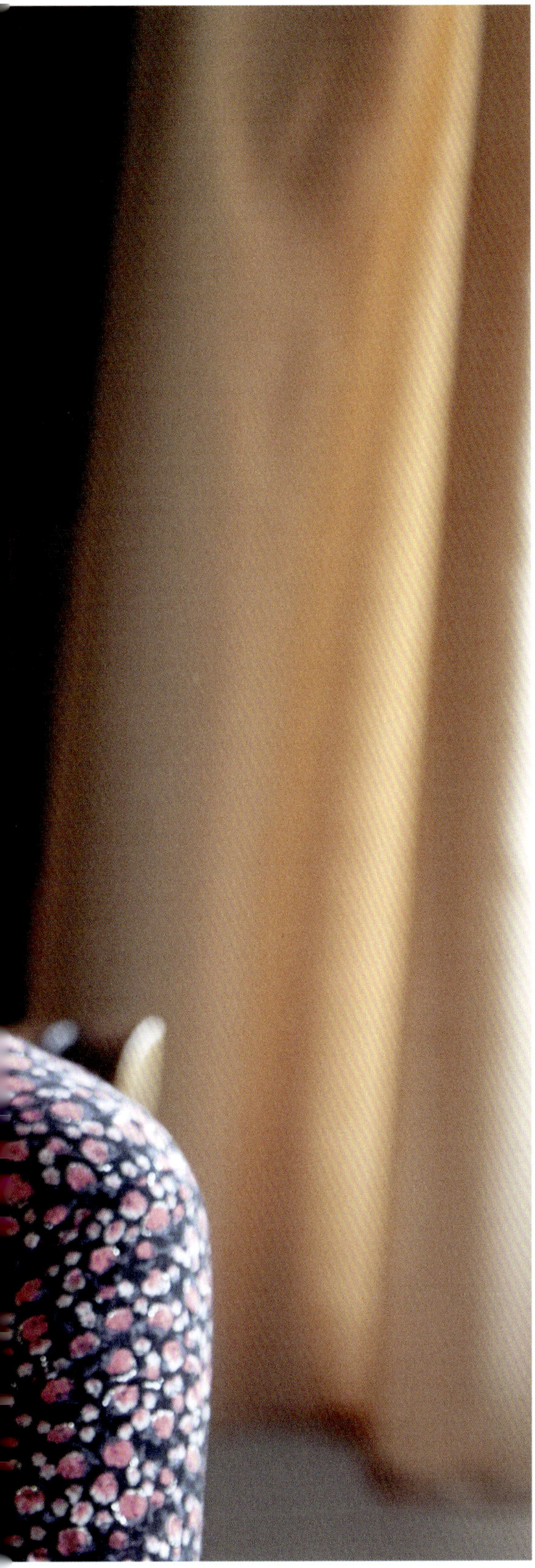

Shirin Parsi

"We are all like trees with roots in this land—that is why we owe something to this soil." Shirin, sixty-five, is deeply connected to the life of a rice farmer. Her profound love for her homeland brought her back after studying French literature in Nancy. She met her husband, Mohammad-Reza, there, who had previously studied architecture in Germany. In 1979, after six years in France, they returned to Iran. Choosing to settle in the north by the Caspian Sea, her husband's hometown, they embraced a life tied to the land. Shirin's father-in-law, the first university graduate in agricultural technology in the western part of Gilan province, owned farmland in the village of Shanderman. Moved by a heartfelt wish of her father-in-law, they decided to cultivate the land together with the family. Shirin reflects with tears in her eyes: *"When I was nineteen years old, my father passed away. My father-in-law became like a father to me. I loved him dearly."*
Back then, Shirin had limited knowledge about agriculture and even less about the northwestern Iranian language spoken by the local Talesh people. Originally from Tehran, she faced significant challenges adapting to life in Shanderman. However, her love for working in the countryside motivated her to overcome these initial difficulties. She learned the language, gained the trust of the locals, and gradually developed a deeper understanding of agricultural practices. Shirin reflects: *"Rice farming is hard work. During the planting season, women stand in rubber boots, almost knee-deep in water and mud in the rice fields, planting the rice bundles individually in the muddy soil—sometimes in high temperatures and humidity."*
Together with her husband and two sons, they optimized work processes over the years and streamlined cultivation. Both sons, Soroush and Ahmad, pursued studies in agriculture-related fields. She believes: *"It's crucial for us to practice sustainable farming. The soil must have the opportunity to regenerate in order to provide us with quality rice each year. However, we won't achieve this by relying on chemical aids."*

Shirin and her family initiated a gradual transition to natural farming methods. *"We avoid the use of chemical fertilizers and pesticides in rice production. Every step toward organic farming standards contributes to our environment and our health."*

The rice seeds are cultivated in rice seedling nurseries in mid-April. Shirin treats her little seedlings with great love and dedication, checking on her treasures daily to ensure their well-being. It takes about a month for the seedlings to reach a size of approximately 15 centimeters. For transferring the plants to the main field, it is necessary to prepare the paddy field by plowing and paddling. In early May, the plants are transferred to the main field and transplanted by machine on the hill approximately 20 centimeters apart. By early August, the rice plants are colored yellow and are ready for harvesting. Until then, Shirin visits the fields daily with her workers to check the water level of the rice fields and irrigate them if necessary.

In Iran, several tons of rice are now being imported, sold at half the price of domestically produced rice. *"We need to educate people about consuming local Iranian rice varieties."* Shirin reaches into a bag of rice, takes out a handful, smells it, and says contentedly: *"This is rice!"*

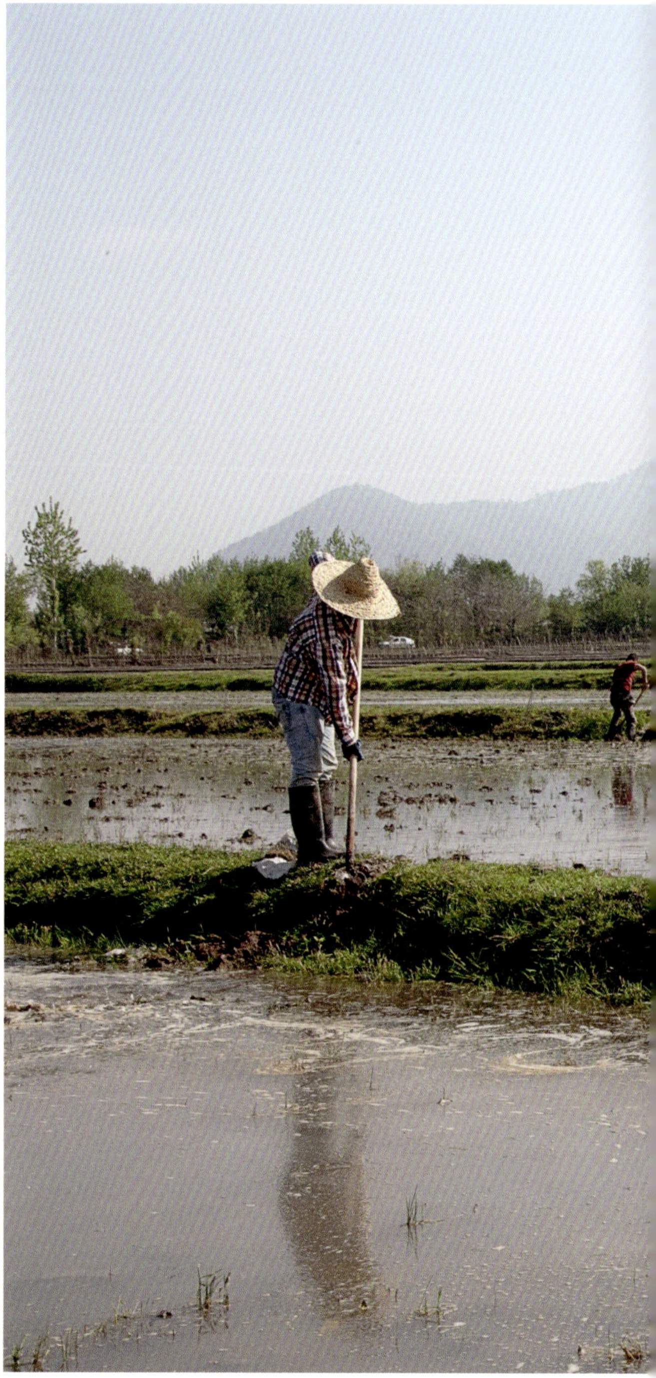

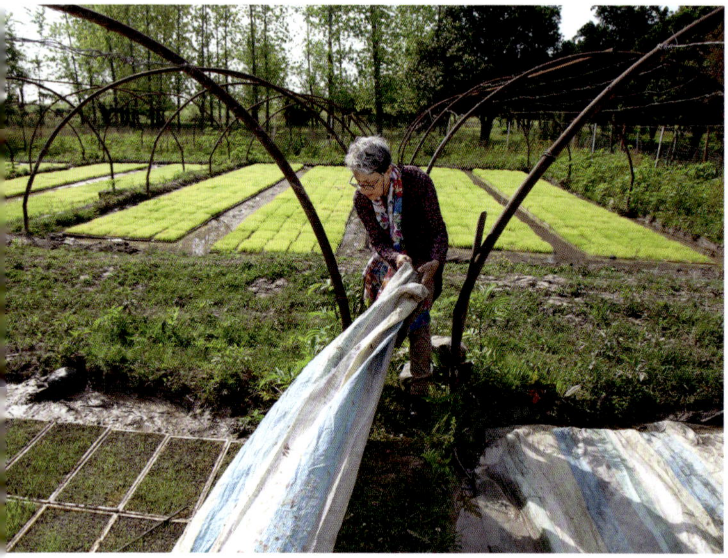

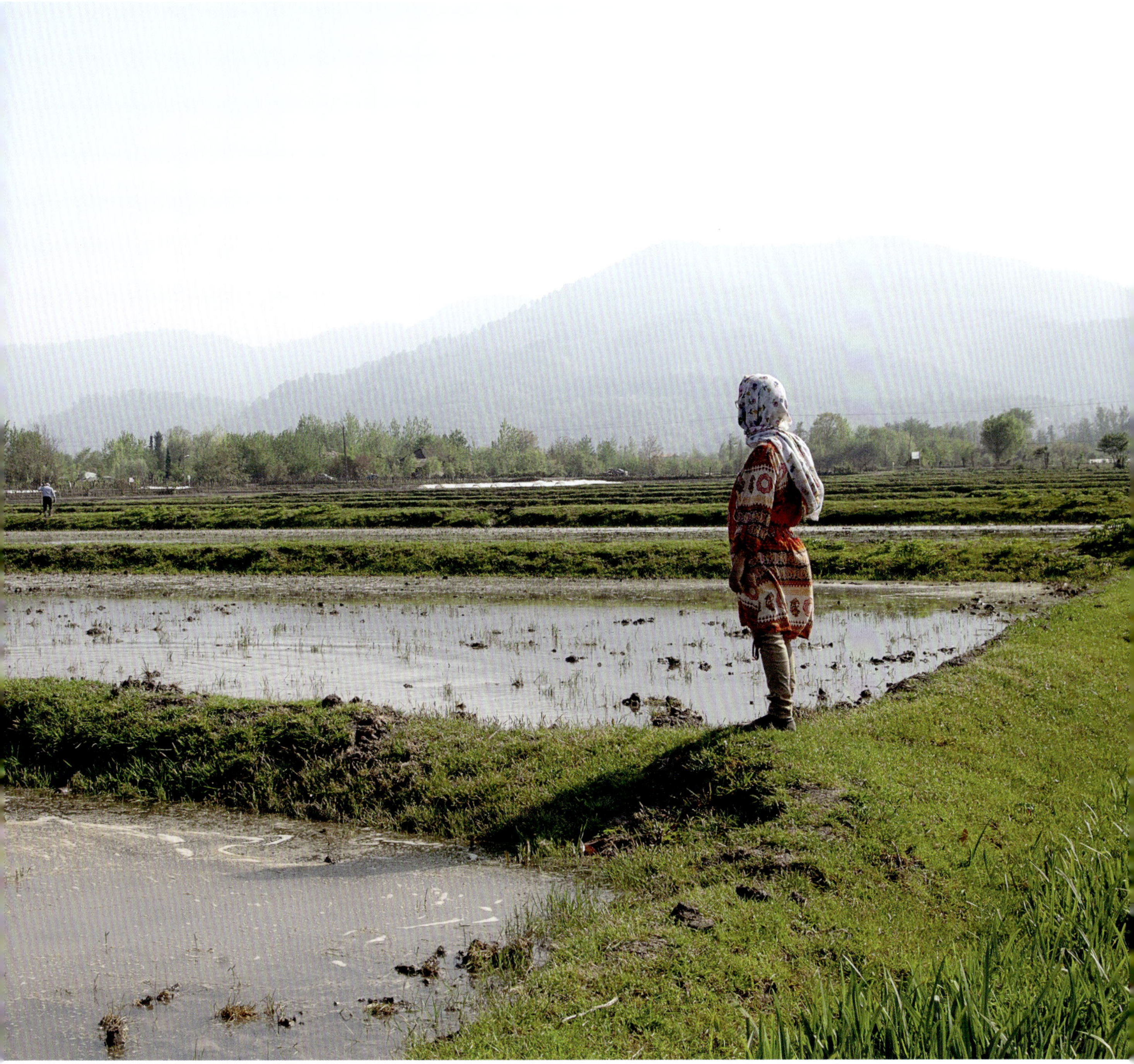

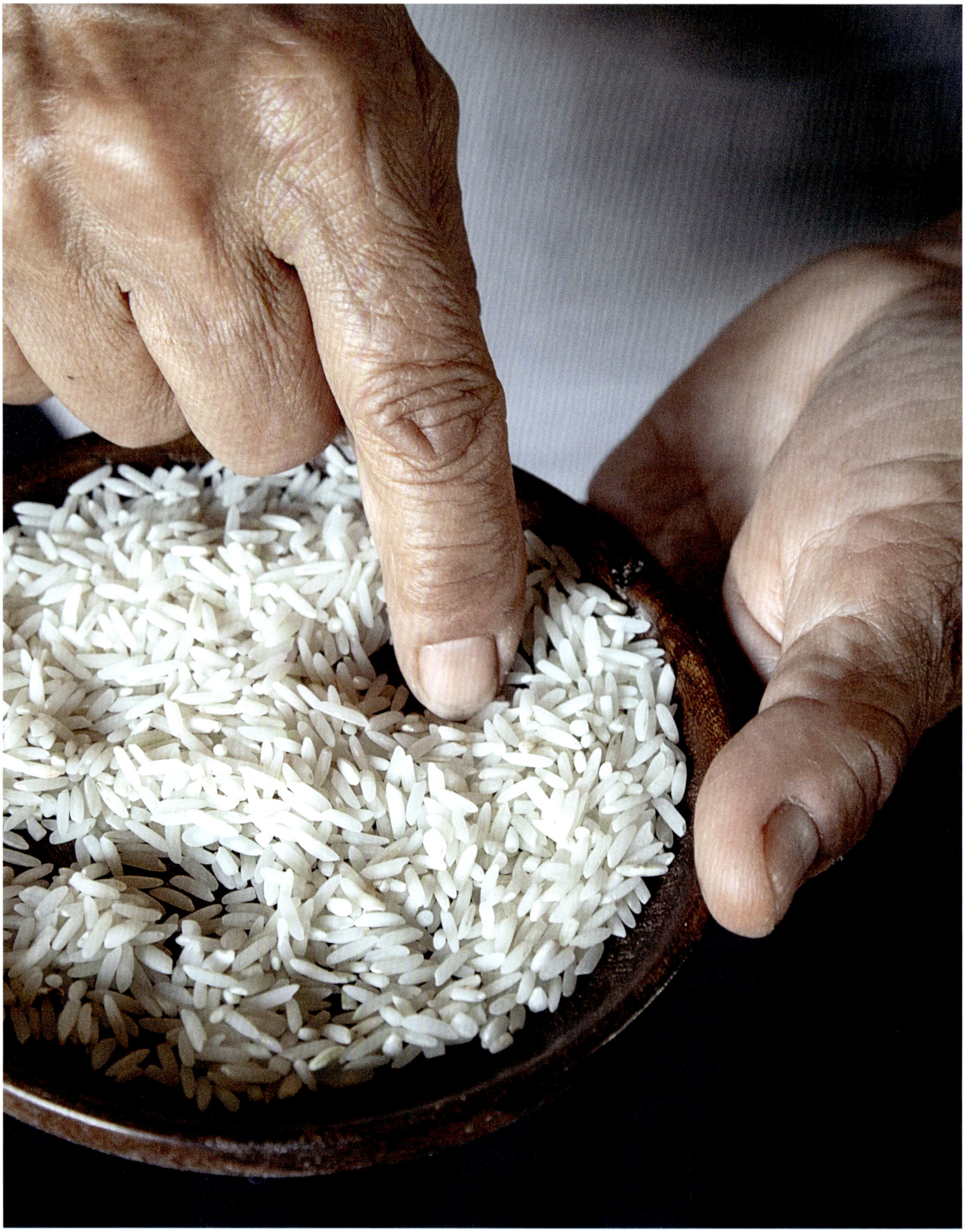

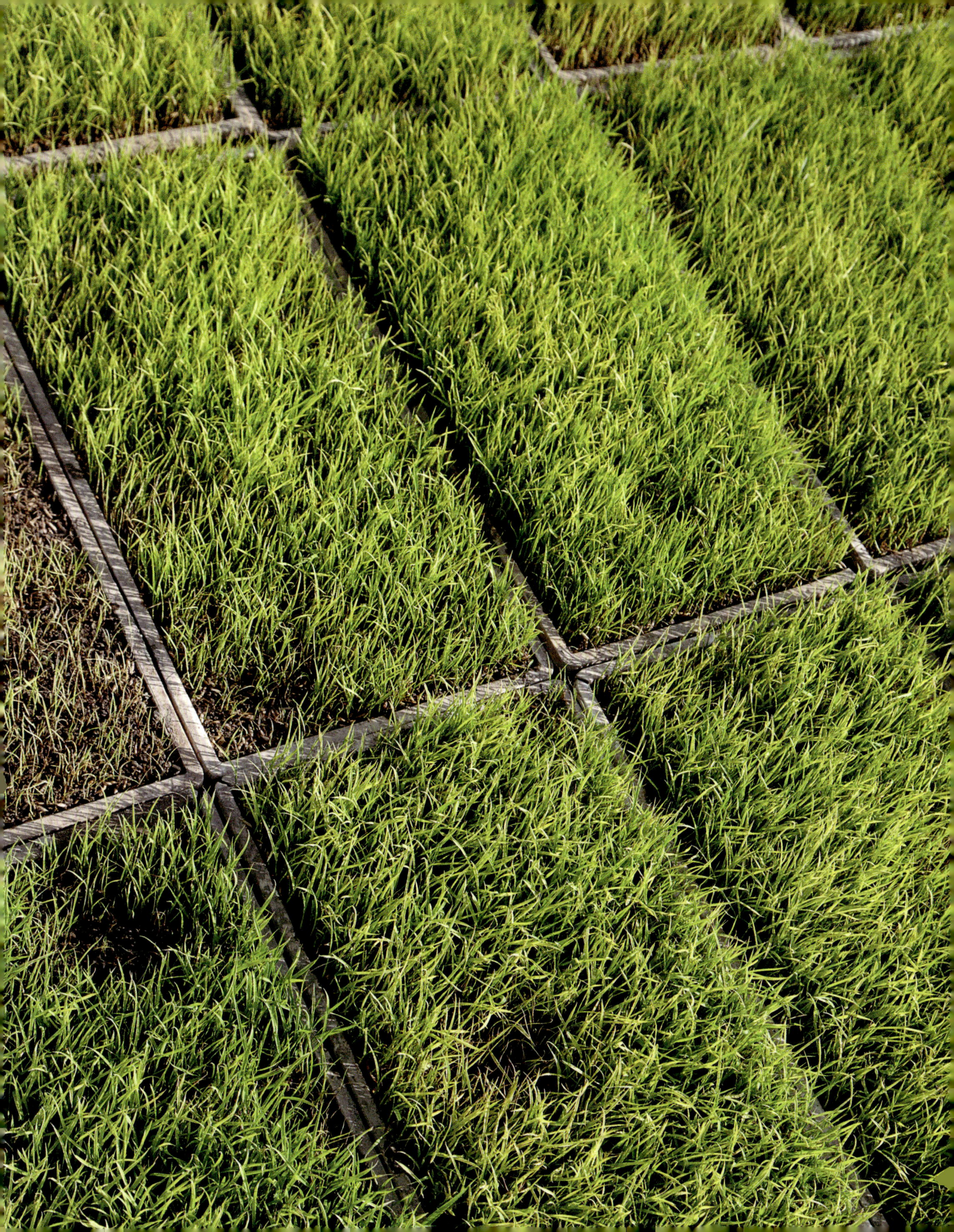

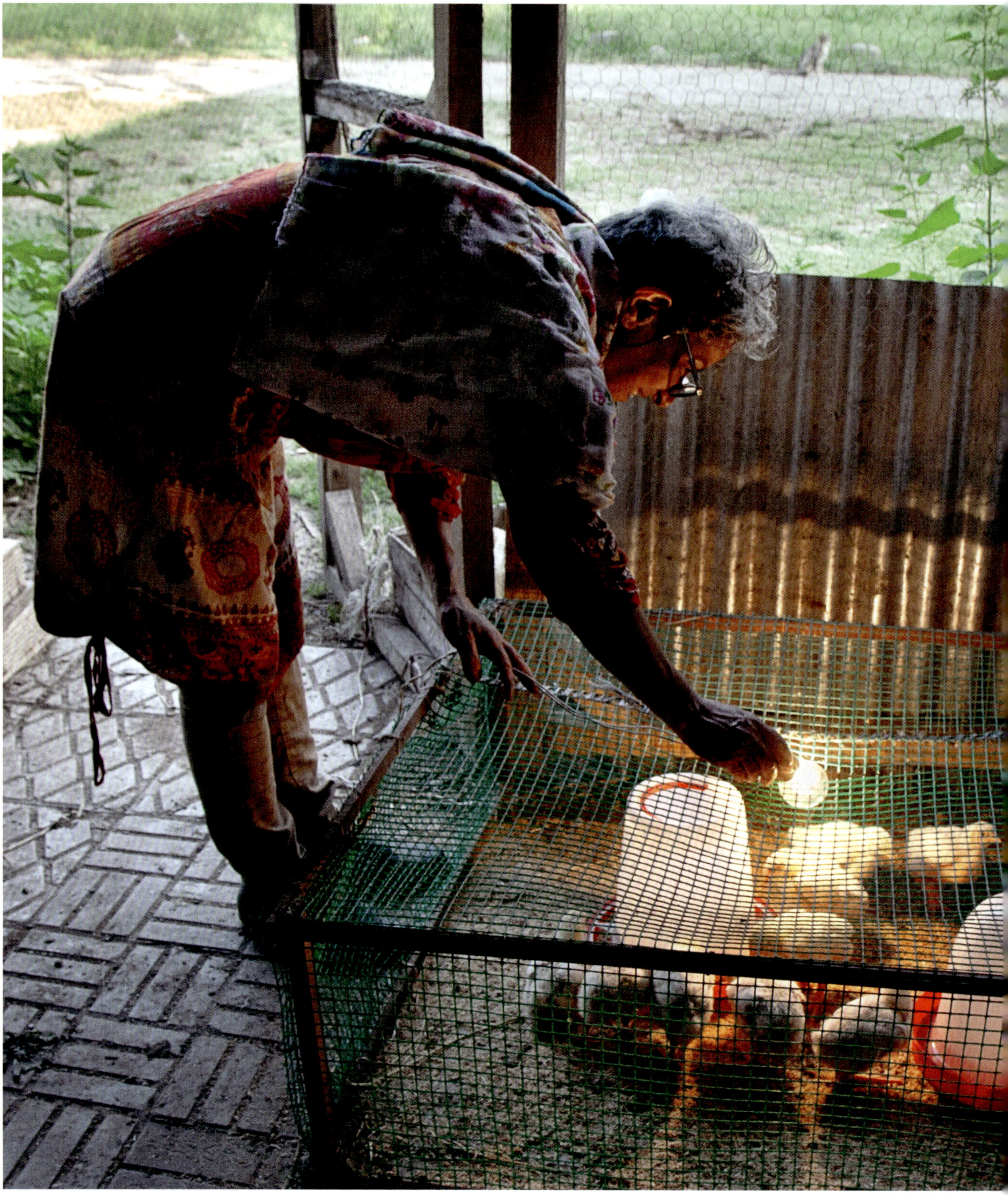

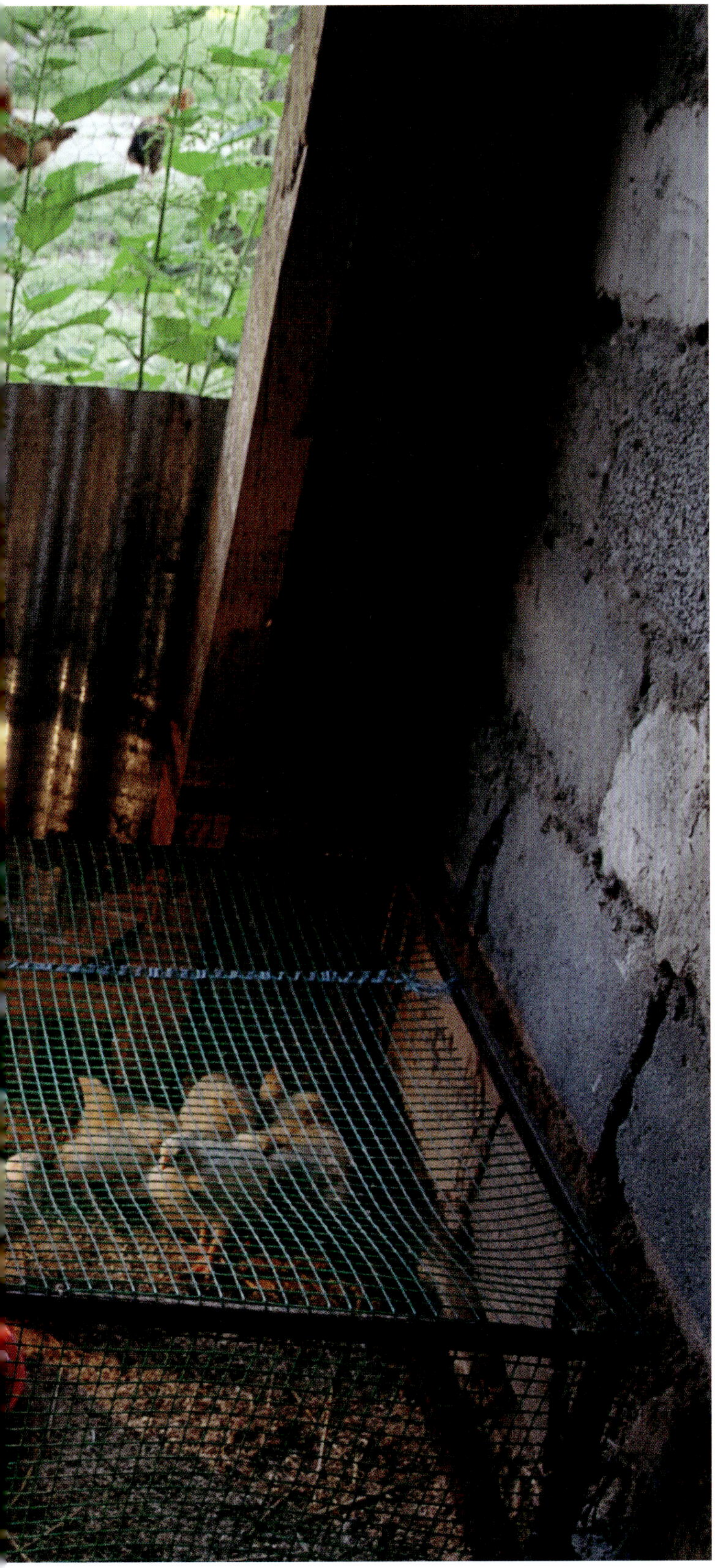

Next to the rice field, Shirin and her family grow vegetables, chickens, and fruit for domestic consumption. *"The chicks currently need a lot of attention. I check on them several times a day to make sure they are doing well."* Her workday starts at six o'clock in the morning and often goes late into the evening.

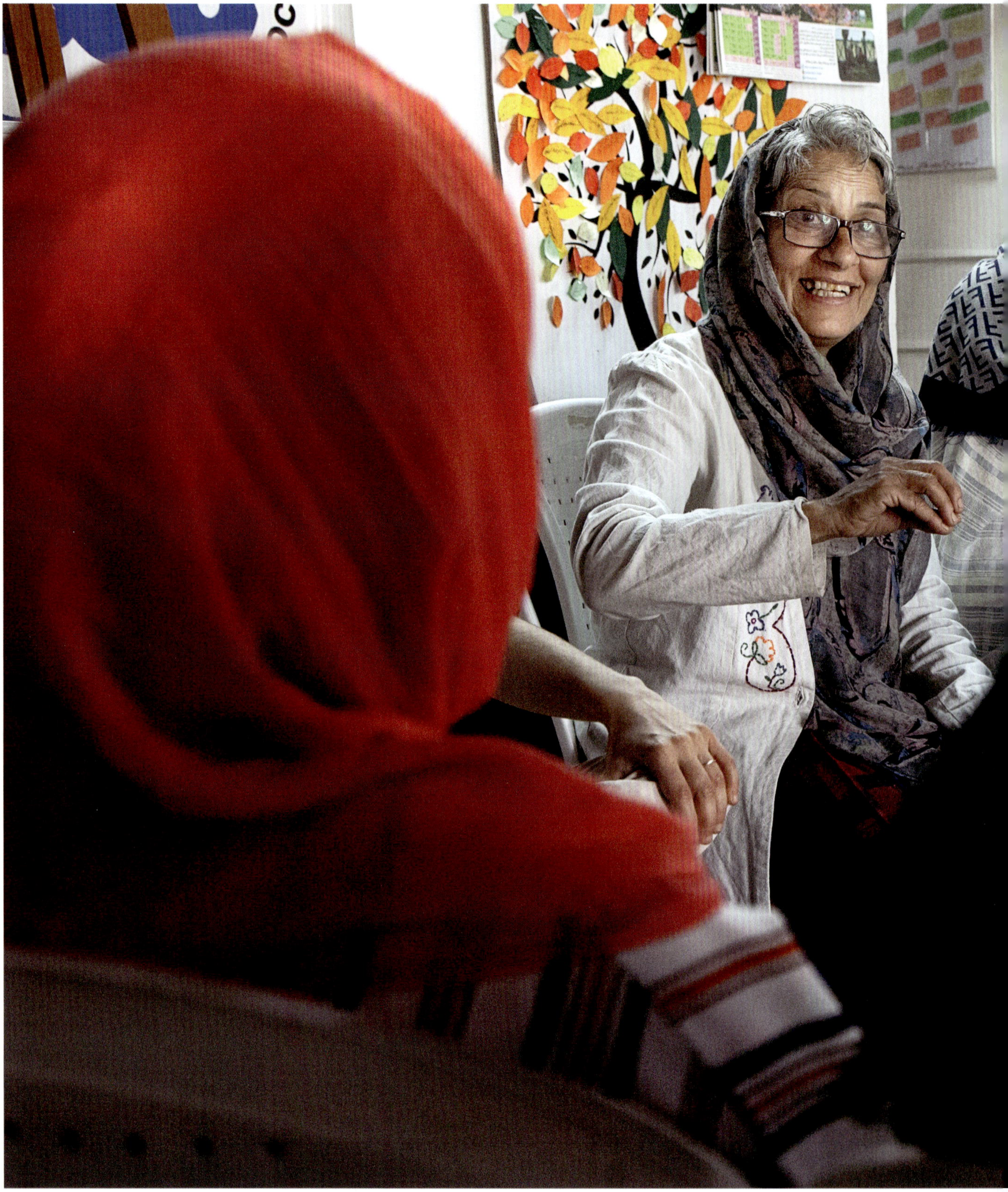

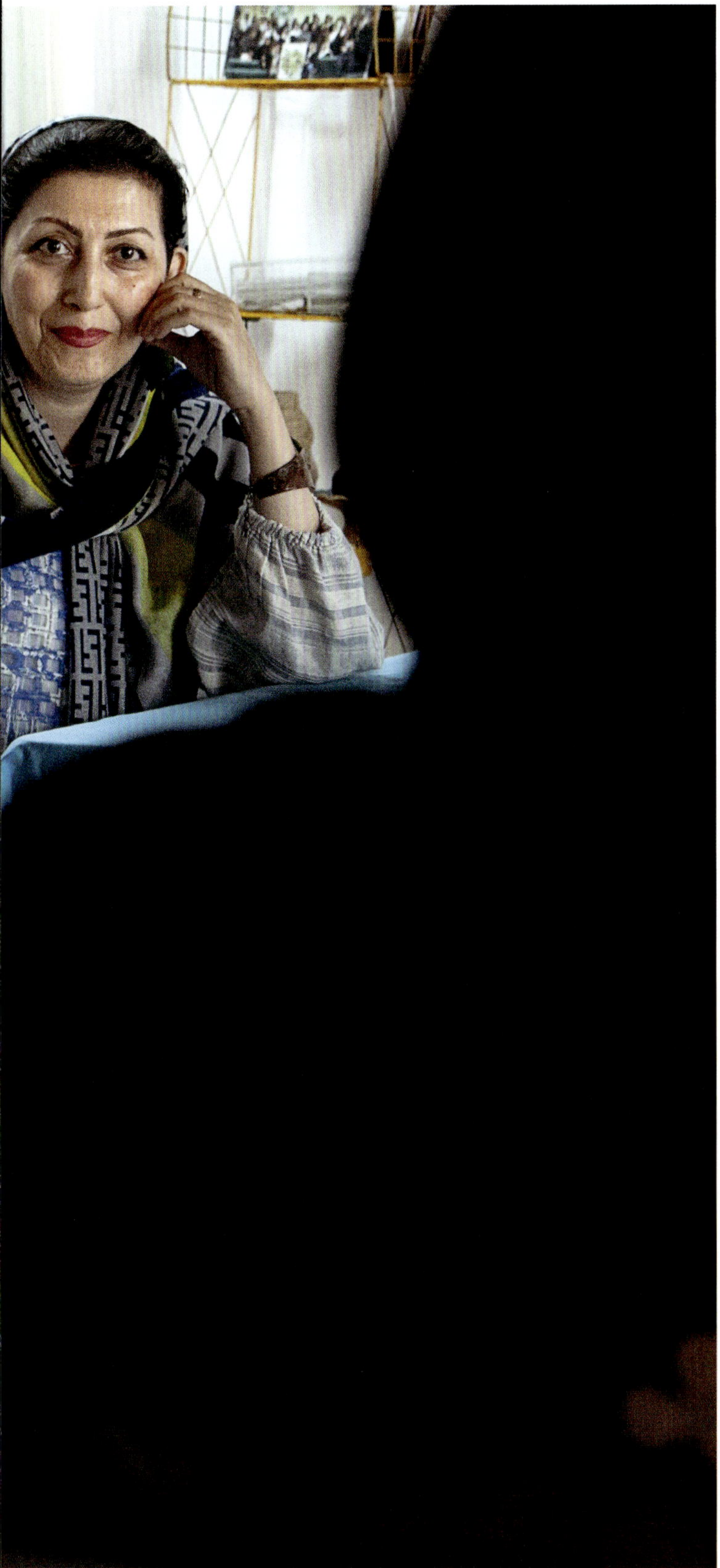

Shirin believes that with enough educational efforts, the people in her village and other regions will come to understand why it's worthwhile to cultivate in an environmentally friendly manner. Therefore, she organizes training sessions for the women in her village to teach them about the interconnections of an ecosystem and to strengthen awareness of nature and the environment. For several years, she has also been a member of the nongovernmental organization Association of Female Environmentalists of Gilan, which is based 60 kilometers away in the provincial capital of Rasht. They are working on different aspects of environmental protection like waste separation, recycling, composting, and the reduction of plastic consumption.

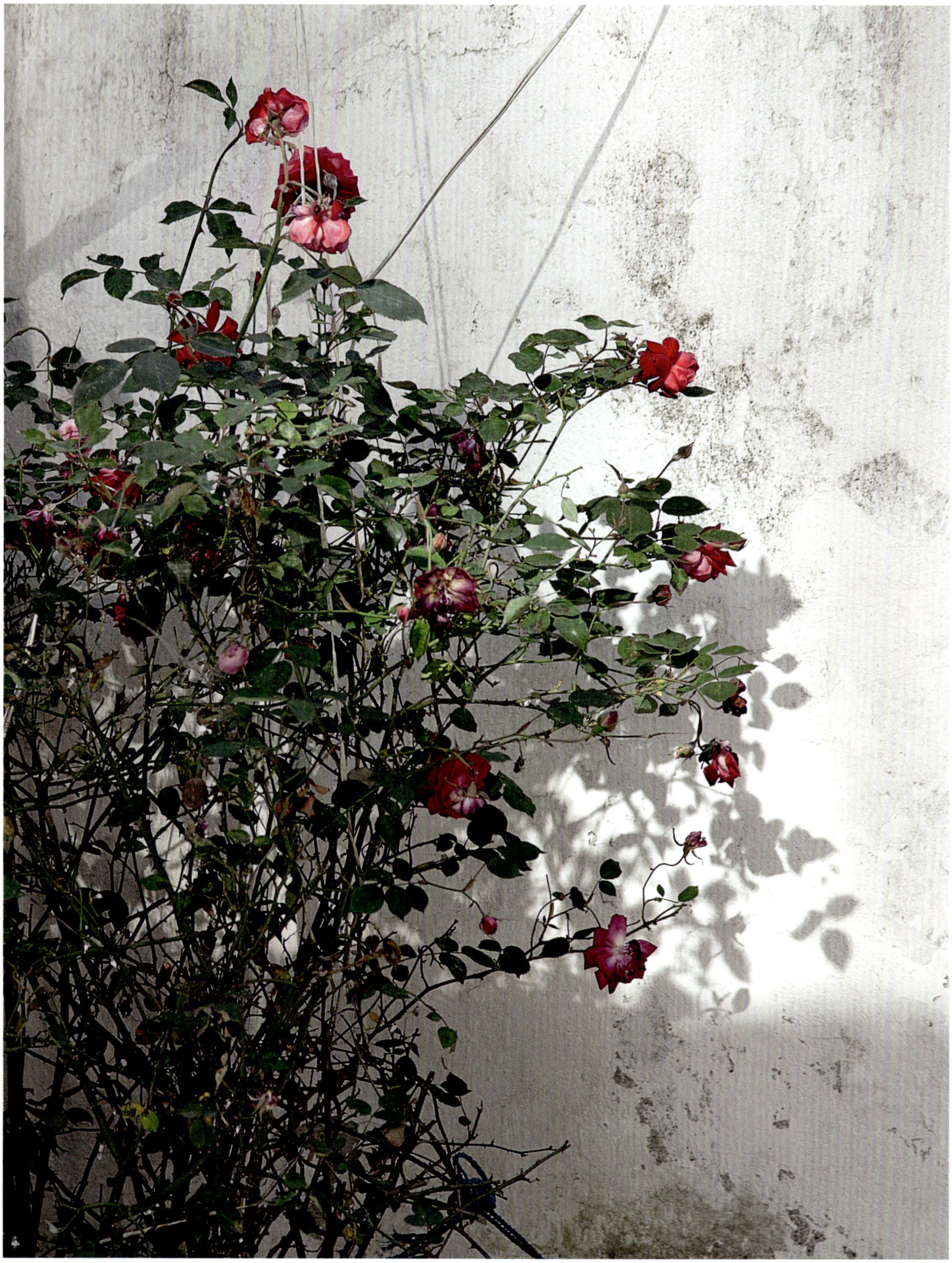

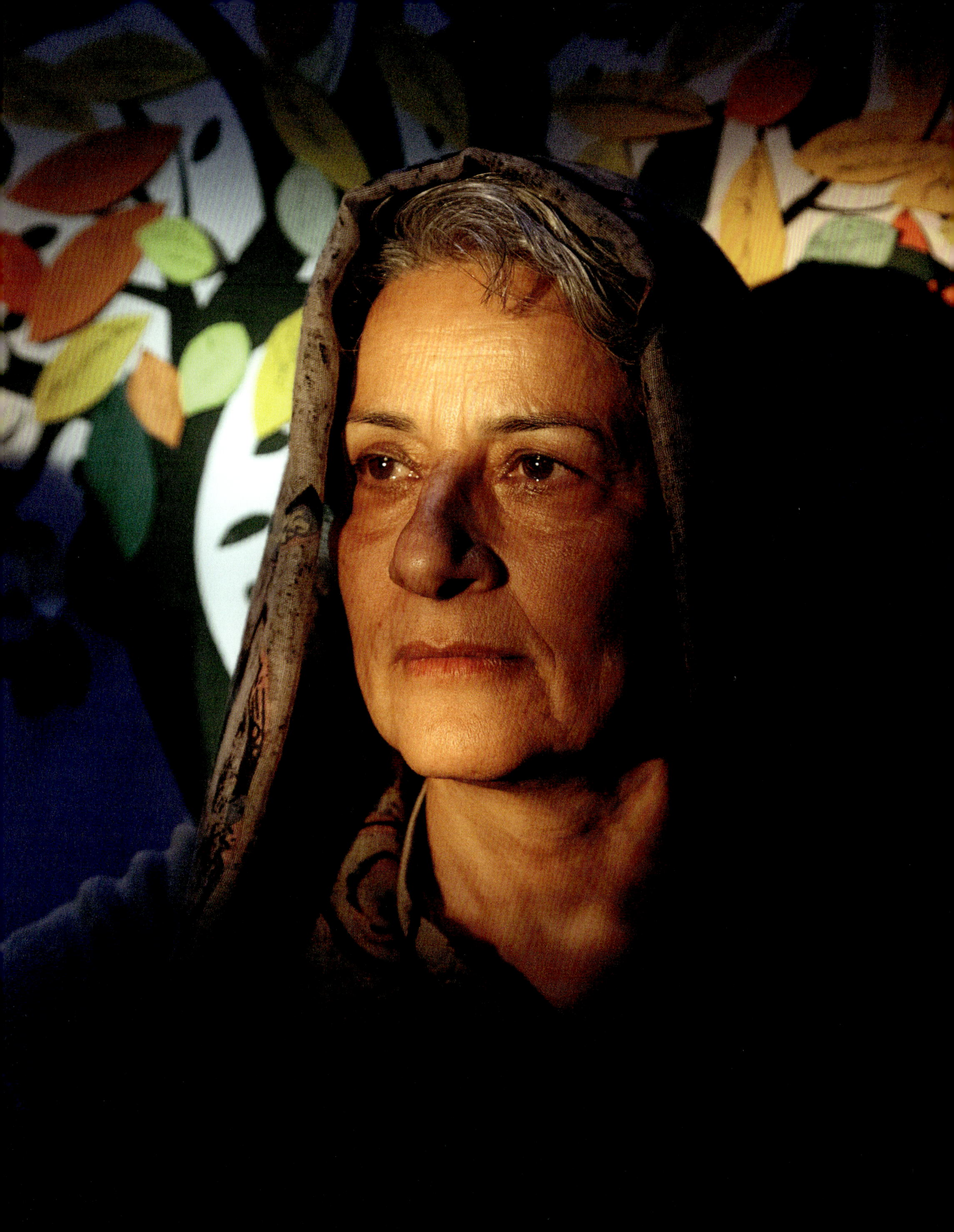

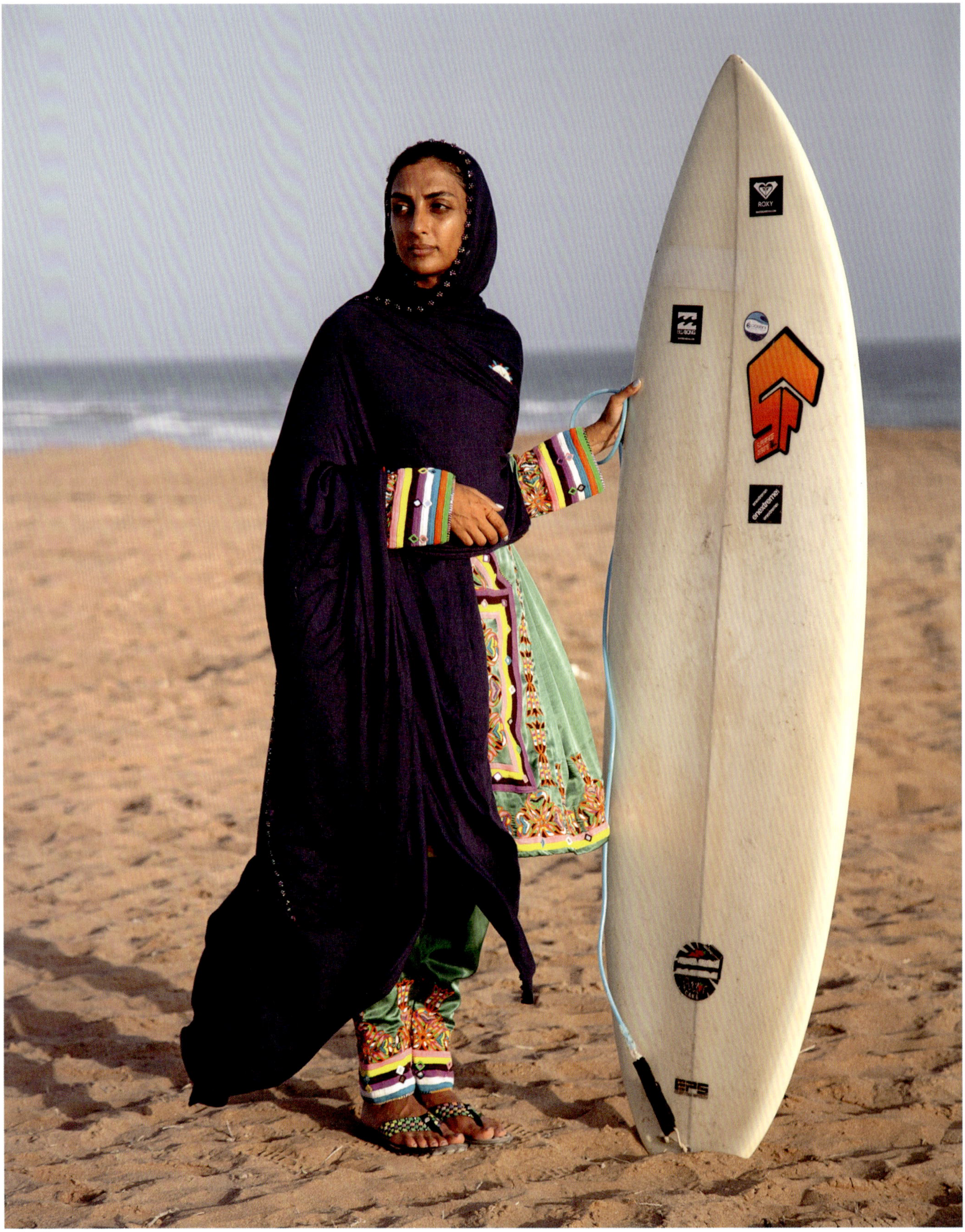
ROXY

Shahla Yasini

Shahla is among the first women in Iran to have stepped onto a surfboard and ridden the waves in the Gulf of Oman at the beaches of Chabahar. This small but regionally significant port city is located in the Sistan and Baluchestan province in southeastern Iran. Until 2010, there was no documentation about surfing as a sport being practiced in Iran. It was only with the Irish marine researcher and surfer Easkey Britton, who surfed there during a research trip to Iran, that the locals became aware of it—and followed the Irishwoman onto the waves. In 2013, particularly young women followed the example of Easkey Britton and started to take an interest in surfing. Thus, the sport first established itself among young Iranian women, who continue to be pioneers in it. With Easkey's efforts, a small surfing community was established in Iran. One of the first Iranian women was the then twenty-one-year-old Shahla Yasini, who had previously preferred to spend her time in and under the water as a professional lifeguard and hobby diver. When a surfing club was founded, she served as its vice president for a year. *"Since I was eighteen, I have been working to be financially independent. My father, and also my mother, who is a housewife herself, always encouraged us to stand on our own feet."*

The twenty-eight-year-old has been living in Tehran with her sister for several years and is studying sports science. When she still lived with her parents in Zahedan, she regularly traveled to Chabahar, which is a seven-hour drive away, and spent several weeks, or even months, of the year with her friends there.

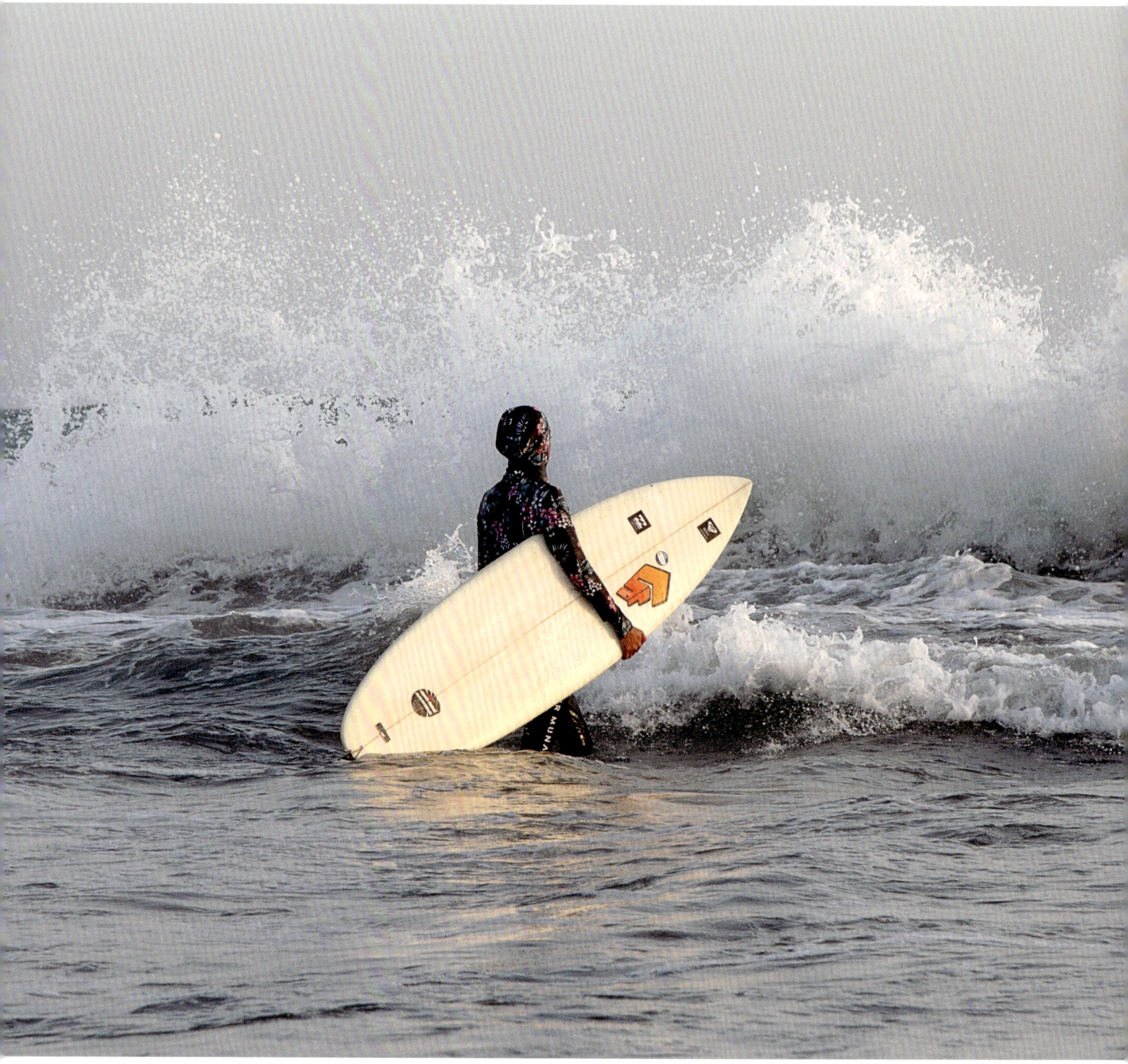

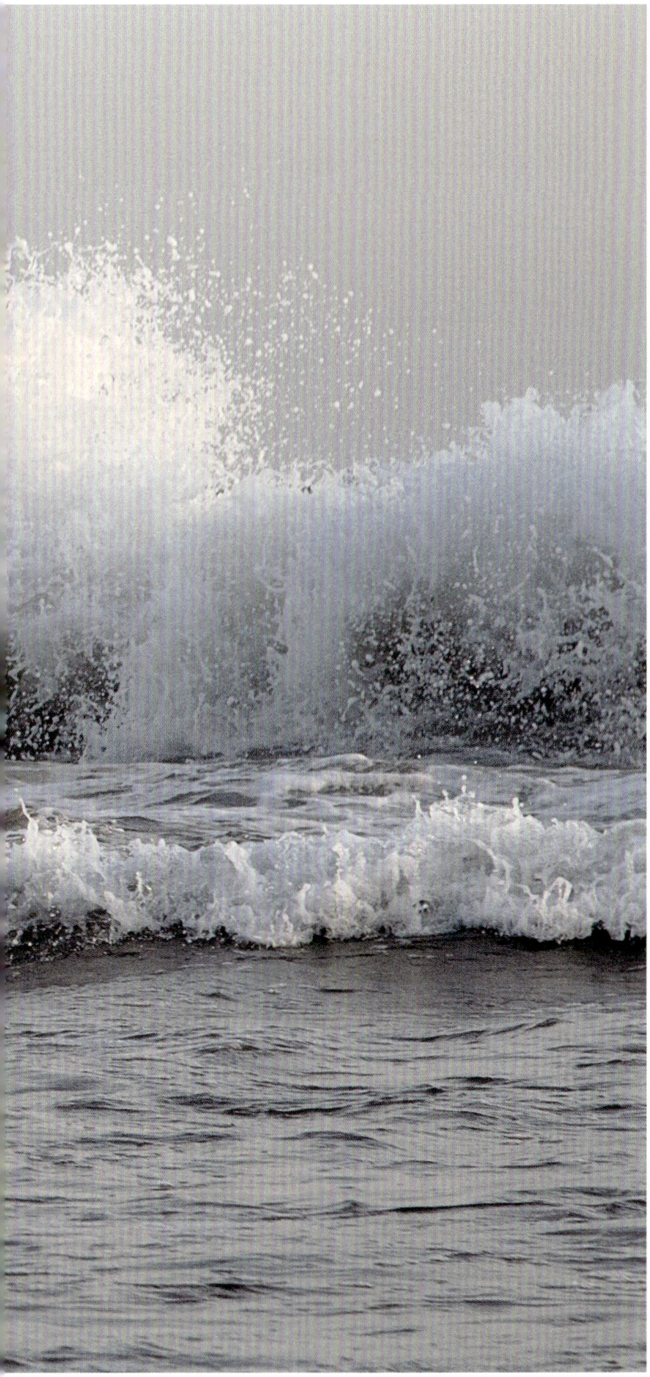

"As a woman in Chabahar—where men hold sway and women have a low presence in society—if you want to surf, you often receive strange looks and encounter unacceptance and shaking heads. Frequently, obstacles are put in your way. It is a very unusual sight in Chabahar to see a woman walking toward the open sea with a surfboard under her arm."

The support of her family and her self-confidence allowed the twenty-eight-year-old to overcome the difficult circumstances and do what she wanted and loved. Shahla talks about girls in her circle of acquaintances who, after marriage, had to reduce their social activities or even quit their jobs. Shahla looks out to the sea and says: *"I will never betray myself!"*

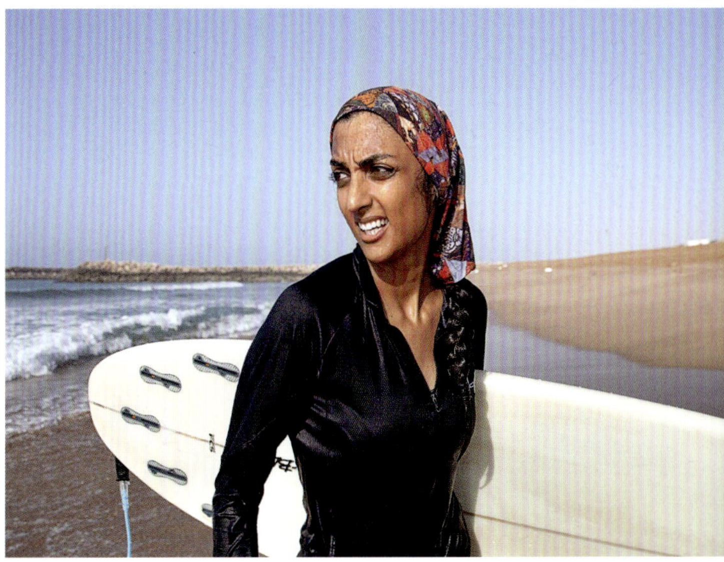

“As a woman in Chabahar–where men hold sway and women have a low presence in society–if you want to surf, you often receive strange looks.”

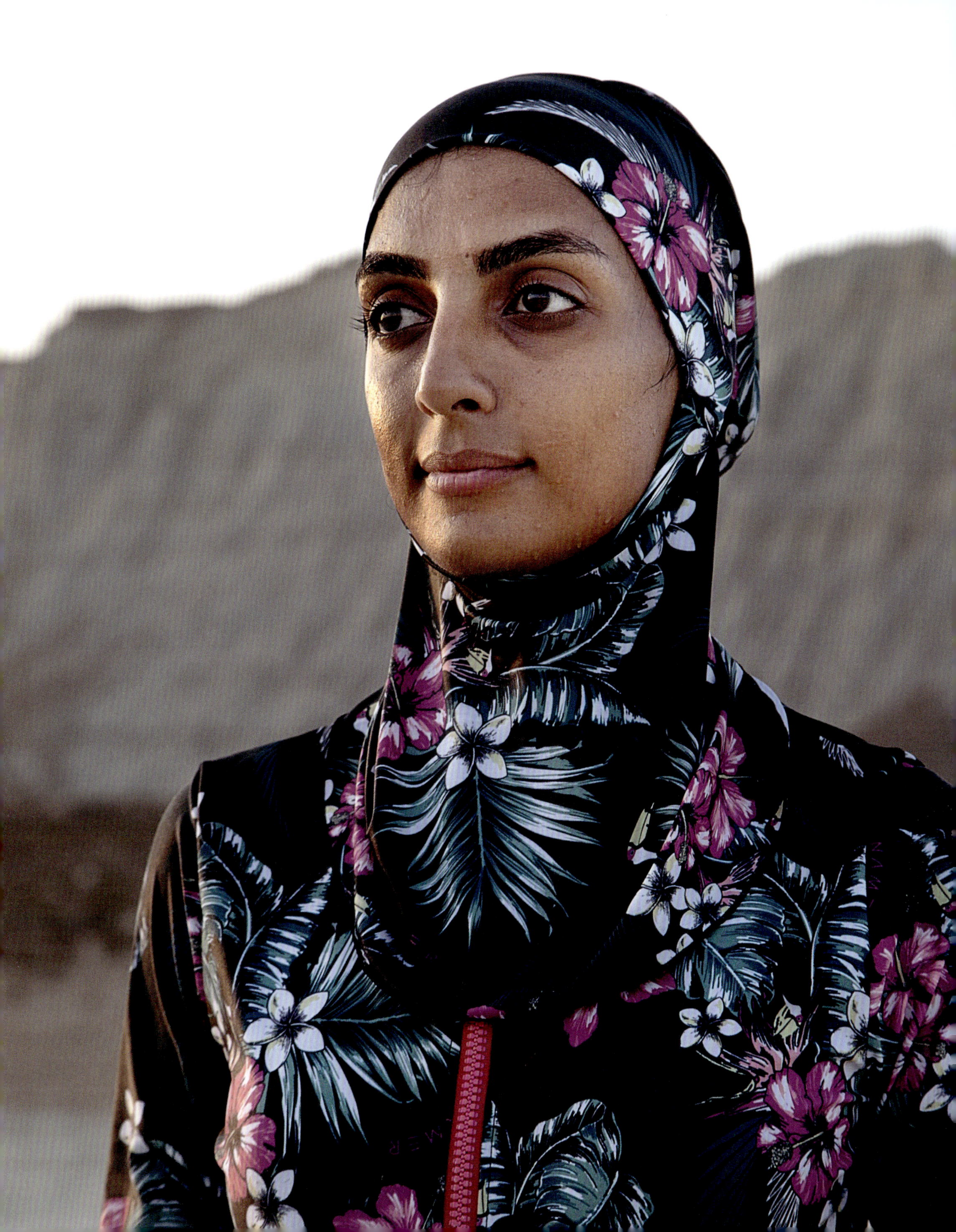

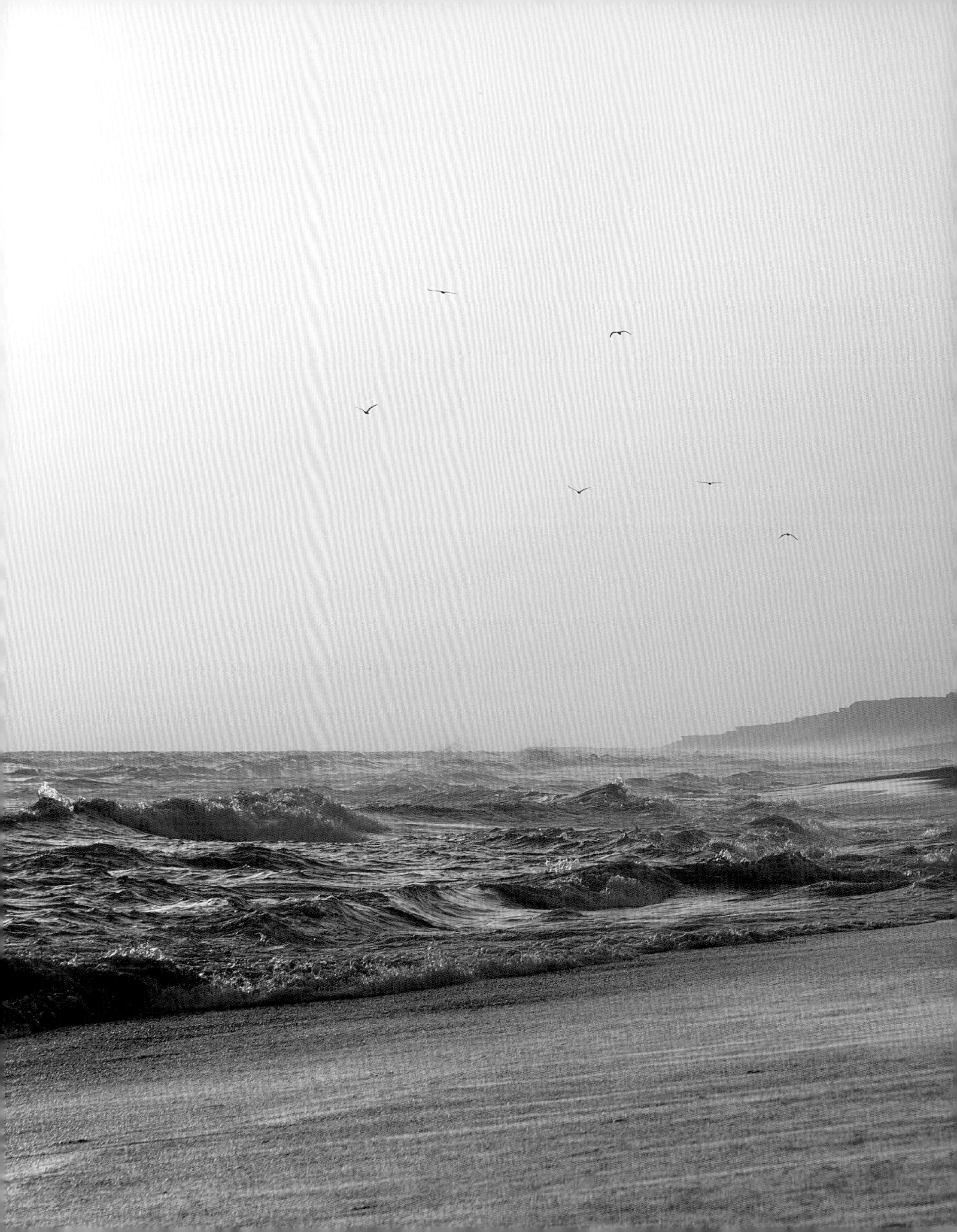

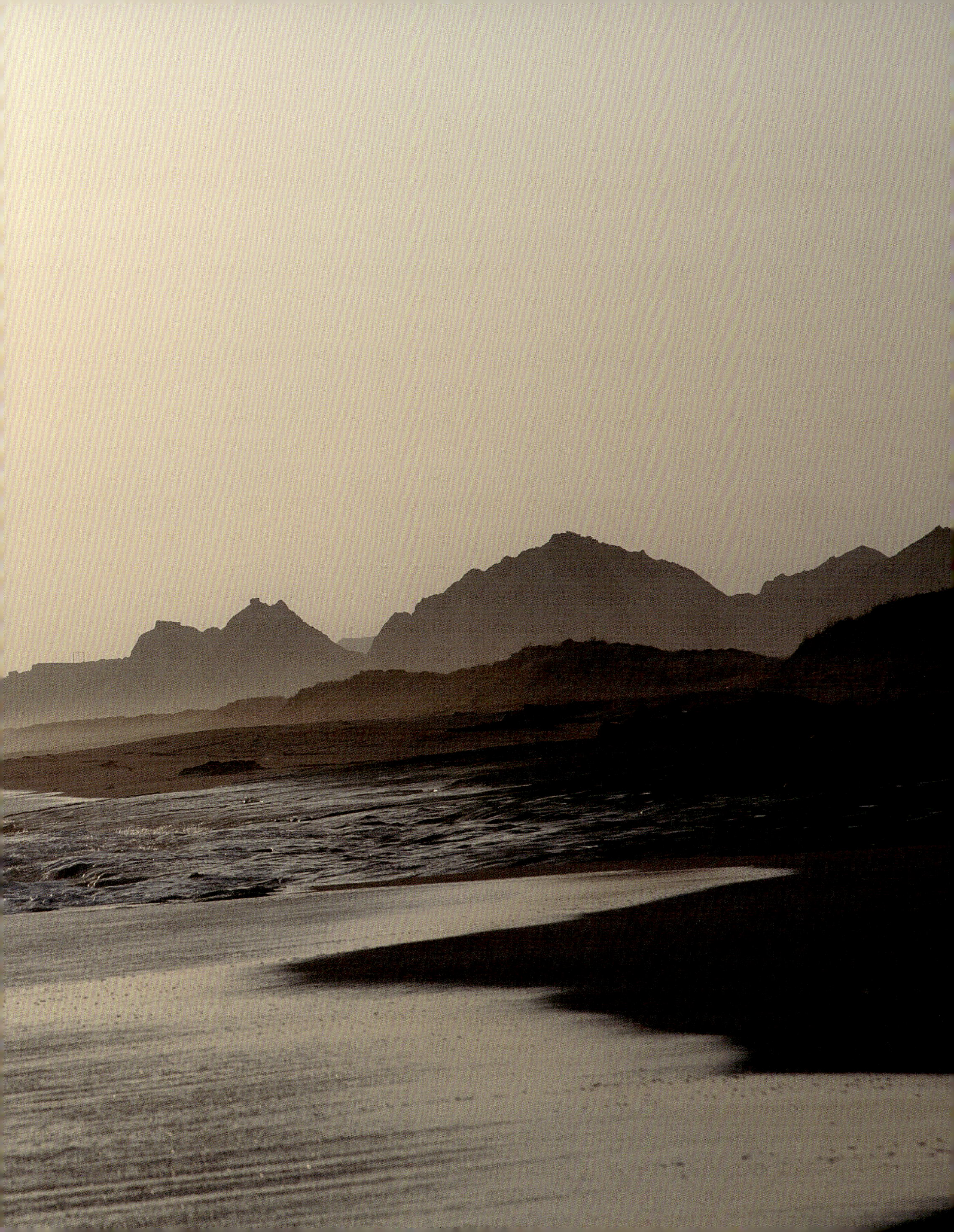

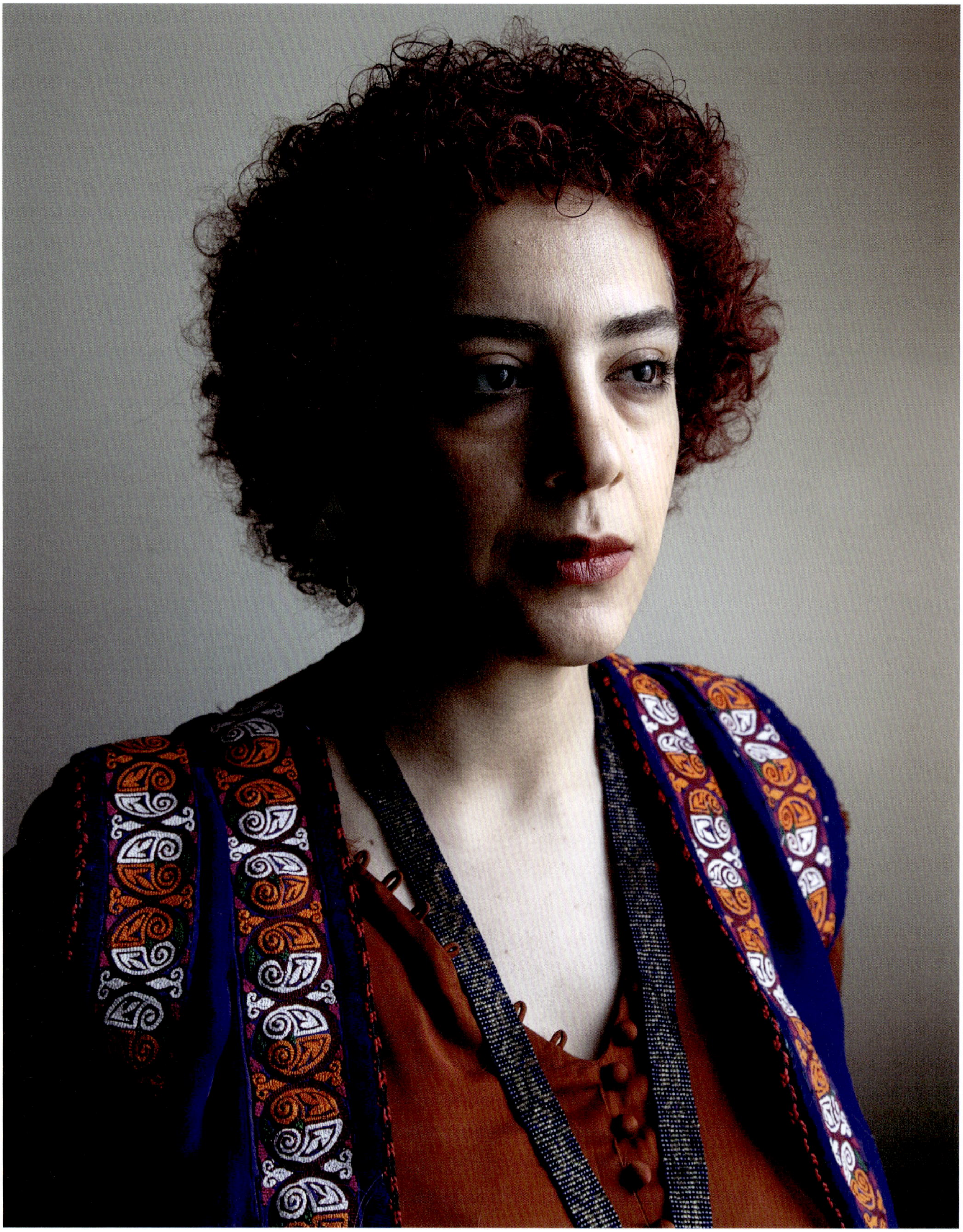

Saghar Radnezhad

"Many women no longer adhere to the public code of conduct—which was almost exclusively formulated by men," emphasizes Saghar, a thirty-nine-year-old graphic designer by training and also an actress, with a serious tone. Saghar is currently working as a freelance textile designer at a film production agency in Tehran. For her, it is important to work independently and break free from the outdated societal norms. Saghar wants to be independent and free in her decisions, and to be perceived as an active member of society.
"In our society, there are now many women who actively engage in economic and political life and distance themselves from the conservative image of women. But there are just as many who have only superficially and one-dimensionally changed. They may not let others dictate to them anymore, but they don't show that they can also be active members of society," Saghar explains, sounding frustrated. *"But perhaps this is a process that our women must go through, both within and outside their own families, in order to grow from it. The more women know about themselves, their world, and the possibilities, the more it helps them to grow intellectually, understand their new self-perception, and perhaps one day be accepted as equal members of society."*
Her family raised her to be very open-minded and encouraged her to become a confident woman, as Saghar describes her upbringing. She was allowed to make her own decisions but also had to live with the consequences. *"When I started acting in theater as an actress, my parents were not thrilled. They were only familiar with traditional employment and firmly believed in regular working hours and structured routines. Acting is the complete opposite,"* Saghar smiles as she recounts her memories. *"But despite their different opinion, they didn't stop me, and now they are happy to see me on stage."* Saghar thoroughly enjoys her acting profession—however, she looks at the situation realistically and knows that one cannot solely make a living from it. She says: *"Leading an independent life is becoming increasingly challenging for young people in Tehran. The cost of rent has risen drastically, and due to the absence of tenant protection regulations, rent can be adjusted annually. That's why many of them take on two or even three jobs to secure their livelihood."*

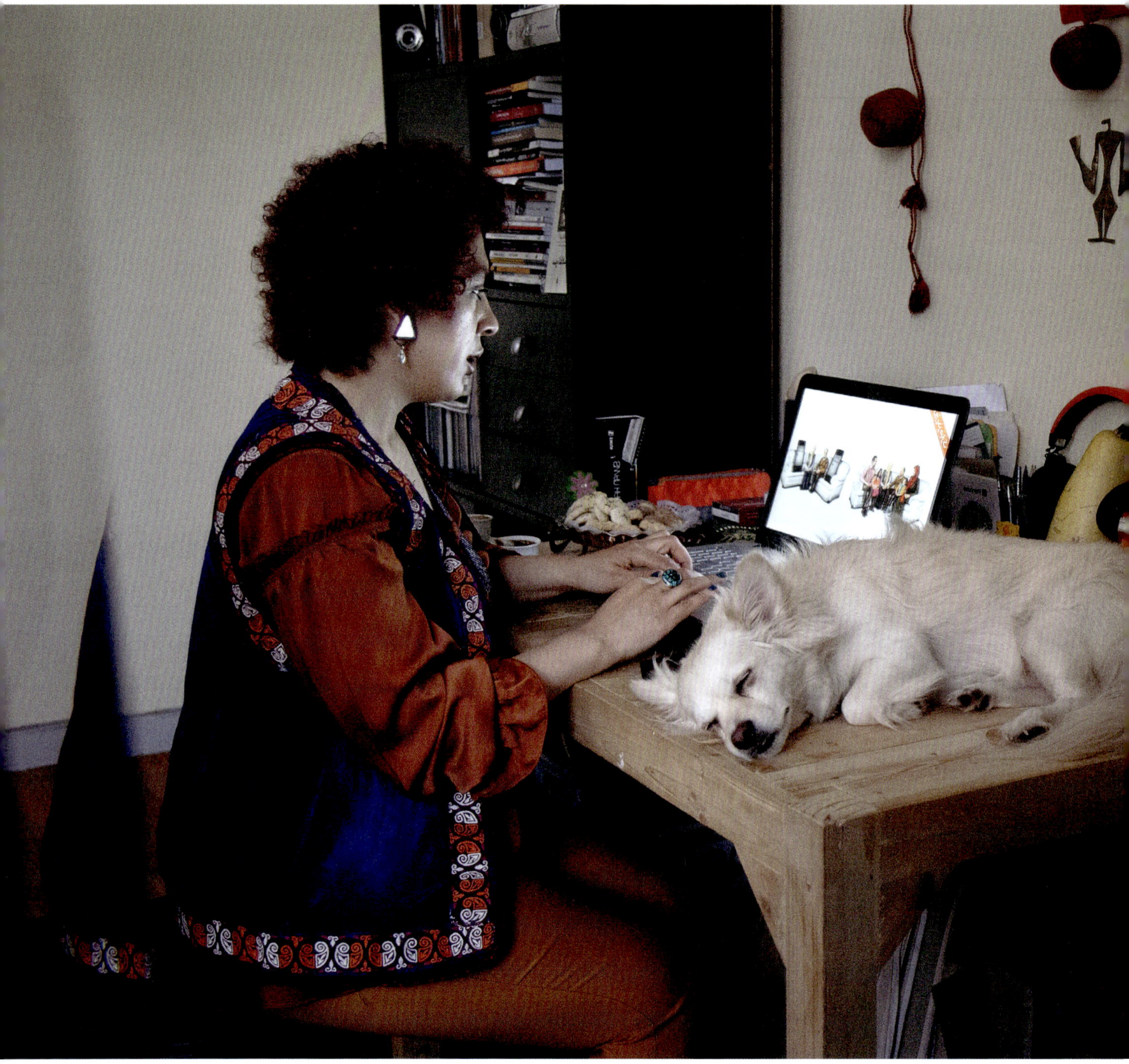

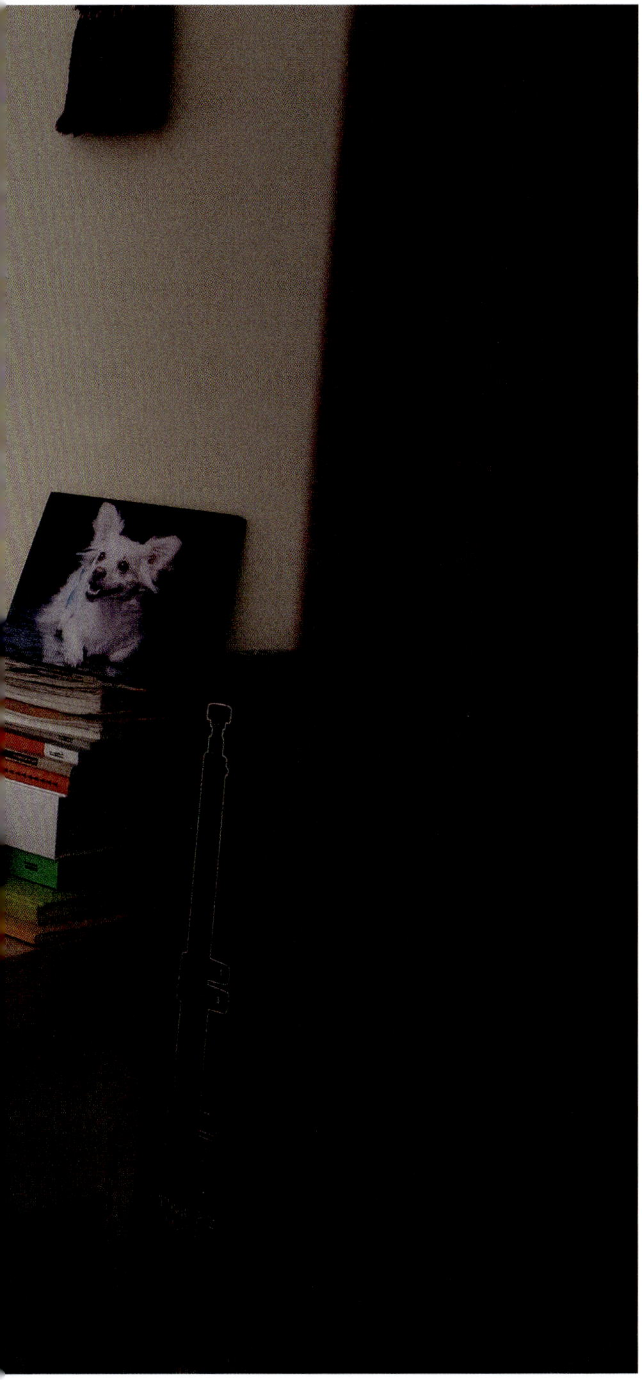

Saghar describes her current situation while working on a new poster design for an advertising agency in Tehran: *"The biggest challenge of working as a woman in Iran is the discrimination in job allocation. Unfortunately, men are still given preference. This makes it even harder for us female freelancers to land the next job, which increasingly burdens the psyche. I can imagine being even more creative if I knew I wouldn't be disadvantaged."*

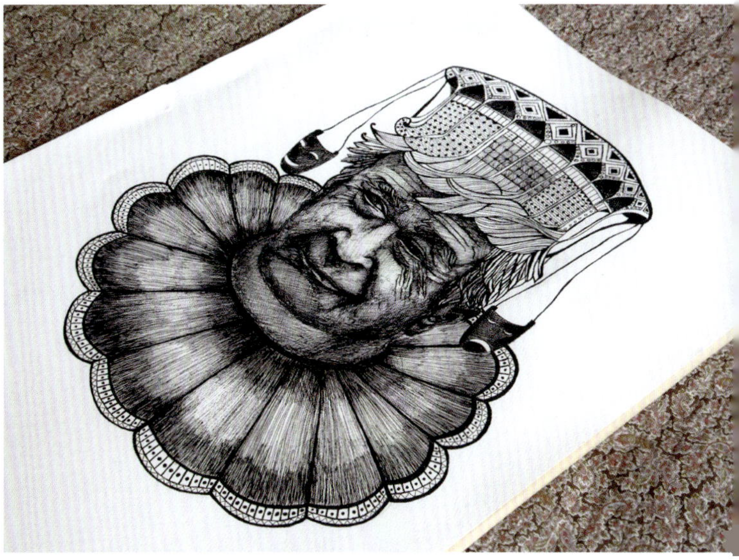

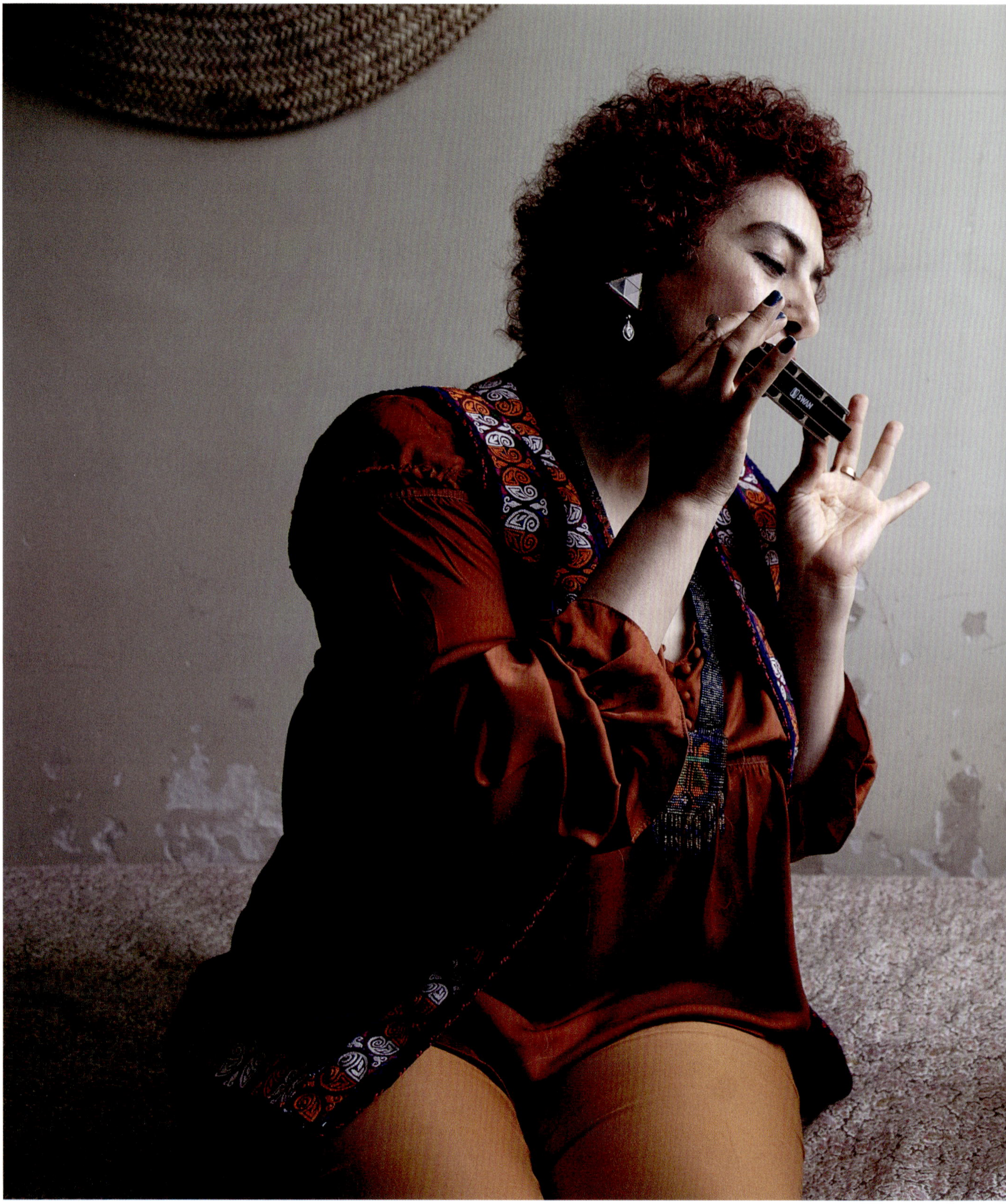
SWAN

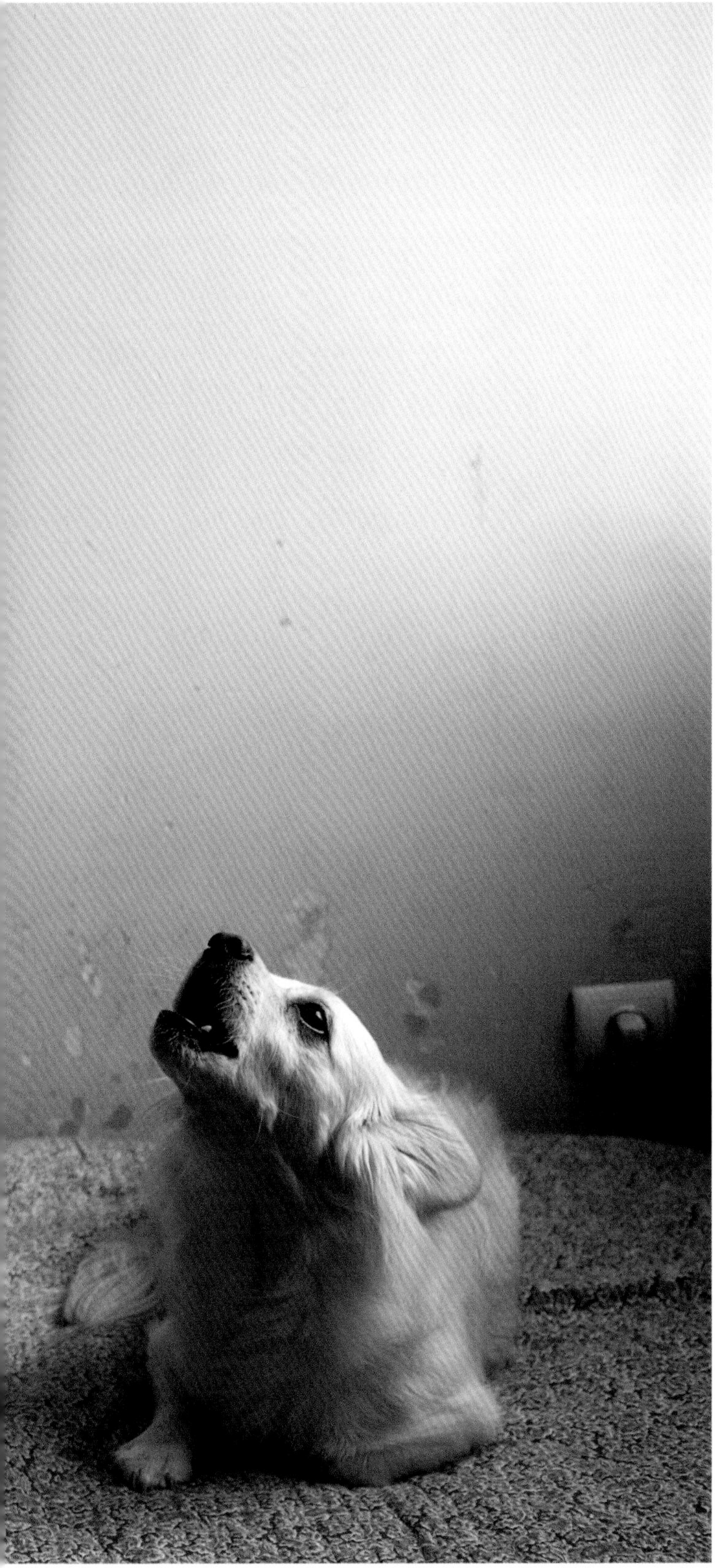

Saghar enjoys playing her harmonica. *"This instrument is pure nostalgia for me; it takes me back to my childhood. But I don't know why. Maybe I watched cartoons back then where the harmonica was used for the soundtrack. But actually, it doesn't matter. I just like it."* And it's not just Saghar who loves the sounds of the harmonica—her dog Happy also enjoys accompanying her. *"I love dogs. They are the most loyal and friendly beings there are."* In Iran, dogs are considered impure among devout people, who believe they would defile the place of prayer within their homes. That's why you rarely find dogs or other pets in households. Although Saghar's mother prays at home, Happy is allowed to be inside.

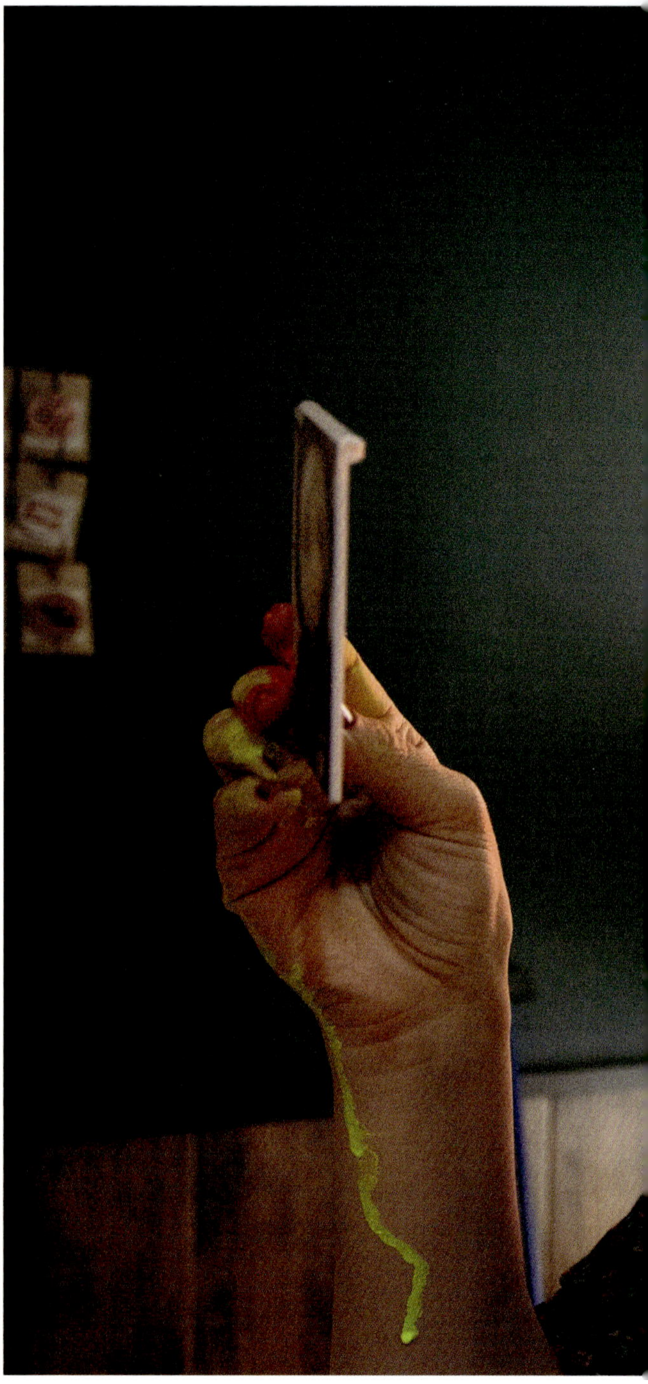

The thirty-nine-year-old is at an artist gathering in a café—this event takes place in different locations in Tehran each time. *"This concept of organizing the meeting in a different place every time always makes it very exciting and stimulates my creativity."* The theme of today's gathering: object collage made from waste or reused materials. Everyone brings something—even collected leaves from the street.

The materials are spread out on the tables, and everyone can choose something to put together on a canvas. Saghar picks an old newspaper, leaves, aluminum foil, and watercolors. Instead of using the A3-sized paper in front of her, Saghar decides to use her face as the canvas.

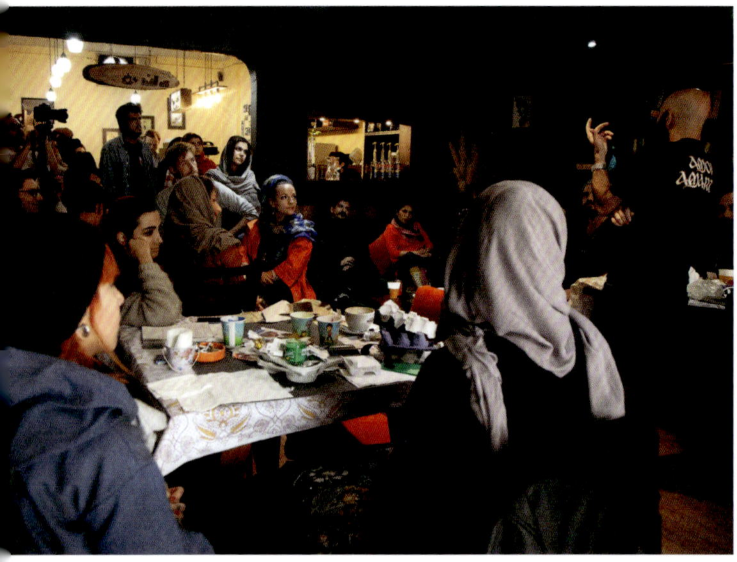

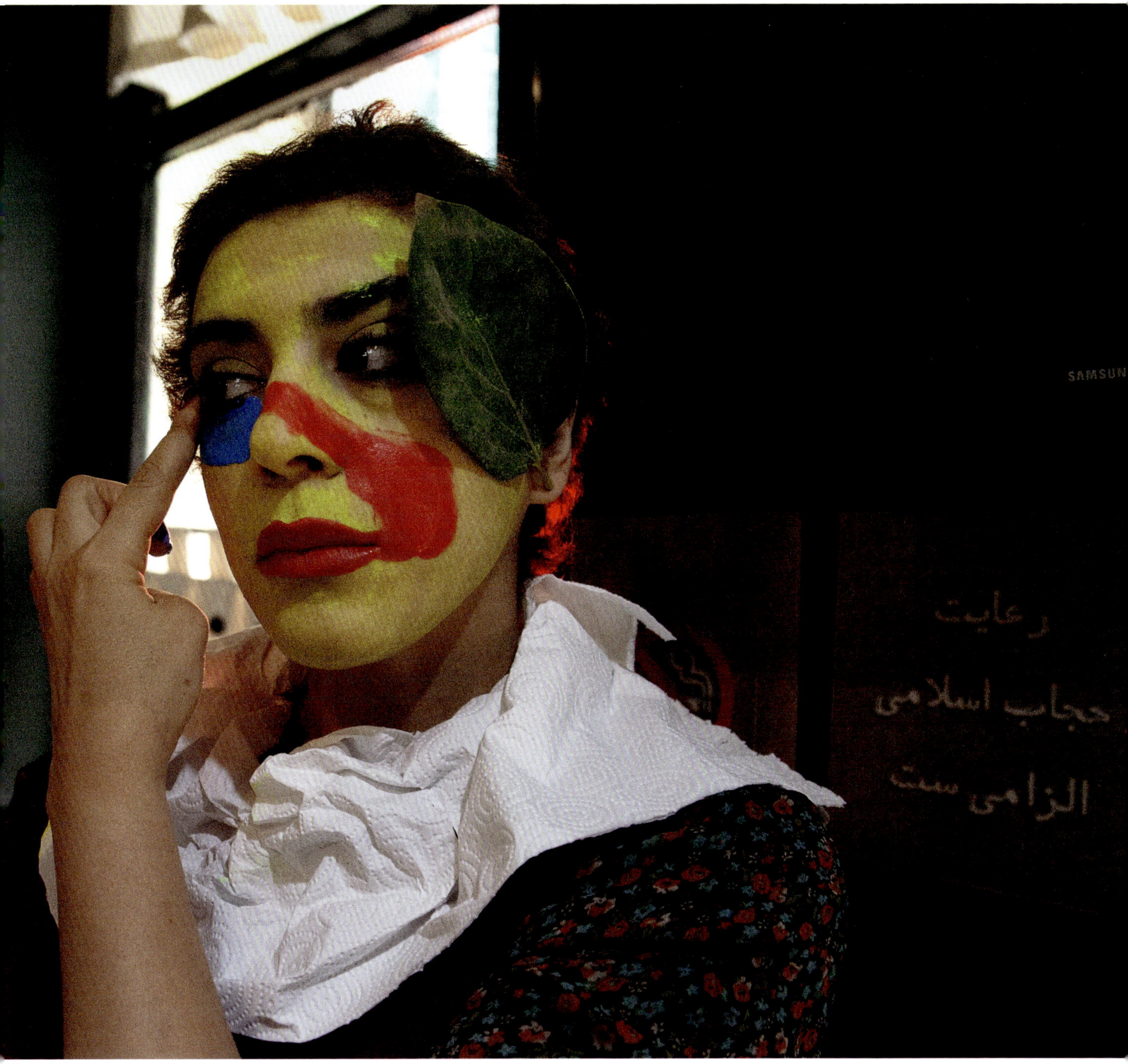
SAMSUN
رعایت
حجاب اسلامی
الزامی ست

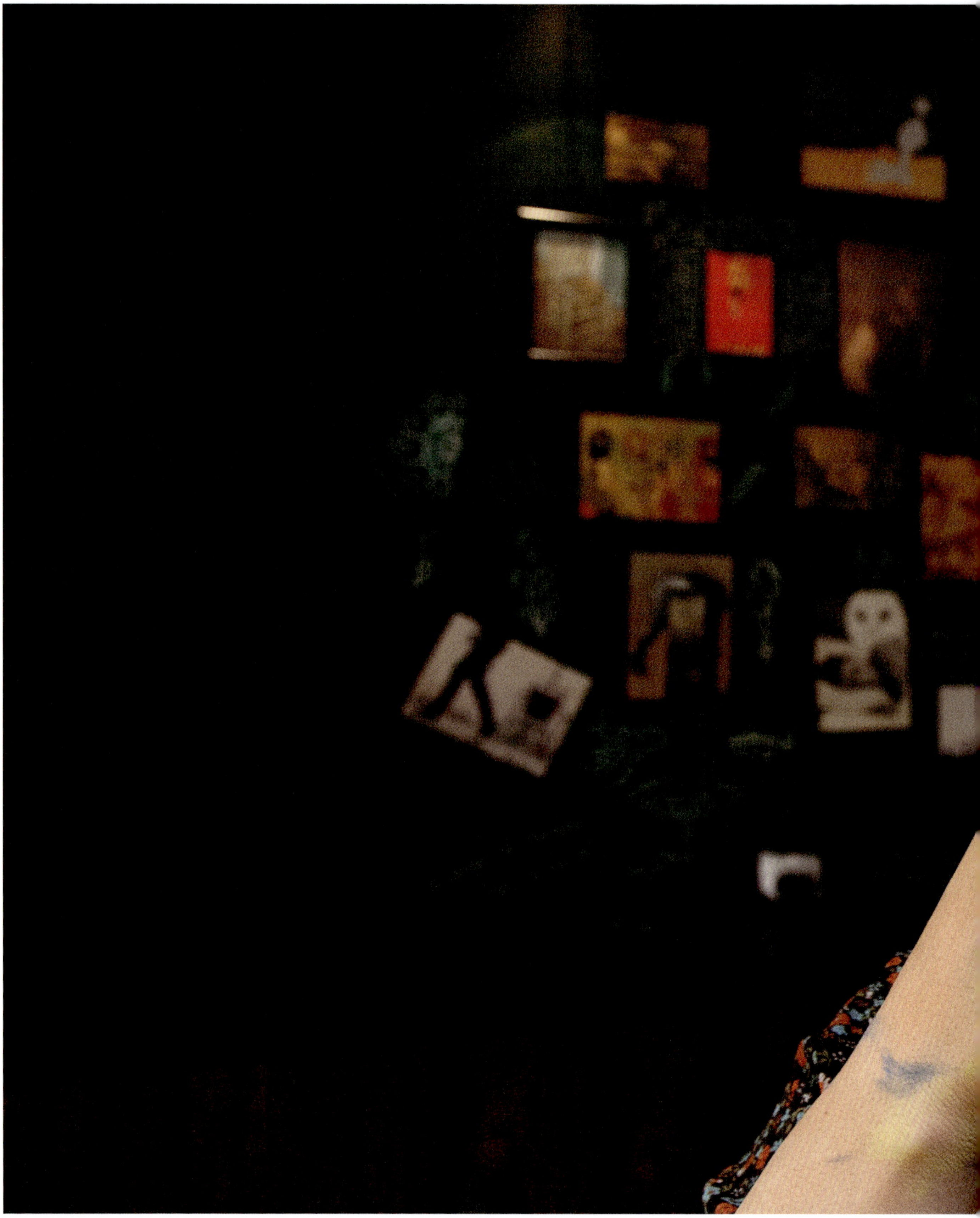

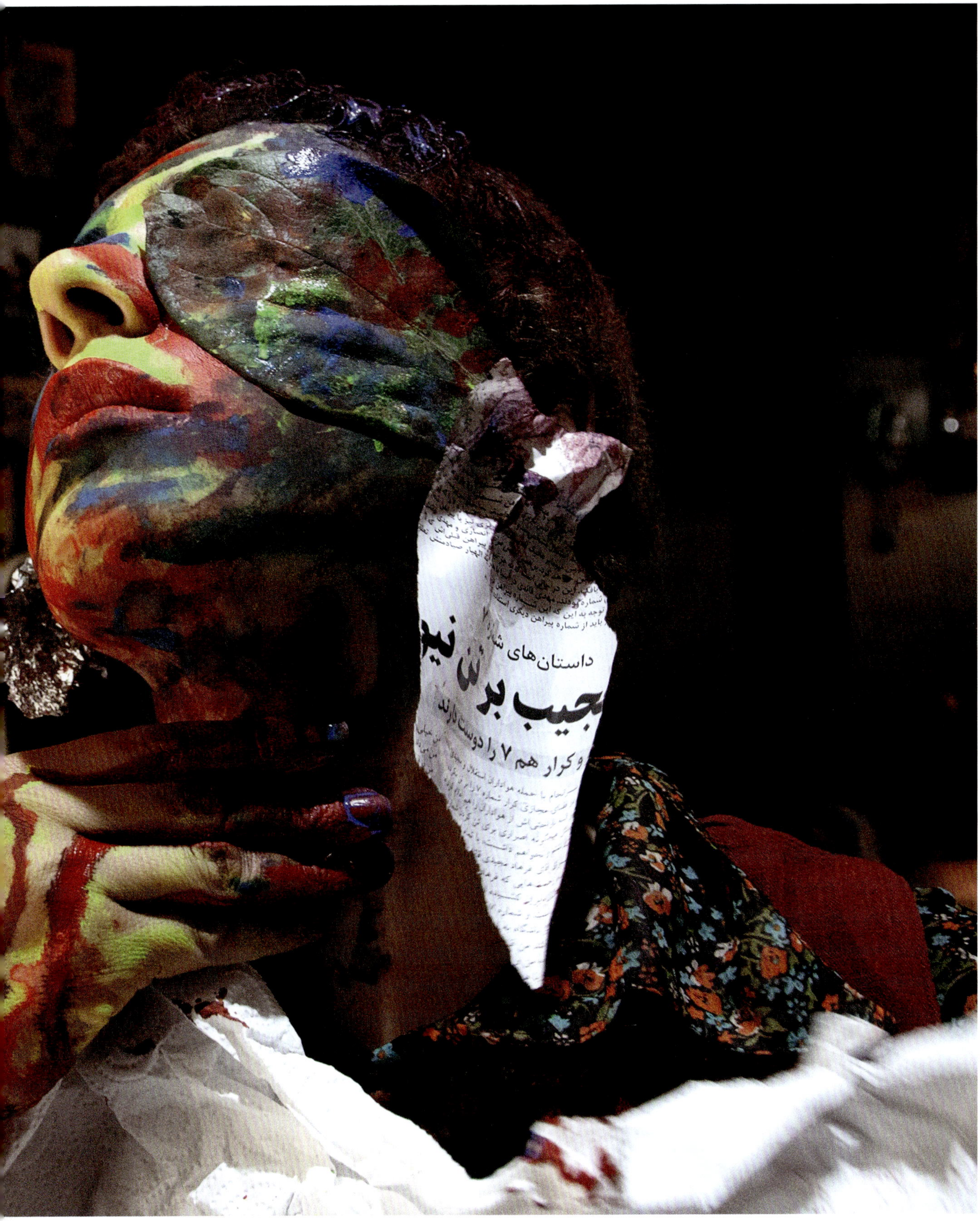

Neda Amiralaei

Since 2002, Neda has been the head of the International Office at the University of Art in Tehran. Two years prior, she worked as an advisor for international affairs at the university. *"Due to my proficiency in English and my experience as an advisor, it was easy for me to establish contact with people from different nations and maintain these relationships,"* says the fifty-year-old. *"One of my most significant achievements in the early years of my career as the head of the International Office was a cooperation agreement with two universities in England for the collaboration of doctoral students on research projects."* The Iranian Ministry of Science, Research, and Technology recognized her achievements and entrusted her with greater responsibilities. Neda explains that in her role there are often obstacles that can only be overcome with strong determination and courage—especially as a woman. *"There are some people who believe that working in the International Office is merely a decorative position. Unfortunately, they fail to grasp the importance of international exchange for research and education."* In 2006, she decided to pursue her own PhD alongside her work.

As a PhD student at Allameh Tabataba'i University in Tehran, she continued her position as the head of the International Office. Neda also had the opportunity to do a research residency in Canada during her PhD studies. *"Although I received a broad range of good job offers during my research residency in Canada, love for my homeland prevailed. And, of course, the connection with my family was another reason for me to return to Iran."* The University of Art in Tehran maintains numerous collaborations worldwide, many of them in Europe. *"Since I've been employed as the head of the International Office at the University of Art in Tehran, I've seen nine university presidents come and go. Each of them came with their own ideas and teams, but my position remained untouched, which I consider to reflect an appreciation for my work."* Neda is firmly convinced that exchange is important at every level. She believes that students and professors should not be deprived of what is happening at other universities around the world.

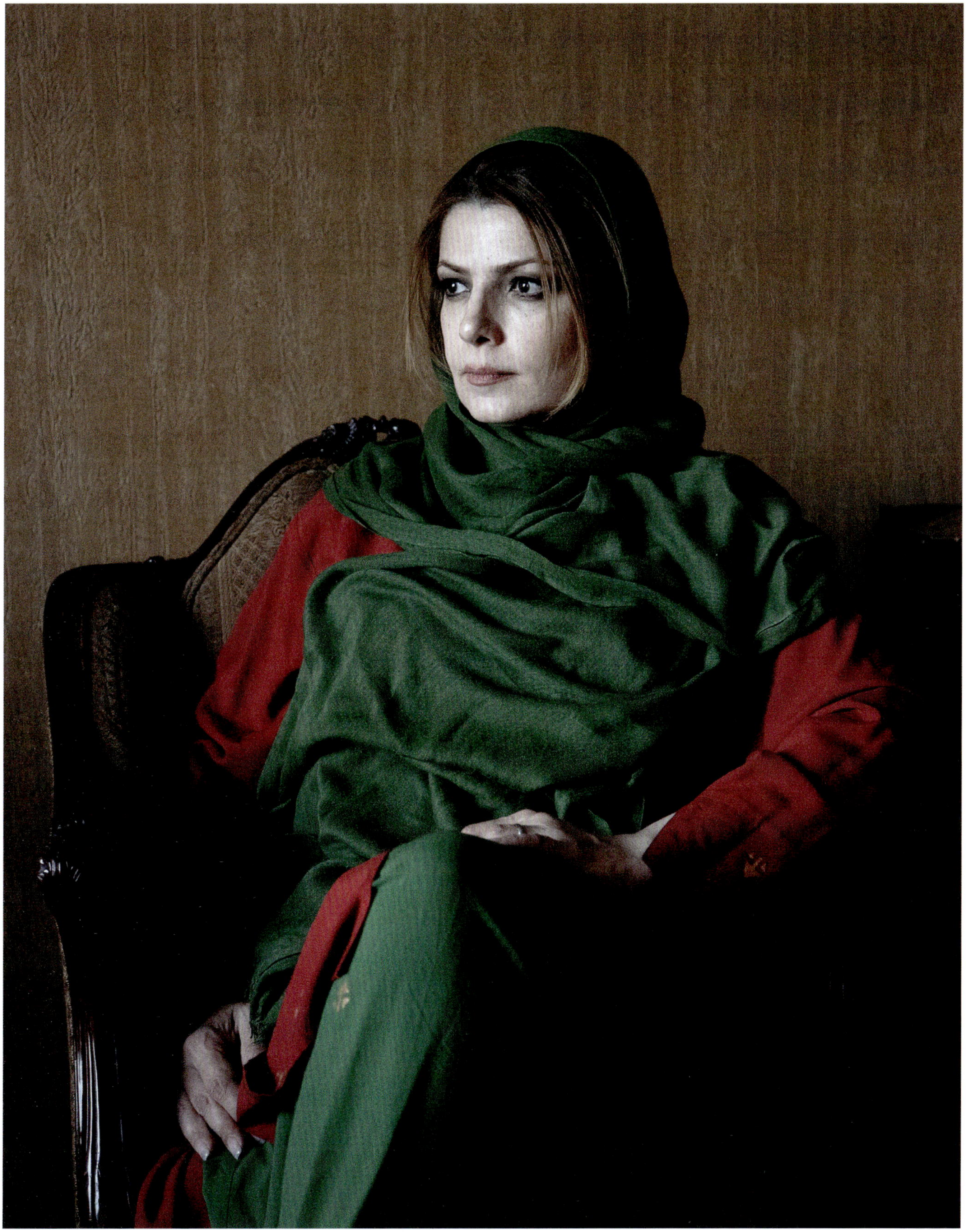

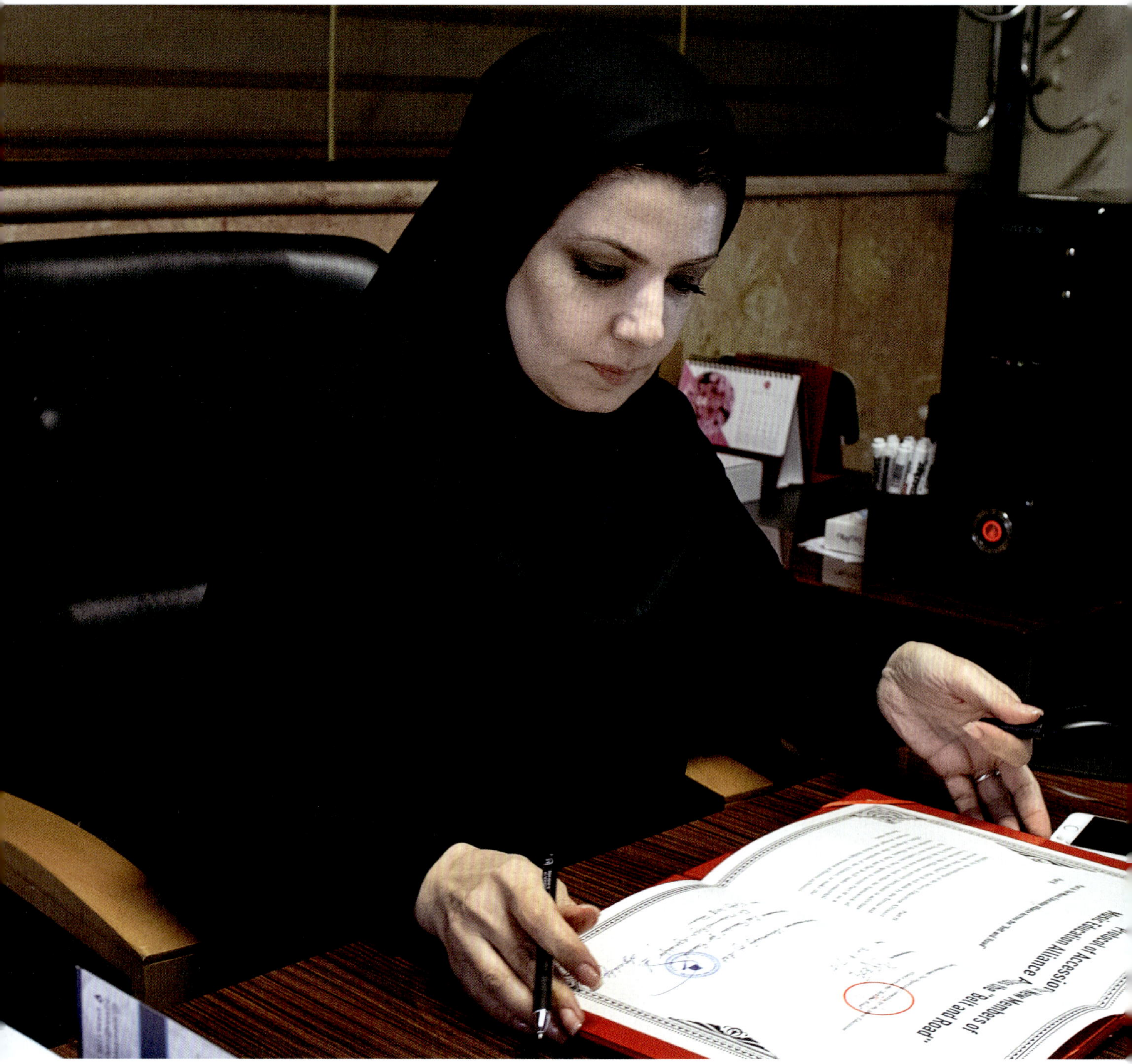

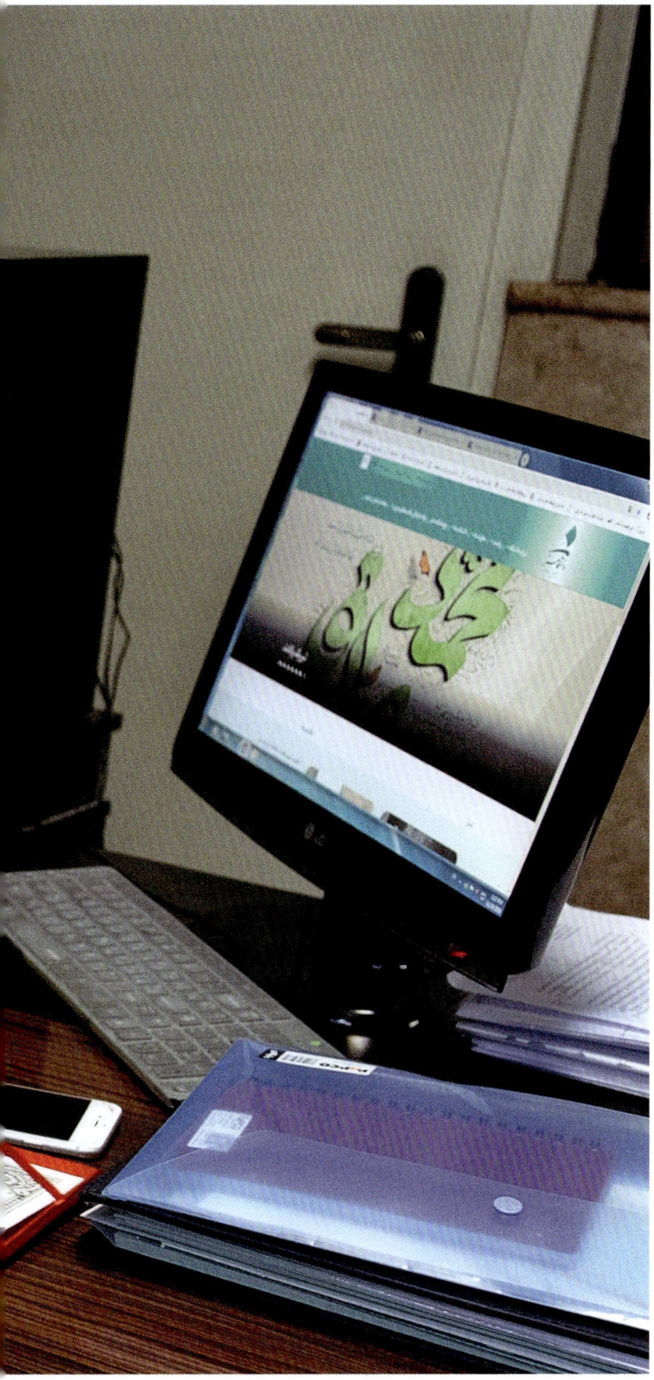

May 2 is Teacher's Day in Iran. Neda shows the plants that her students brought her and says: *"I have great faith in Iranian women and their abilities. If you look at the statistics of recent years, you can see that 60 percent of those admitted to universities are women. This demonstrates how important it is for women to learn and be present in society—even though there are still more social restrictions for women than for men. For example, in some villages, 100 kilometers away from big cities, there are no secondary schools for girls. If there were equality, Iranian women and girls might be even further ahead than our men."*

Neda shares an anecdote about an experience with a German academic delegation that she welcomed at the airport and took to their hotel. Neda was asked in surprise: *"Are women allowed to drive in Iran?"* The guests had previously worked extensively with some Arab countries where women were not allowed to drive. That's why they were surprised that a woman greeted them alone at the airport and organized the entire week's program without any male intervention. When they also learned that men on her team even worked for Neda, their amazement grew even larger. *"It is very gratifying when our foreign guests return with a completely different impression of the role of women in Iran. It makes me proud when they have a better understanding of Iranian society and the active role of modern Iranian women."*

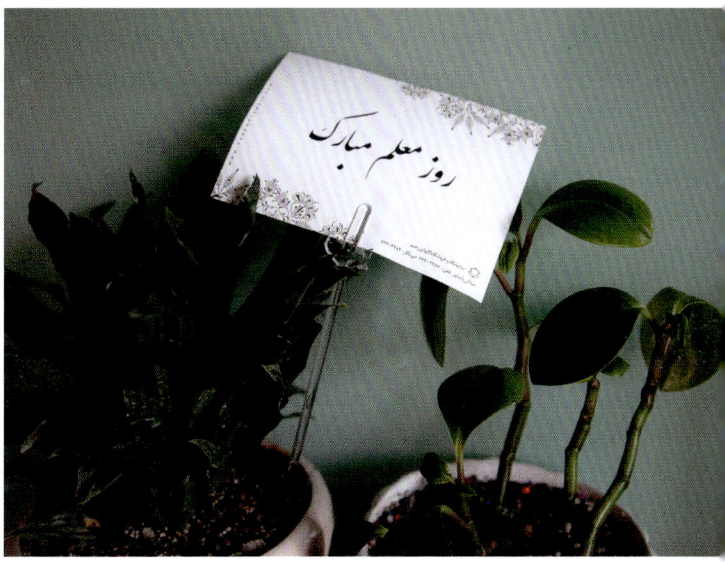

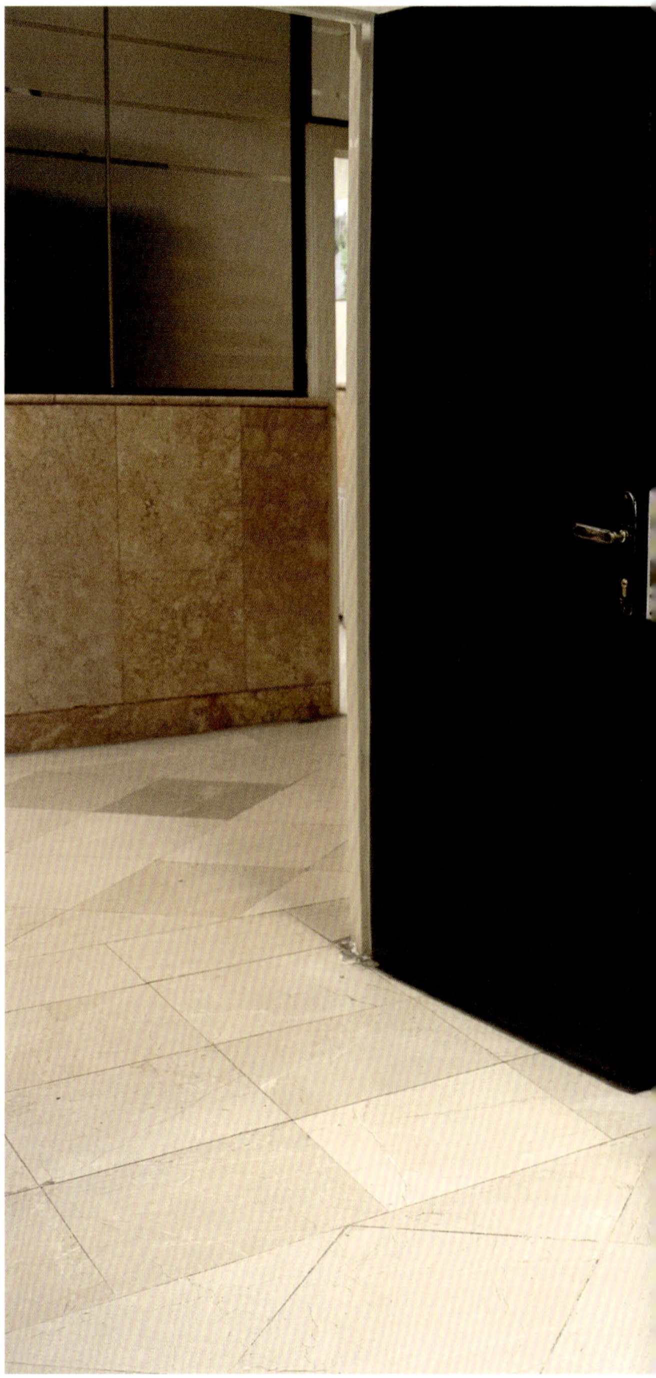

Despite her acute leg injury, Neda attends her appointments at the university. Today, she is hosting professors from Germany. The meeting is held in the conference room, together with the university president. Before entering the room, Neda explains the procedure to the press photographer. The pictures and a brief report of today's meeting will be published on the university's website shortly thereafter. As a gesture of Iranian hospitality—especially when foreign guests are present—Neda has ensured that the table is abundantly set with traditional sweet pastries and tea during the meeting. Additionally, each guest is gifted with a few books about Iran and traditional Iranian sweets like Gaz.

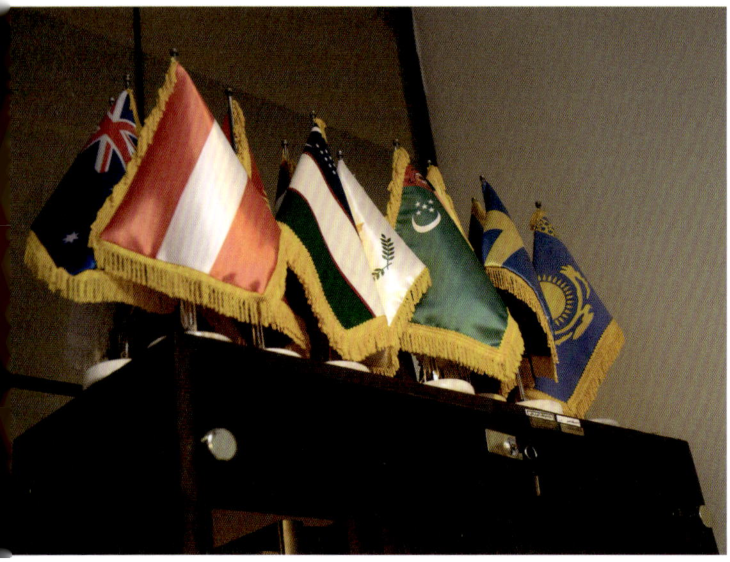

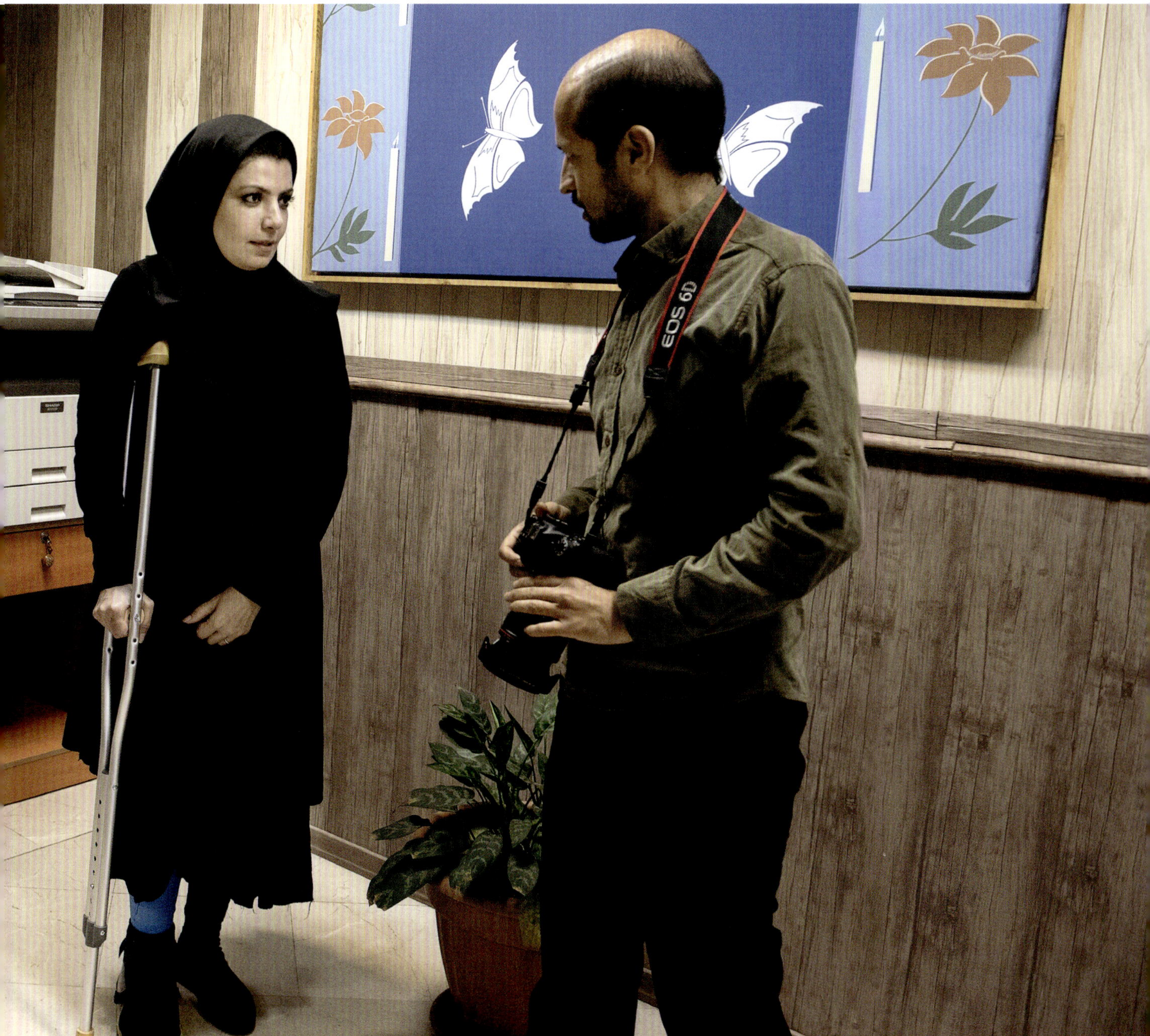
EOS 6D

“I have great faith in Iranian women and their abilities. If you look at the statistics of recent years, you can see that 60 percent of those admitted to universities are women.”

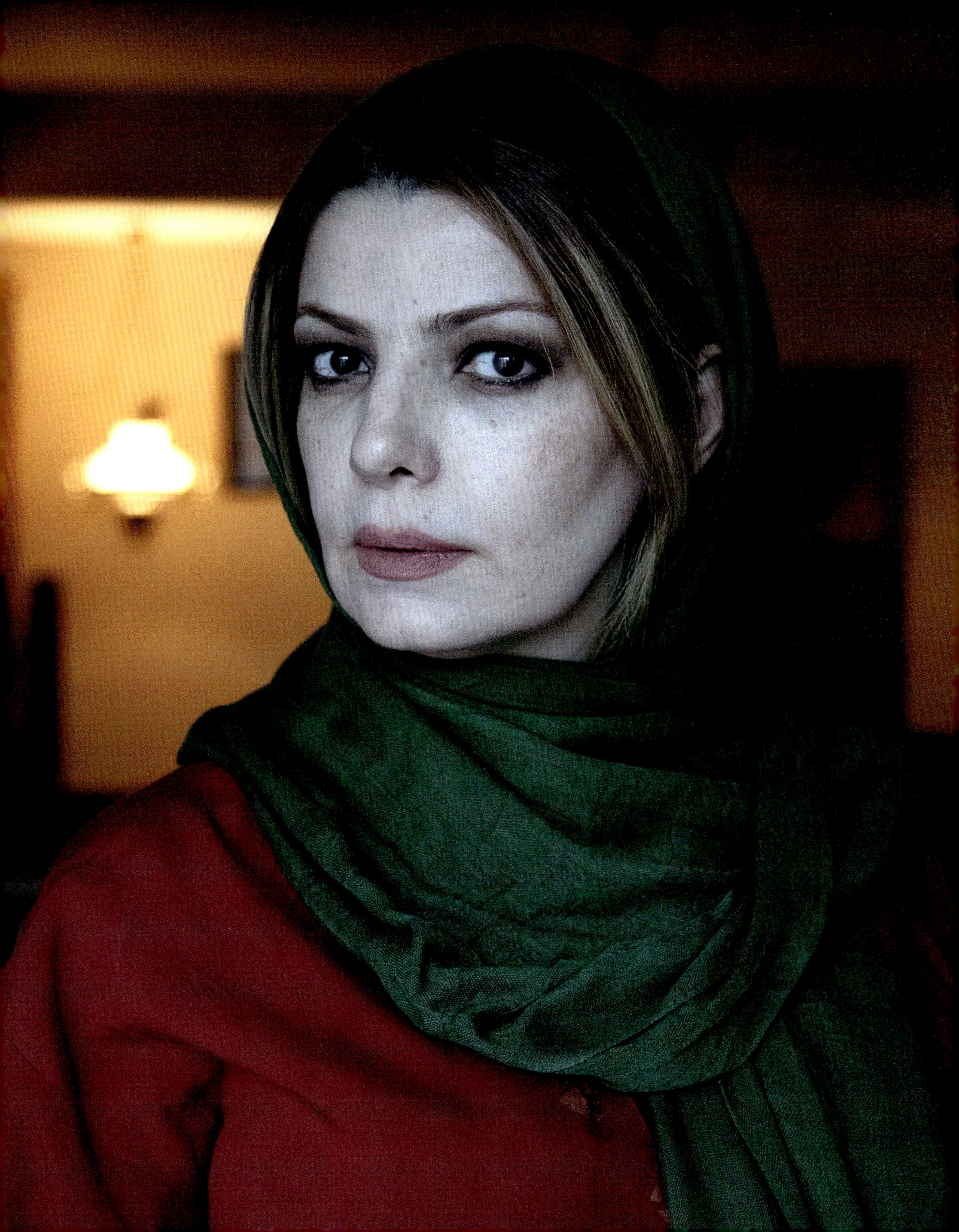

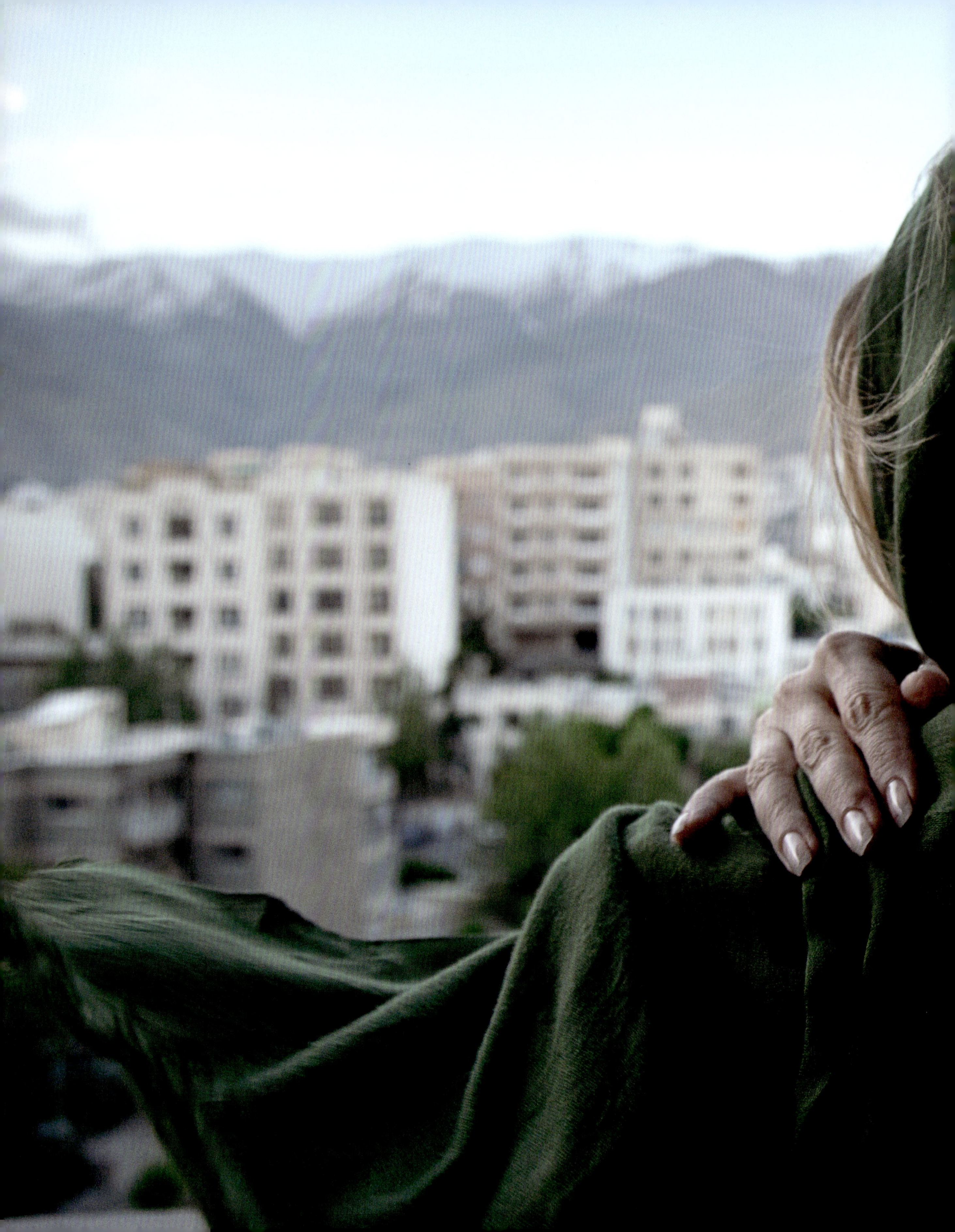

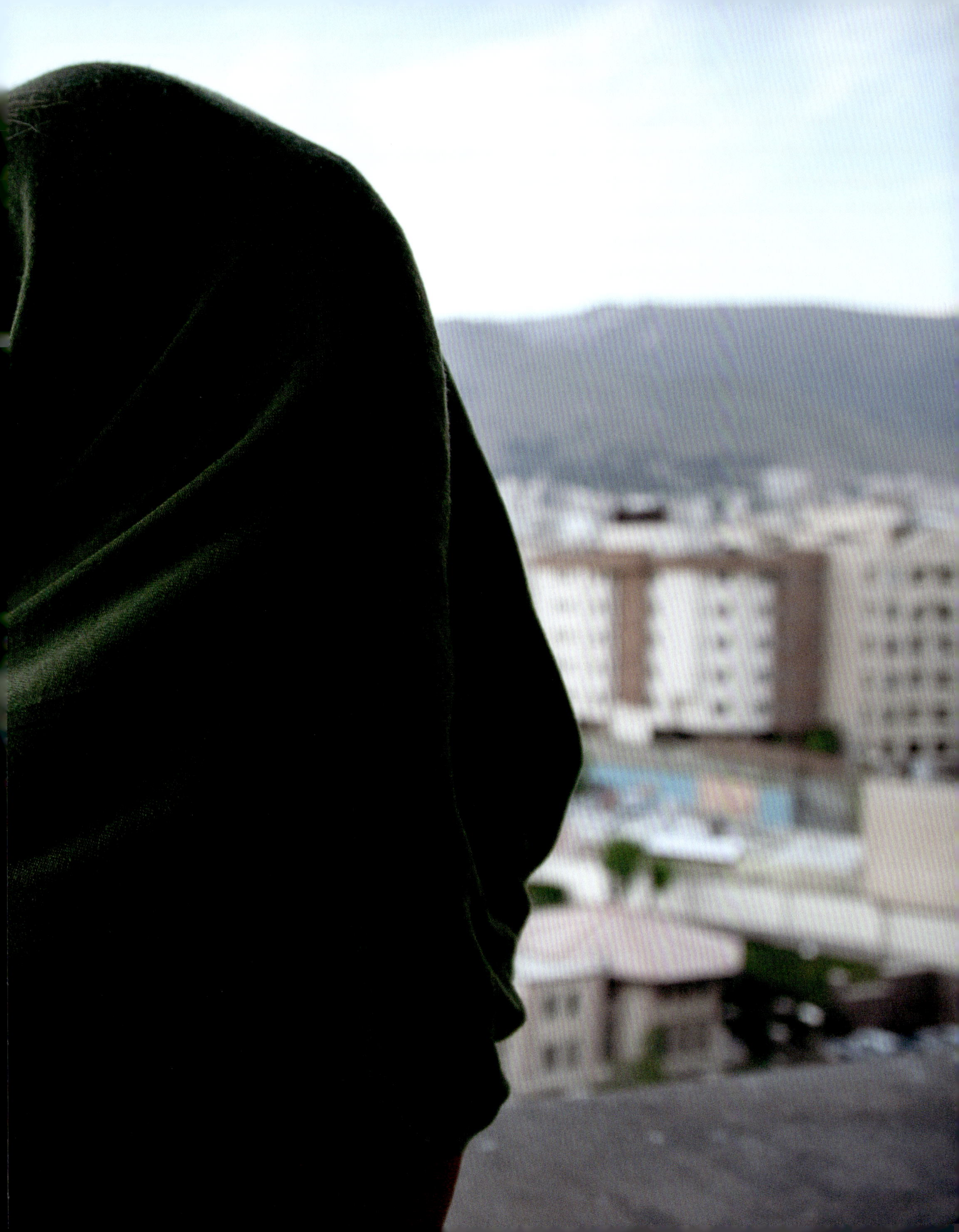

Somayeh Arjmandkia

Somayeh is a cheerful and lively woman who enjoys laughing and bringing joy to others. Raised in a devout family, she veils herself with a chador out of religious conviction. The forty-year-old is convinced that everything in life must be kept in balance, or else one quickly loses joy. *"A successful person is someone who pays attention to both spiritual and material development. I myself try to live in balance every day, and it's not that easy."* Somayeh, her husband Mohammad, and their daughter Reyhaneh live in an affluent area in Mashhad. Her husband works as the head of the PR department at a state telecommunications company. Somayeh sees the upbringing of her nine-year-old daughter as her most important task: *"I don't necessarily have to be an active part of society to make my contribution."* She refers to her more traditionally defined role as a woman. *"I want to raise my daughter to be a confident woman so that she can forge her own path. What my daughter considers success is her decision. My decision was to be a mother and a homemaker—while also working on myself and on the future of my daughter and my family."*

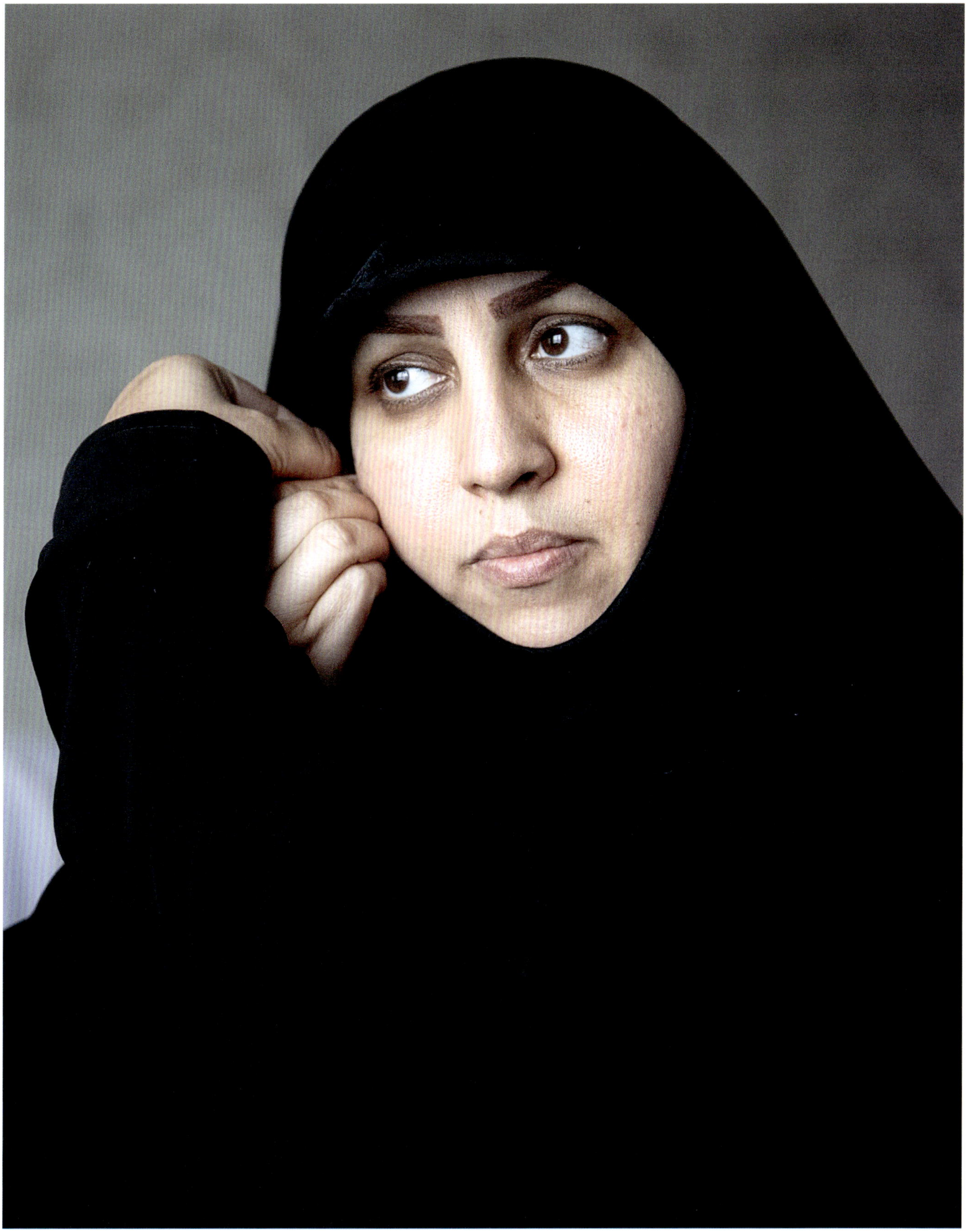

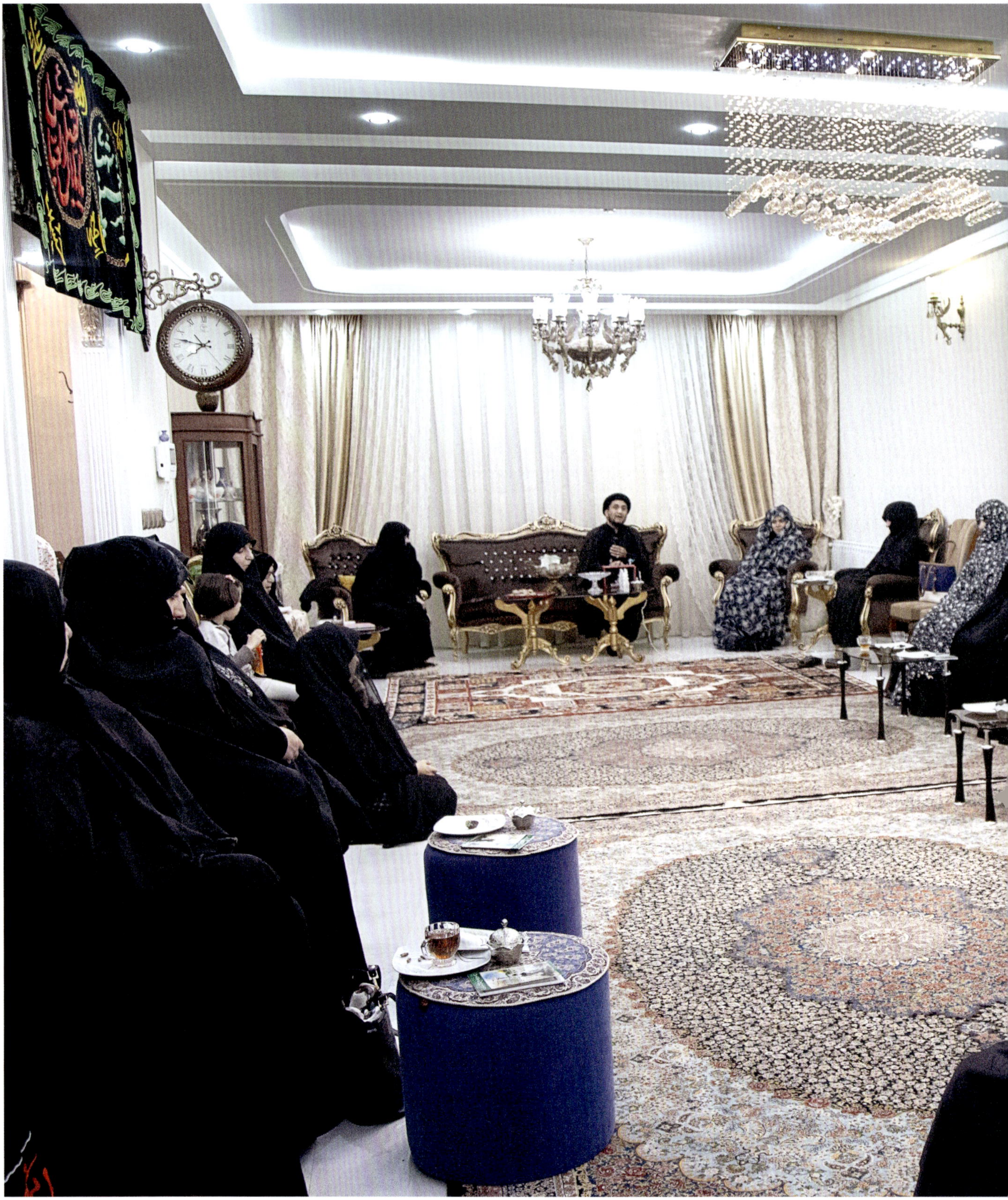

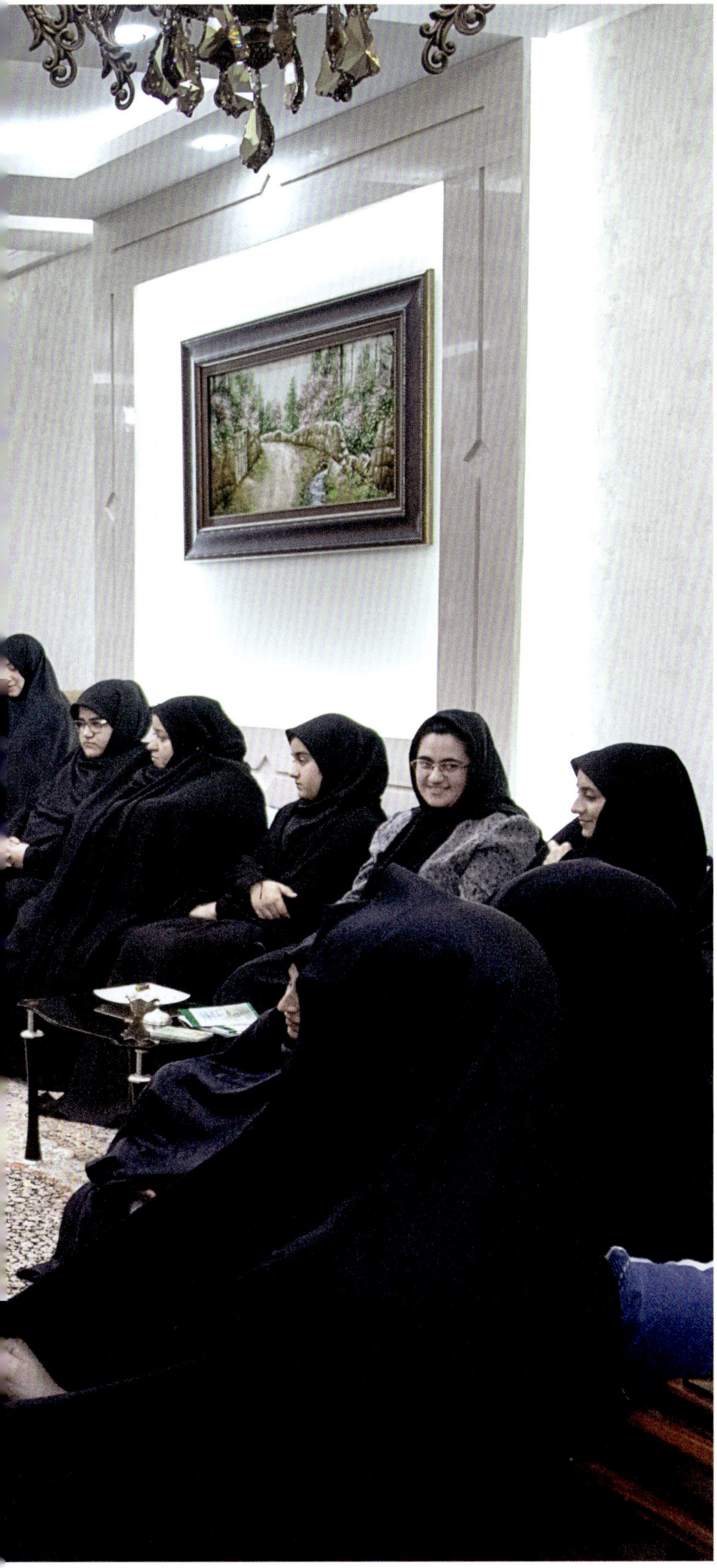

Somayeh organizes religious events in her home. To this end, she has invited a *mullah*, an Islamic jurist and religious scholar, to speak about Islam and provide enlightenment. He narrates the story of Hussein, the third Imam of the Shiites. In Shiite Islam, recognized successors to Prophet Muhammad are referred to as Imams. Imam is an honorary title for outstanding Muslim personalities in Islamic history. Imam Hussein's story is often told in Iran due to his martyrdom.
"Such events bring people closer to religion again. Additionally, we maintain social contacts with friends and family through these gatherings. We share our lives and see how we can help each other in difficult phases of life."
Somayeh's daughter Reyhaneh recently turned nine years old and has now reached the age of *taklif*. In Shiite Islam, from this age onward, women are required to fulfill their religious duties, particularly daily prayers and wearing the hijab. The hijab refers to the covering of the female body, except for the face and hands. Since 1983, the Islamic Republic of Iran has legally mandated the hijab in public, and it is not a free choice for women. However, the younger generations do not agree with the hijab guidelines in their mandatory form and are developing their own fashion appearances. They have found a unique way to express themselves. Reyhaneh proudly tells her cousin that, from now on, she is not allowed to kiss or hug any man—except her father, uncles, grandfathers, and her future husband.

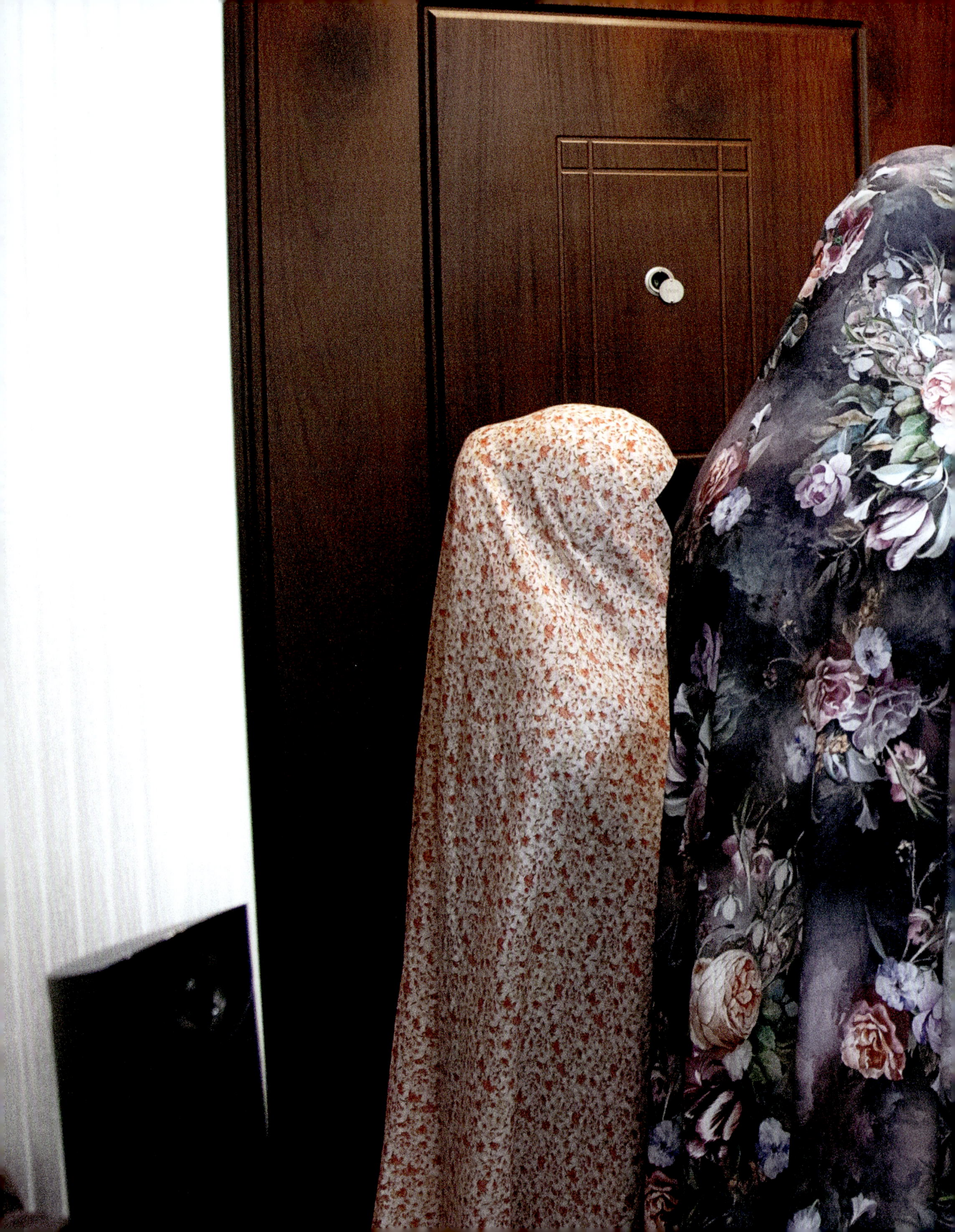

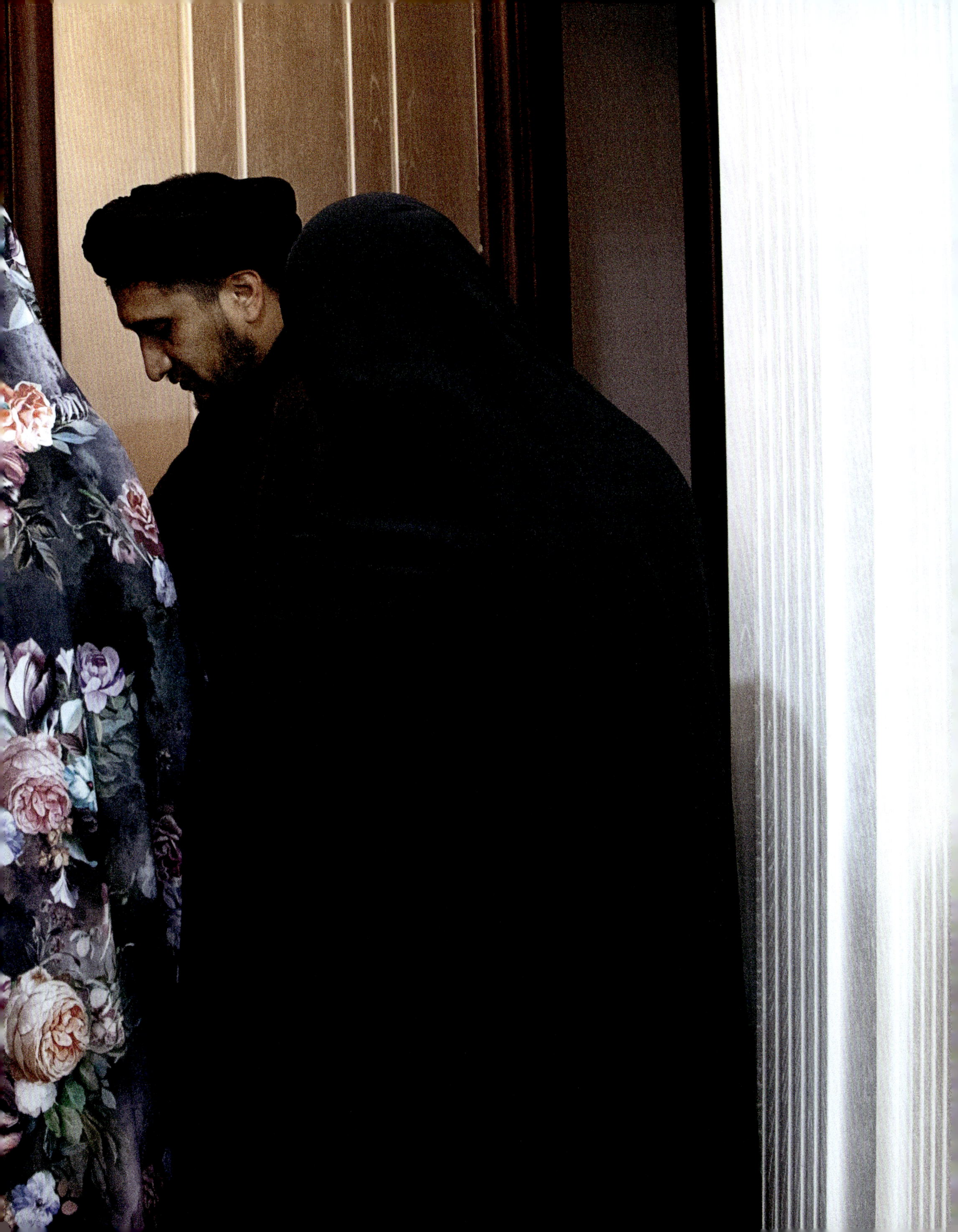

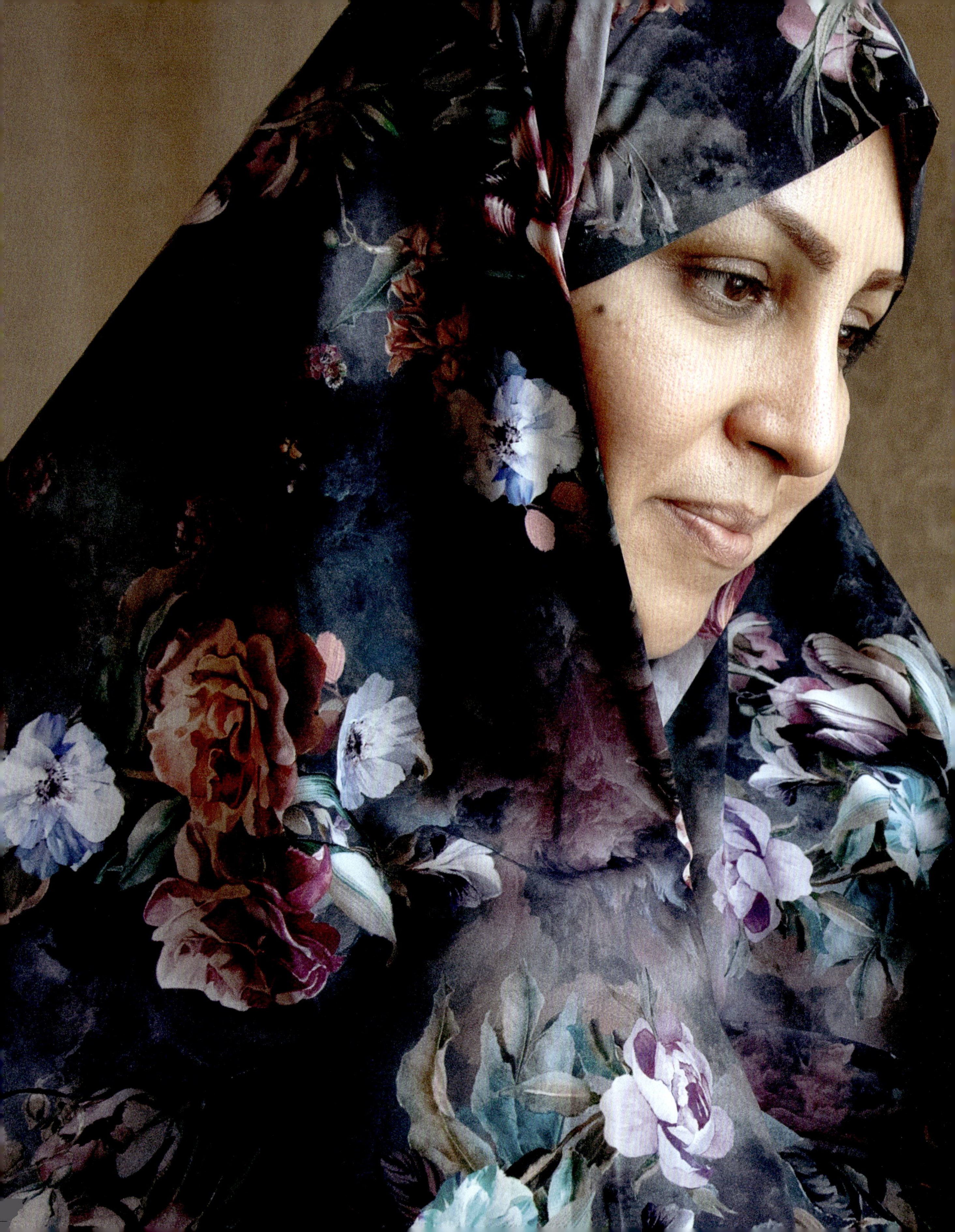

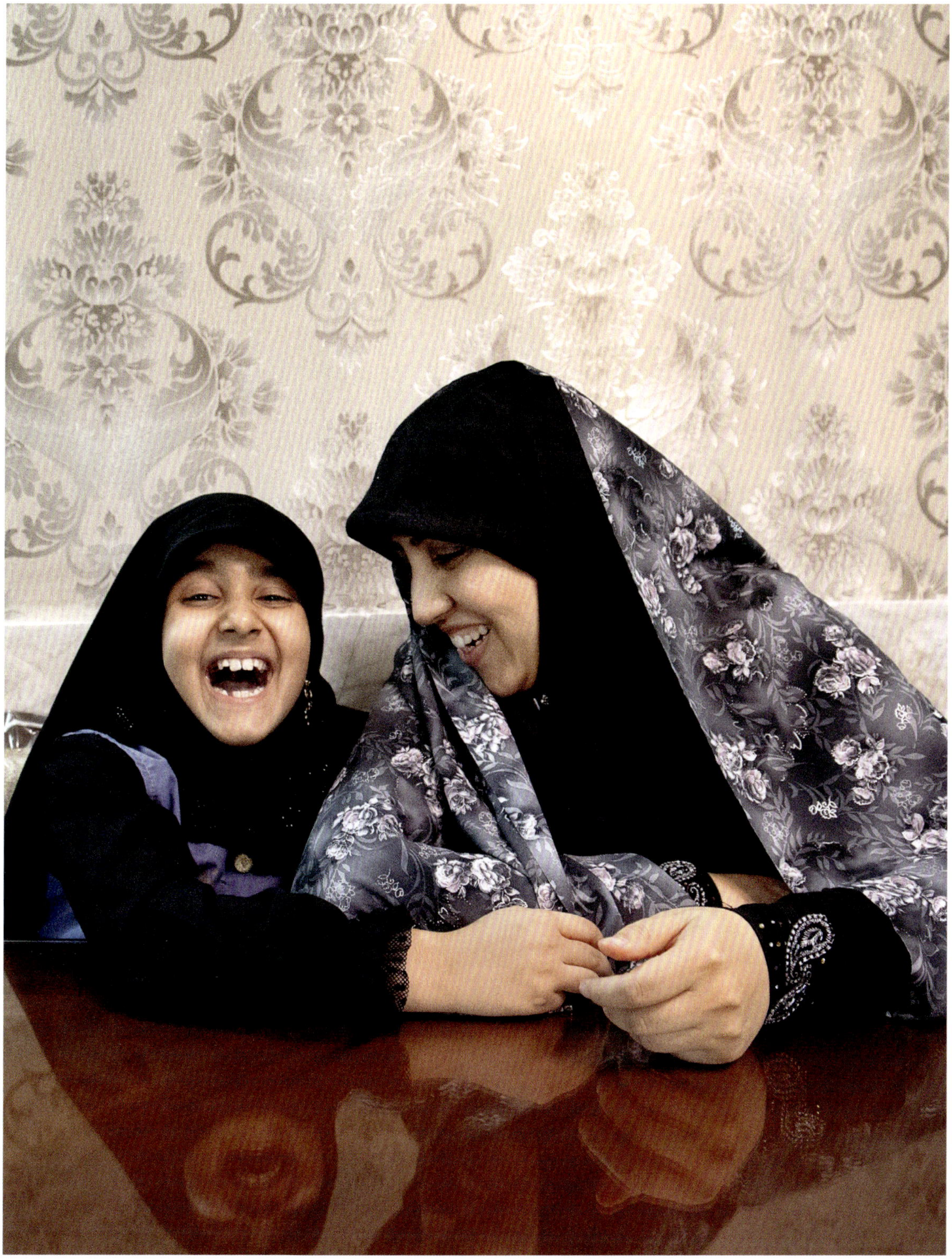

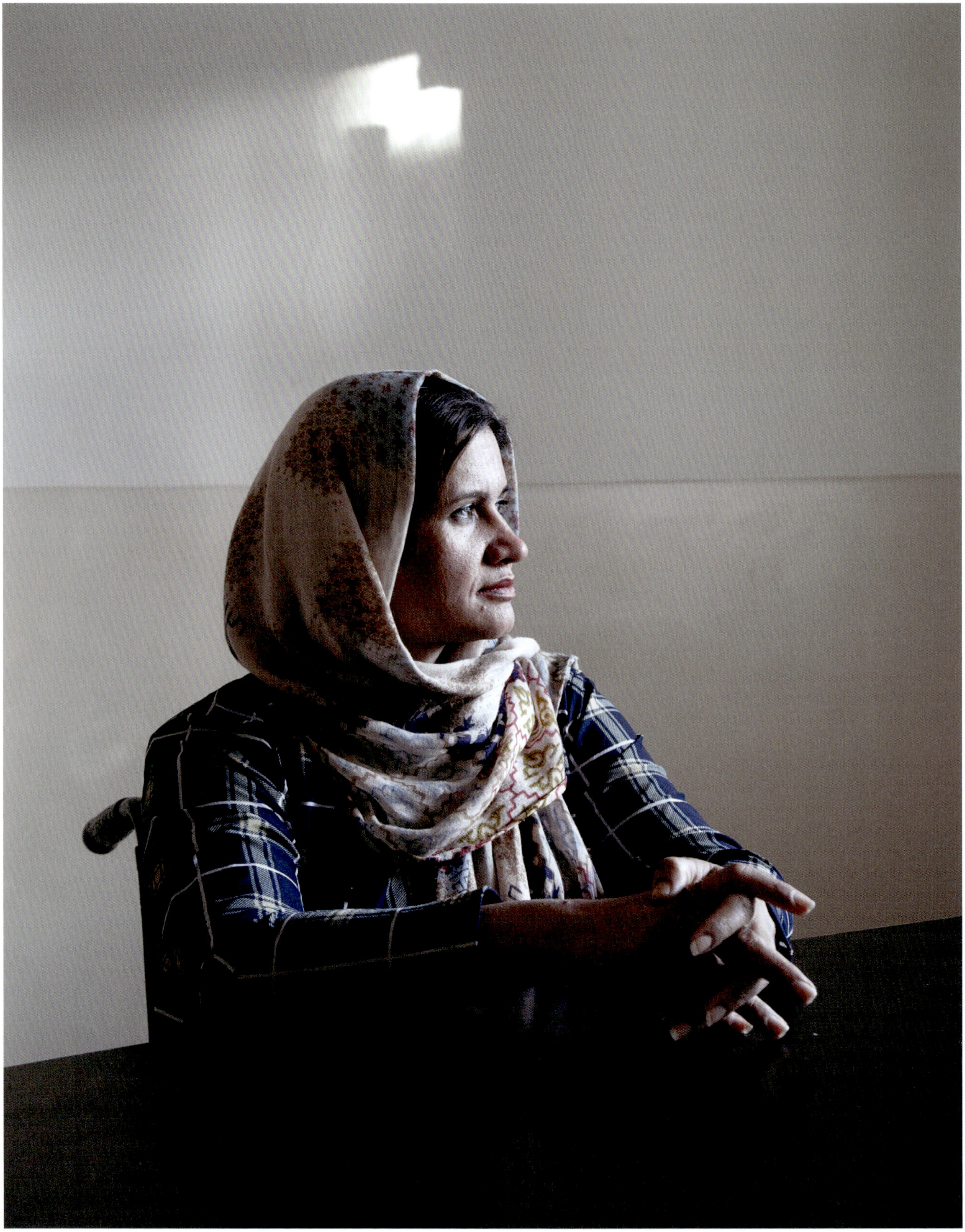

Nesa Khoshniat

Nesa has been in a wheelchair since 2006 after a car accident. She spent a total of one year in the hospital and underwent eighteen surgeries—on her legs, arms, hips, and injured internal organs. Before her accident, she worked as an elementary school teacher in the city of Shirvan, located in eastern Iran near the pilgrimage city of Mashhad. However, since she was unable to work for over a year and is now in a wheelchair, she was terminated with the following explanation: *"It is not possible to create a barrier-free environment at the school."* Nesa shares: *"I often contemplated taking my own life. I was very frustrated and depressed for a long time. But the physiotherapy sessions helped me to meet people with similar fates. This allowed me to rehabilitate not only physically but also mentally. I continued to use a wheelchair, but I also discovered new perspectives and ways of looking at things. Over time, I learned to work with a computer and later found a job where I could teach people how to use one."*

At that time, Nesa lived in Shirvan with her husband and son. For every follow-up examination, she had to travel to the city of Mashhad, which was 200 kilometers away. Shortly thereafter, she moved with her family to the bustling metropolis. *"After a while, my husband divorced me after twenty-four years of marriage. Another shock. After weeks of deep sorrow and many tears, I found my way back to myself and set a big goal for myself."* Nesa, along with her friends, founded the Association for the Support of People with Spinal Cord Injuries. *"Those who suddenly find themselves unable to walk due to an accident need to understand that they cannot return to their old lives. We help them learn to cope with the new situation and find a new way back to life."*

Most of these people are unable to continue their previous professions, which is why Nesa places a lot of emphasis on her association providing support for a new career orientation. They offer various courses such as sewing and carpentry. Nesa says: *"Work is like therapy for me—it gives me a sense of strength, joy, and confidence. The feedback I receive about my work motivates me."*

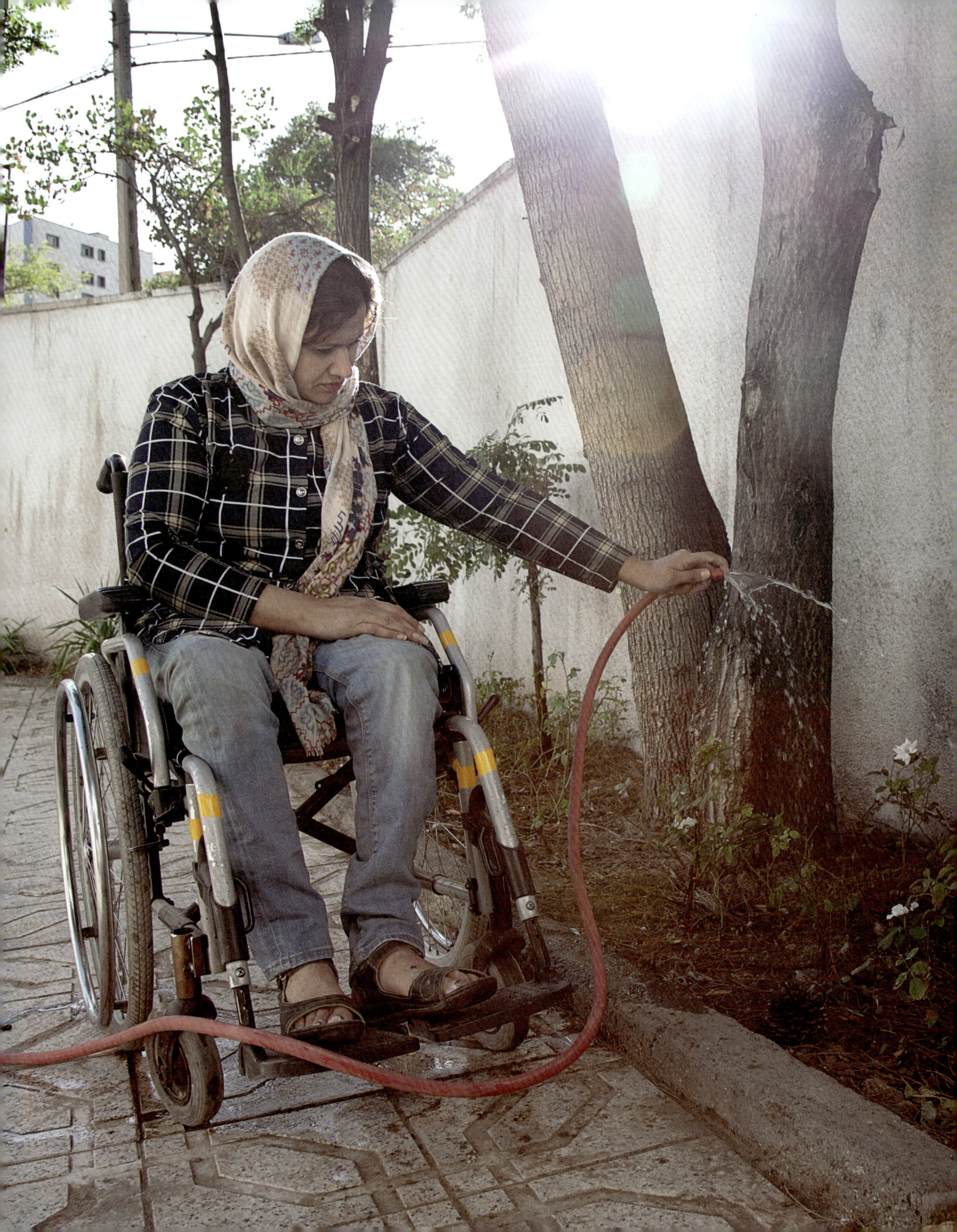

"Work is like therapy for me—it gives me a sense of strength, joy, and confidence."

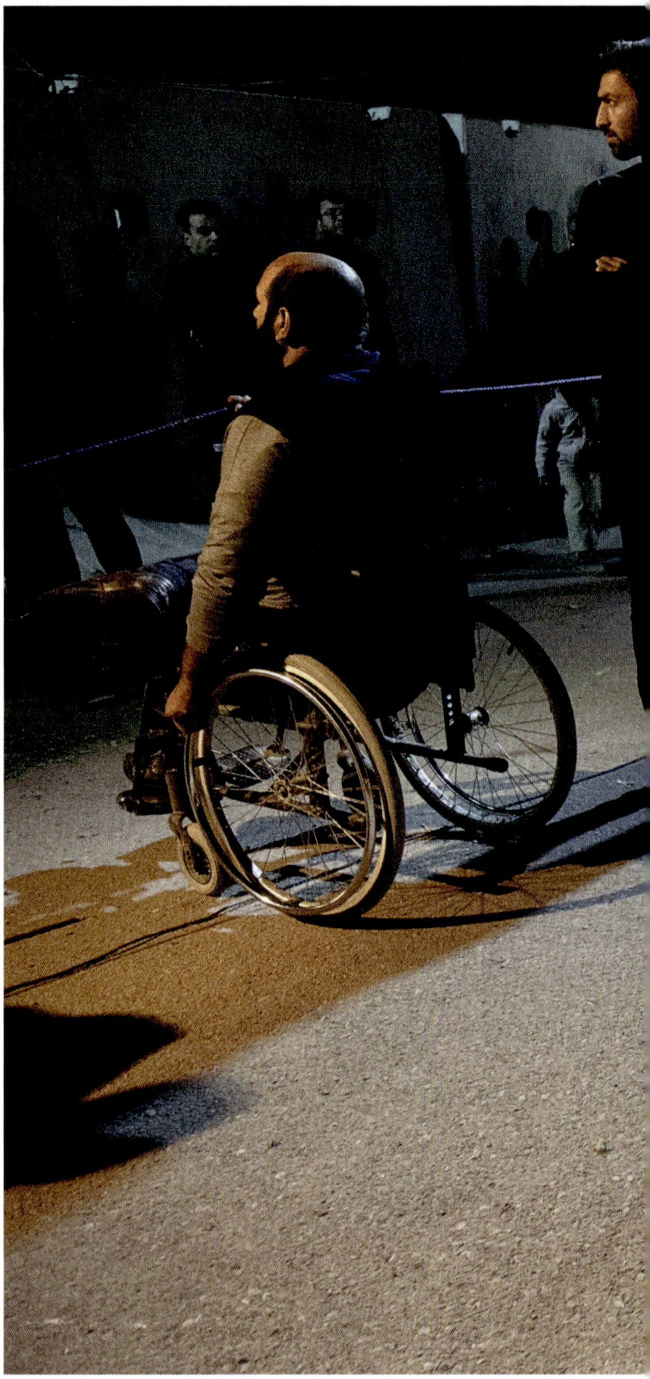

"One of the reasons why people with disabilities in Iran are isolated and have a low presence in society is the inadequate accessibility in public places. We always need assistance from others for simple tasks like shopping in a supermarket or for regular bureaucratic errands. That's why we show people with physical disabilities through our association how they can live independently again despite obstacles. We give them tips on what to do in specific situations to manage their daily lives. But we also exchange experiences and expand our knowledge together," says the forty-one-year-old.

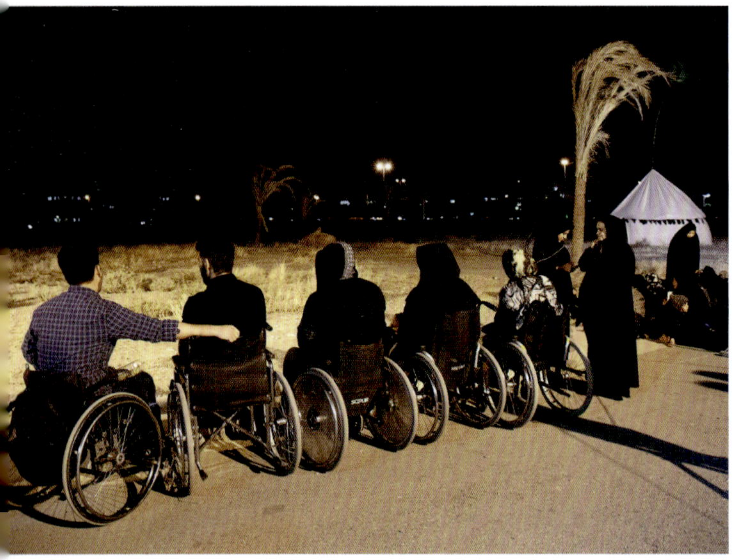

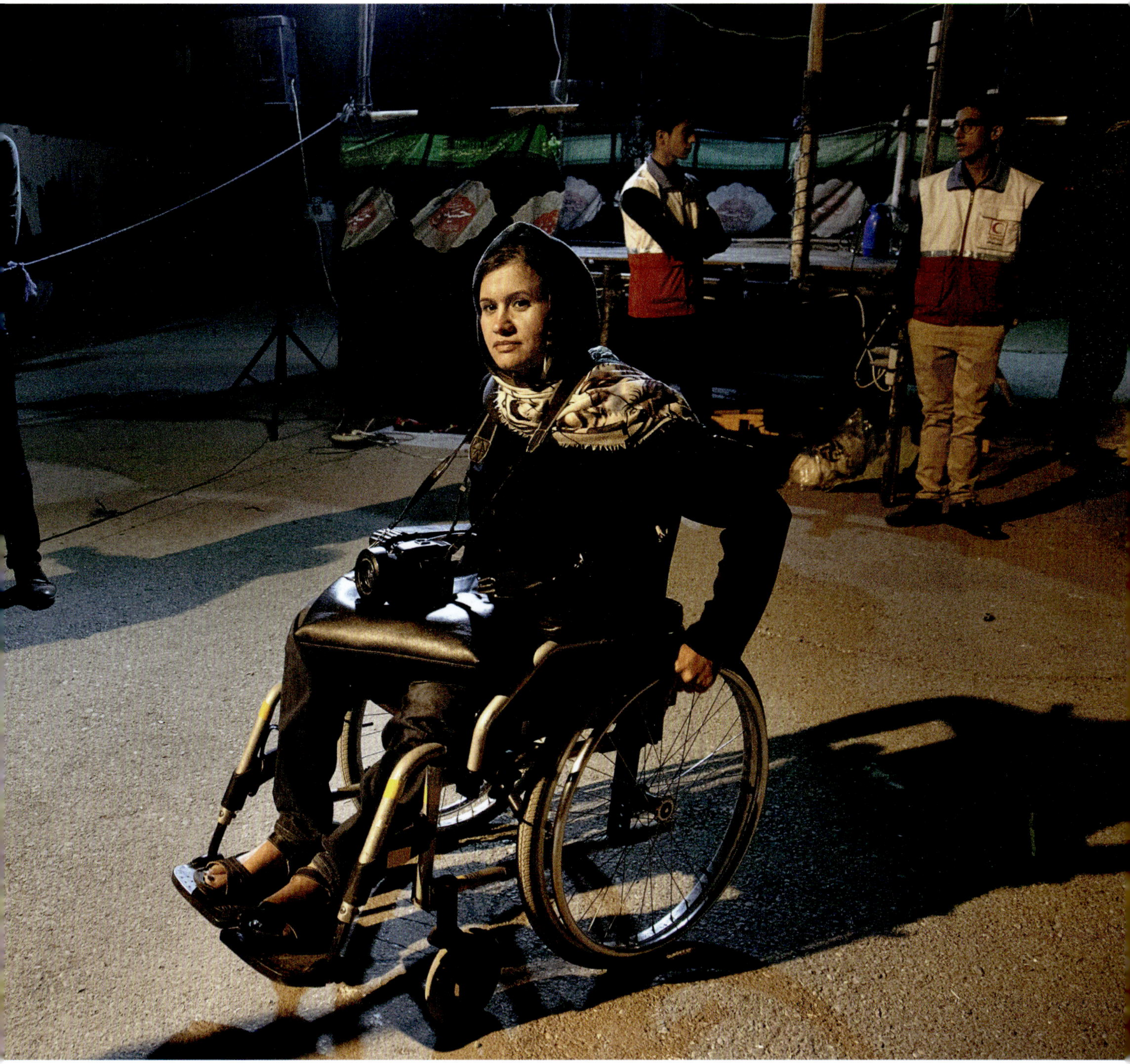

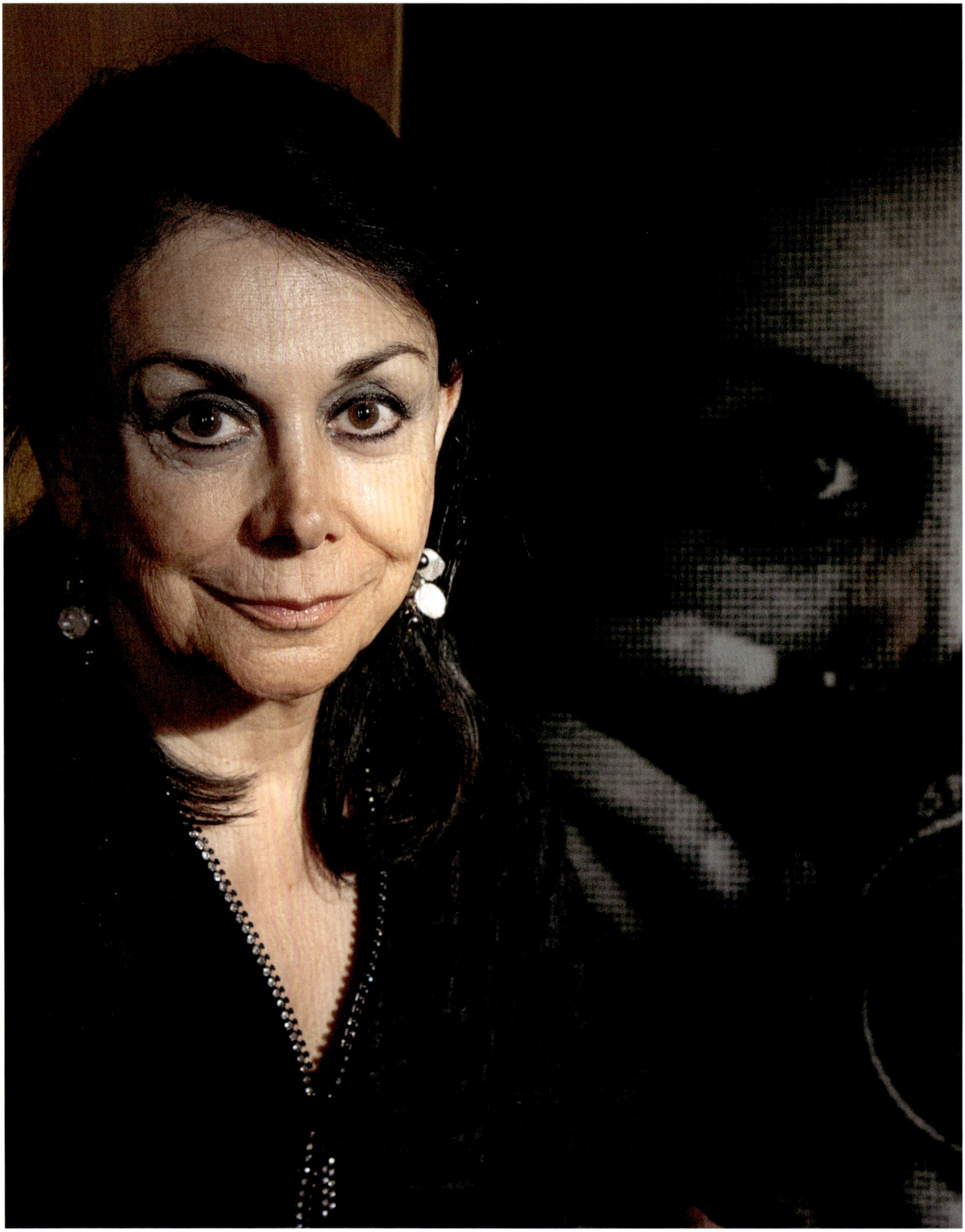

Maryam Zandi

"I have struggled to be recognized in society and had to prove myself in a male-dominated field," says Maryam, a veteran of Iranian photography. In her career spanning over fifty years, Maryam Zandi has published more than fifteen photobooks, starting with her first one, *Turkmen and Sahra*, which was released in 1982. She photographed seminomadic ethnic Turkmen from northeastern Iran near the Caspian Sea. This is the first book about Turkmen and also the first volume on ethnographic photography to be published in Iran.

One of her significant long-term photographic projects, *Chehreh'ha*, which means portraits, began in 1981 and concluded in 2017. This project led to the publication of five photobooks about the contemporary intellectual elite of Iran. In these books, Maryam addressed personalities in the fields of literature, theater/cinema, art, and music. In addition to portrait photography, she has dedicated herself to nature and landscape photography.

In 2005, Maryam, along with twelve other renowned Iranian photographers, cofounded the National Iranian Photographers Society in Tehran and was elected its first chairperson. Throughout these years, she faced many obstacles that her male colleagues were spared. Despite all adversity, she never lost hope and *"worked much harder"* than her male counterparts. Maryam Zandi has made a name for herself in her career and is considered one of the most active and influential photographers in Iran. In 2010, she received an independent award from the Sheed Award as the most influential photographer of the year for supporting the rights of Iranian photographers. Four years later, she won the same award again for advocating the uncensored publication of the book *The Revolution of Iran 79*.

In her book *The Revolution of Iran 79*, she recalls one of her memories from those days: *"In spite of governmental threats and warnings, people were out on the streets, together with their fists and voices, and I was there with my little daughter and my camera. I couldn't stay at home. Events had been taking place for some time and I was roaming the city, camera in hand. I felt responsible. I had to take photographs, to record what was taking place."* And elsewhere, she wrote: *"I still don't know and can't remember how I climbed the stairs of that ten-story building with a baby and a camera. I was able to take pictures that now look to me like they were aerial photographs of Daneshgah Street and the teeming masses of demonstrators."*

The seventy-three-year-old prominent photographer states: *"In my opinion, starting a family has always been a career impediment for women. Once my children were grown, I opted to live alone to concentrate on my photography."*

Maryam Zandi examines the test print of her book *The Government of 80*, printed in 2018 by a publisher named Nazar in Tehran. Forty years after the Islamic Revolution, she presents the second part of her images in this volume, documenting the establishment of the Islamic Republic of Iran and the events after the revolution. In the first part of the photobook *The Revolution of Iran 79*, in turn, she depicts the events just before and during the 1979 revolution. This book waited six years for permission to be published because the Ministry of Culture and Islamic Guidance had asked Zandi to remove thirty images from the series, particularly pictures of protesting women without headscarves. *"I disagreed with omitting or censoring a part of Iranian history because of the narrow-mindedness of some people. Therefore, I fought six years for it."*

Maryam proudly says: *"After all these years of hard work and effort, I can say that I was victorious and successful in this struggle; I have published my images and many books, have organized many exhibitions in Iran—and abroad—and have significantly shaped the Iranian photography community as a prominent photographer."*

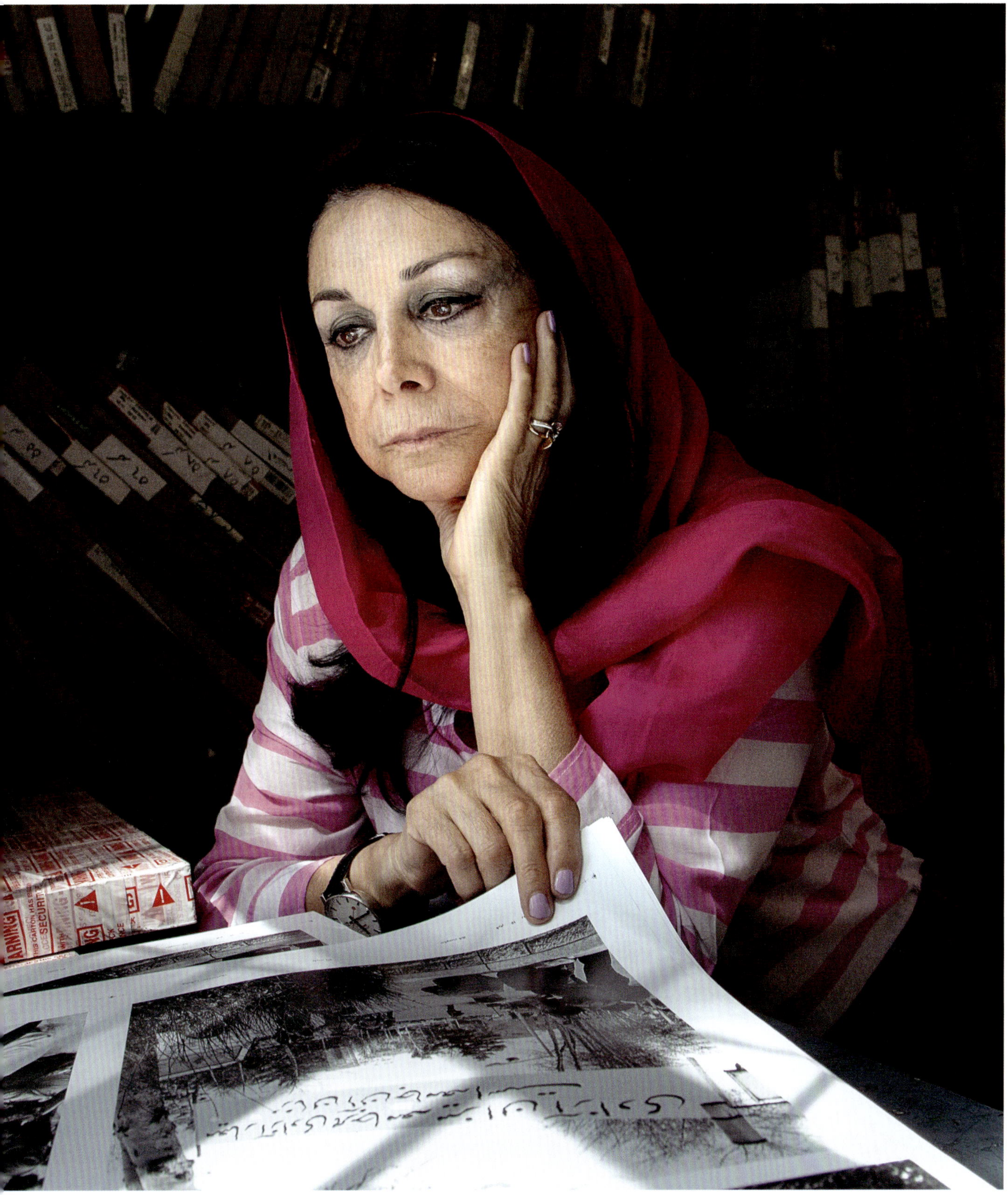

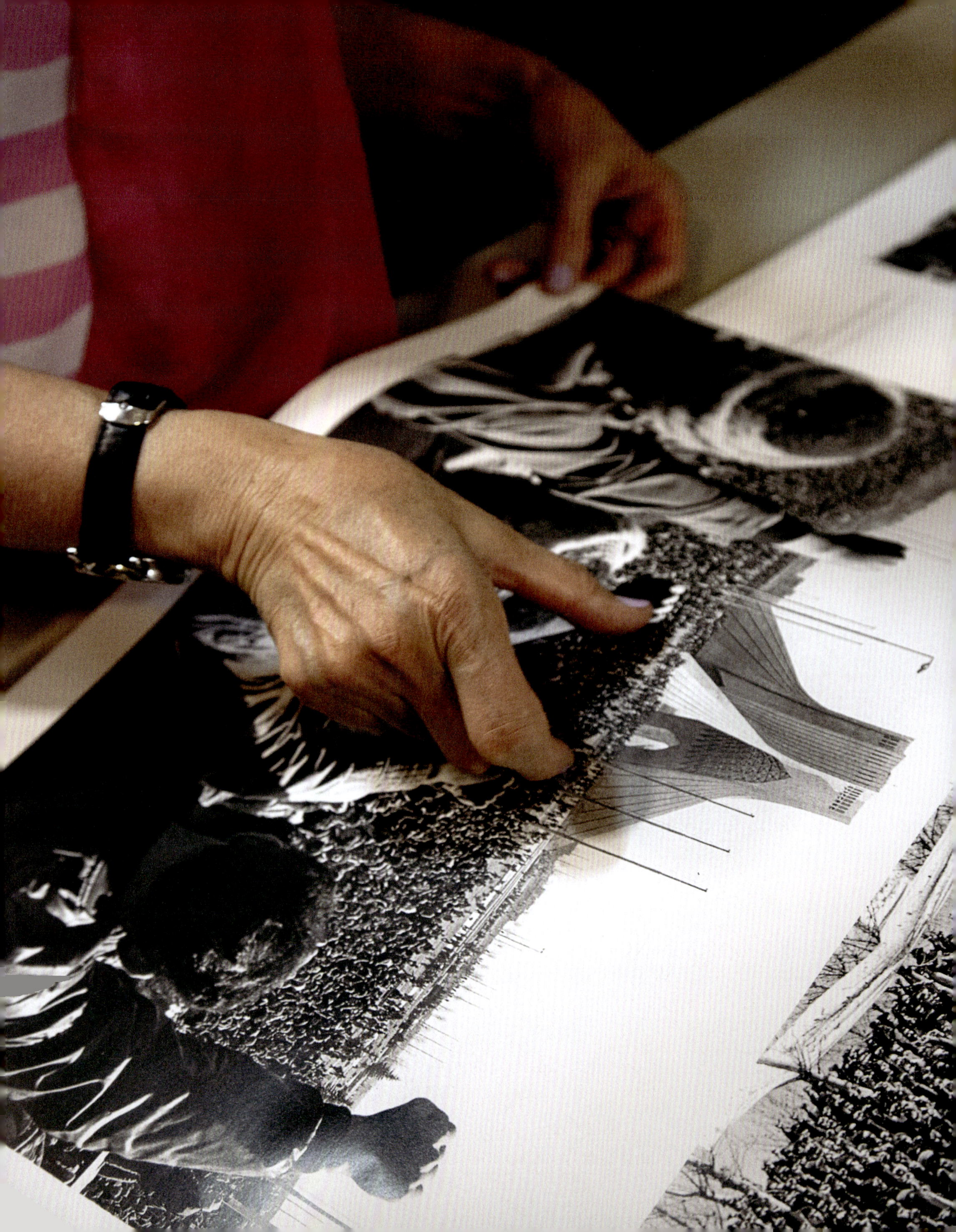

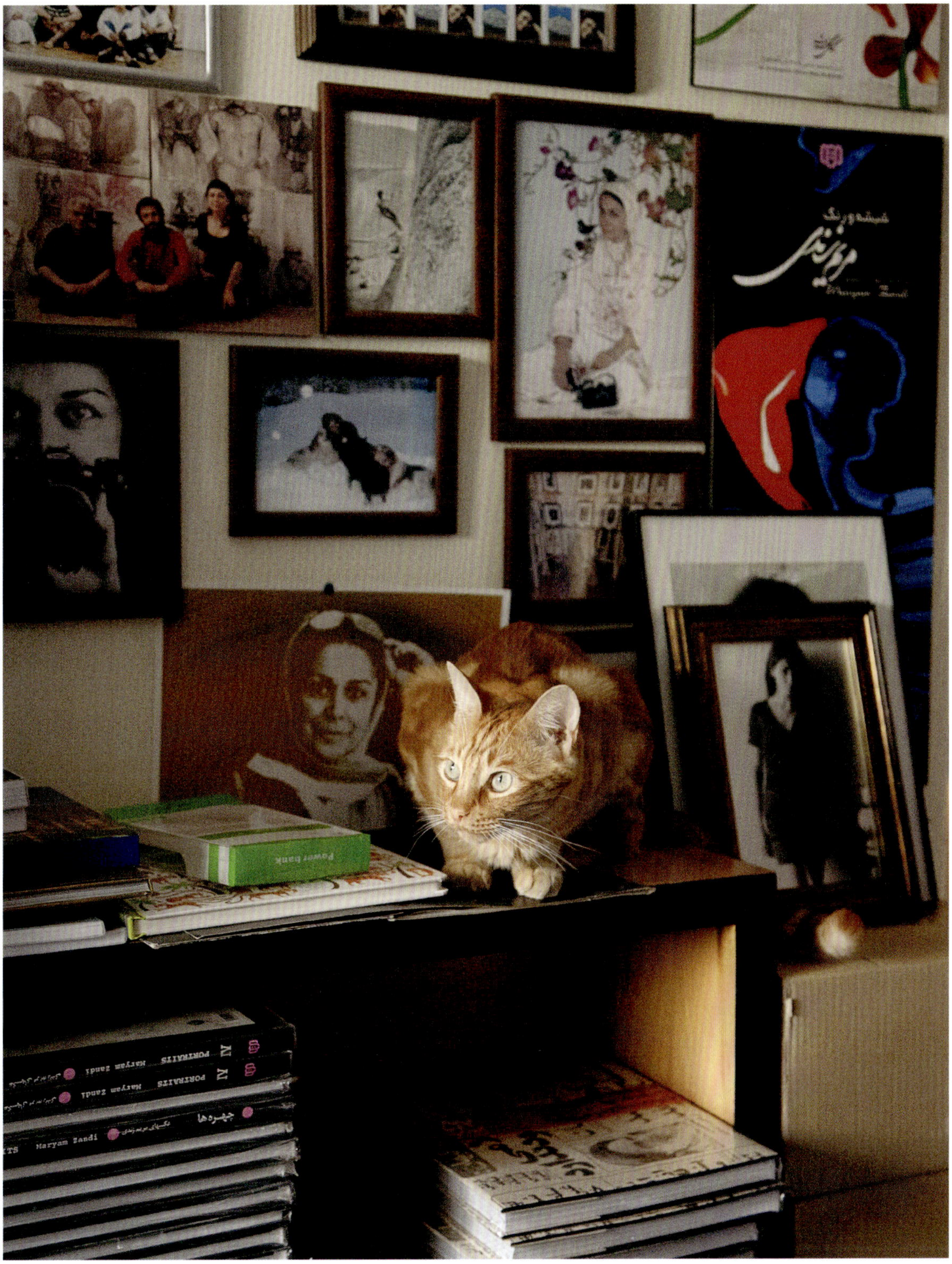

PORTRAITS Maryam Zandi
چهره‌ها
Maryam Zandi

“I had to work much harder than my male colleagues to reach my current position.”

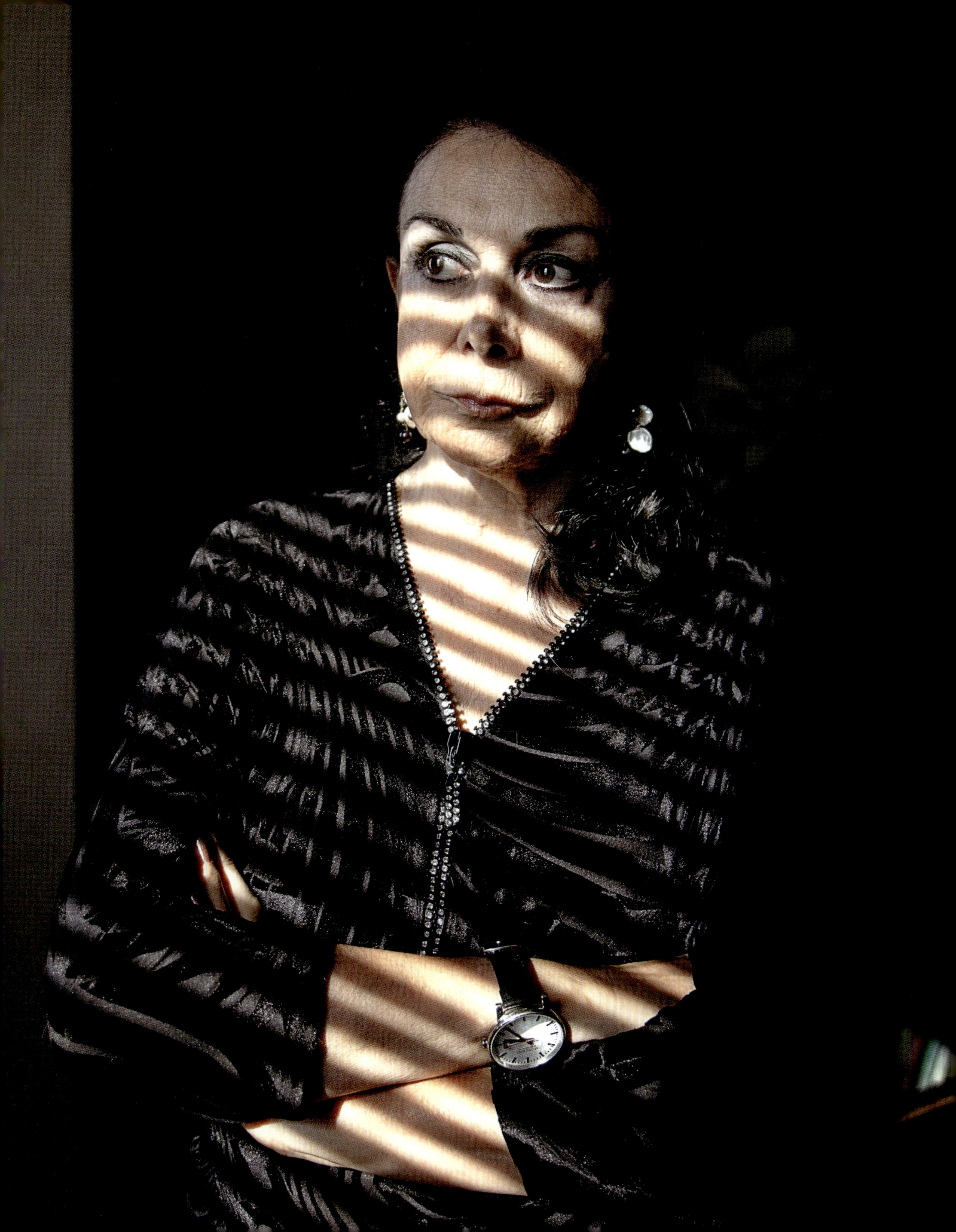

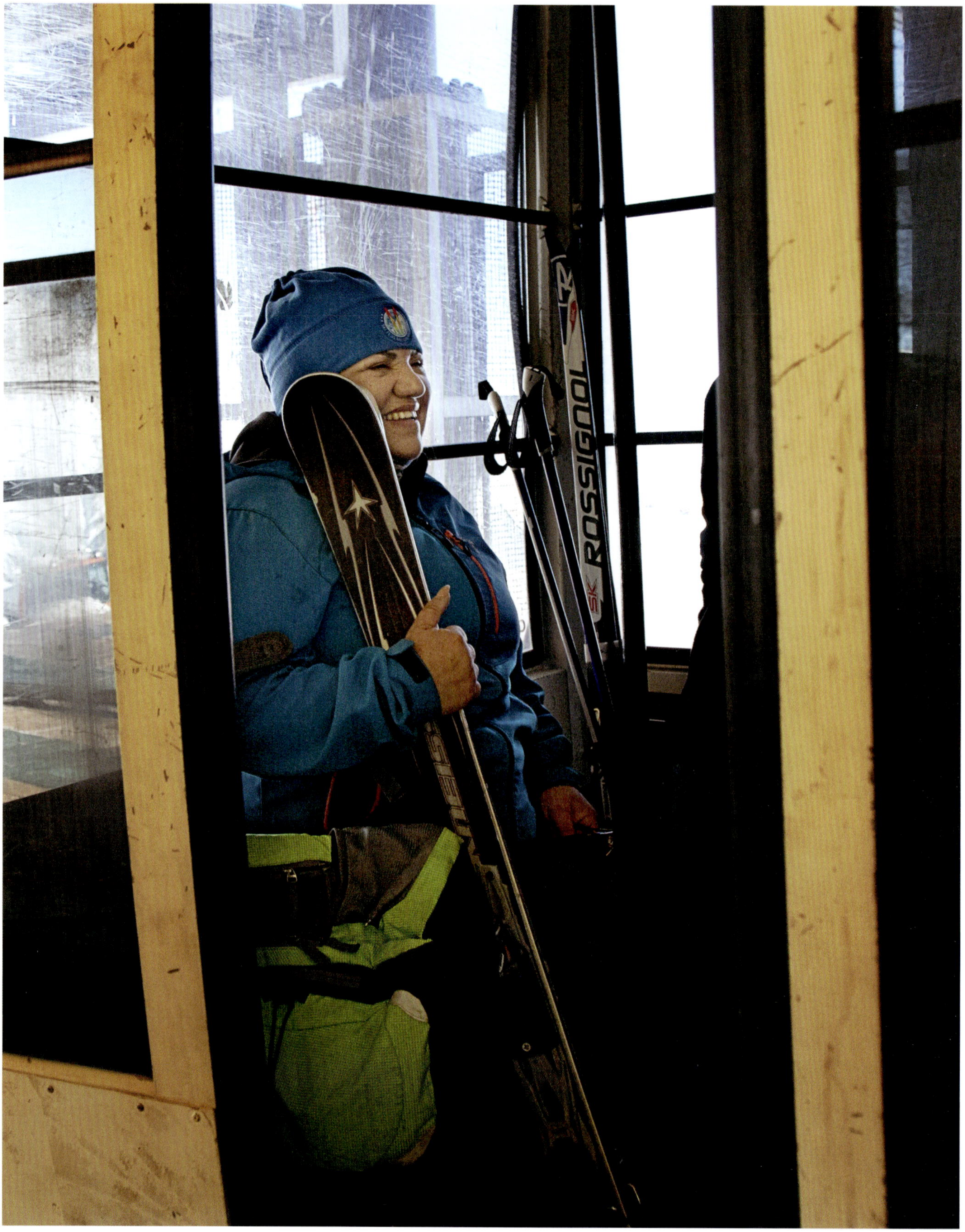
ROSSIGNOL

Masoumeh Kalhor

Masoumeh fondly remembers her first time on skis, trying to navigate down a small hill without falling. It took several days before she could do it without an instructor. Thirty-five years ago, at the start of the Islamic Republic of Iran, male ski instructors were not allowed to teach women, and there were very few female trainers, all of whom worked in other ski resorts. However, the operators of the ski resort recognized the strong interest of women and soon hired female ski instructors. Masoumeh and a few other women from her village were among the fortunate few whose families had no issue with women participating in the sport.

The forty-eight-year-old describes her father's support as her *"great fortune,"* for it allowed her to pursue the sport at the age of fourteen without any hindrance. *"At first, my five brothers were not as enthusiastic, but when they saw how passionately and eagerly I skied, they too encouraged and supported me."* Even later, after she got married, Masoumeh had the full support of her husband, who also enjoys hitting the slopes. At the age of twenty-four, she completed a ski instructor training program, turning her hobby into a profession.

"As the first female ski instructor in the Darbandsar ski resort, I have been working for twenty-four years and now also support young talents in the women's national ski team." As a local and experienced skier, she helps young athletes focus on their training. She takes care of the entire organization and planning of the training season and collaborates with the coaching staff.

Darbandsar is located 60 kilometers northeast of Tehran in the Alborz Mountains and is a popular and well-visited ski resort among locals and tourists alike. Situated at an altitude of 2,550 meters, Darbandsar is among the three most popular winter sports areas in Iran; the other two are Shemshak and Dizin. All three are located within a radius of 10 kilometers. Dizin is also Mahsoumeh's hometown, where her father worked in the nearby Gajereh coal mine. This meant she only had to travel a few meters from home to the ski slope. The Alborz Mountains also include Mount Damavand, at 5,610 meters the highest peak in Iran, which can be admired from the ski resorts. During the ski season, many affluent Iranian tourists come to the mountains for skiing. But even outside the ski season, it is a popular retreat from the hustle and bustle of the city, offering the opportunity to enjoy the fresh, and above all, clean air. Many Tehran residents take advantage of their weekends to hike in the mountains or visit one of the ski resort's many restaurants.

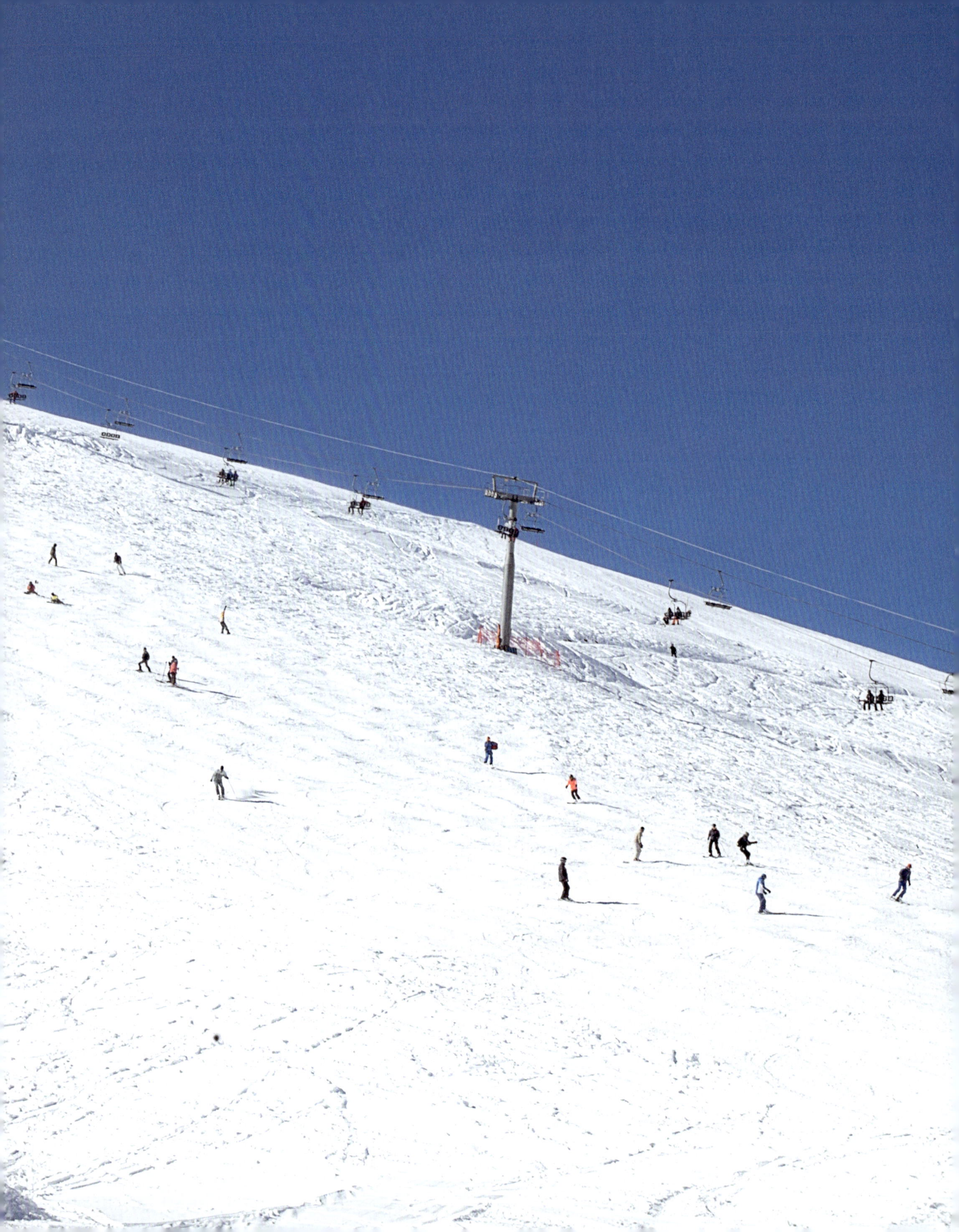

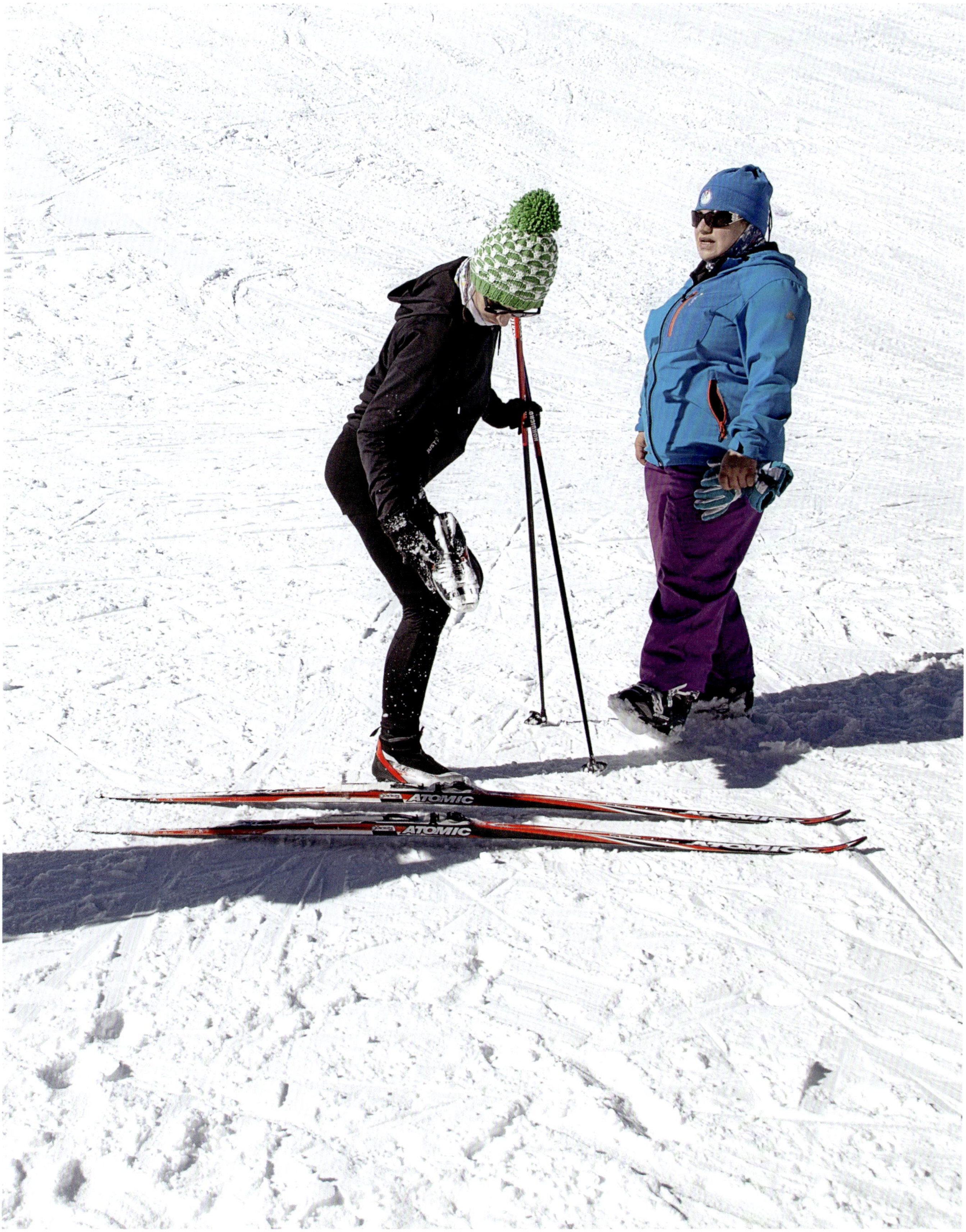
ATOMIC
ATOMIC

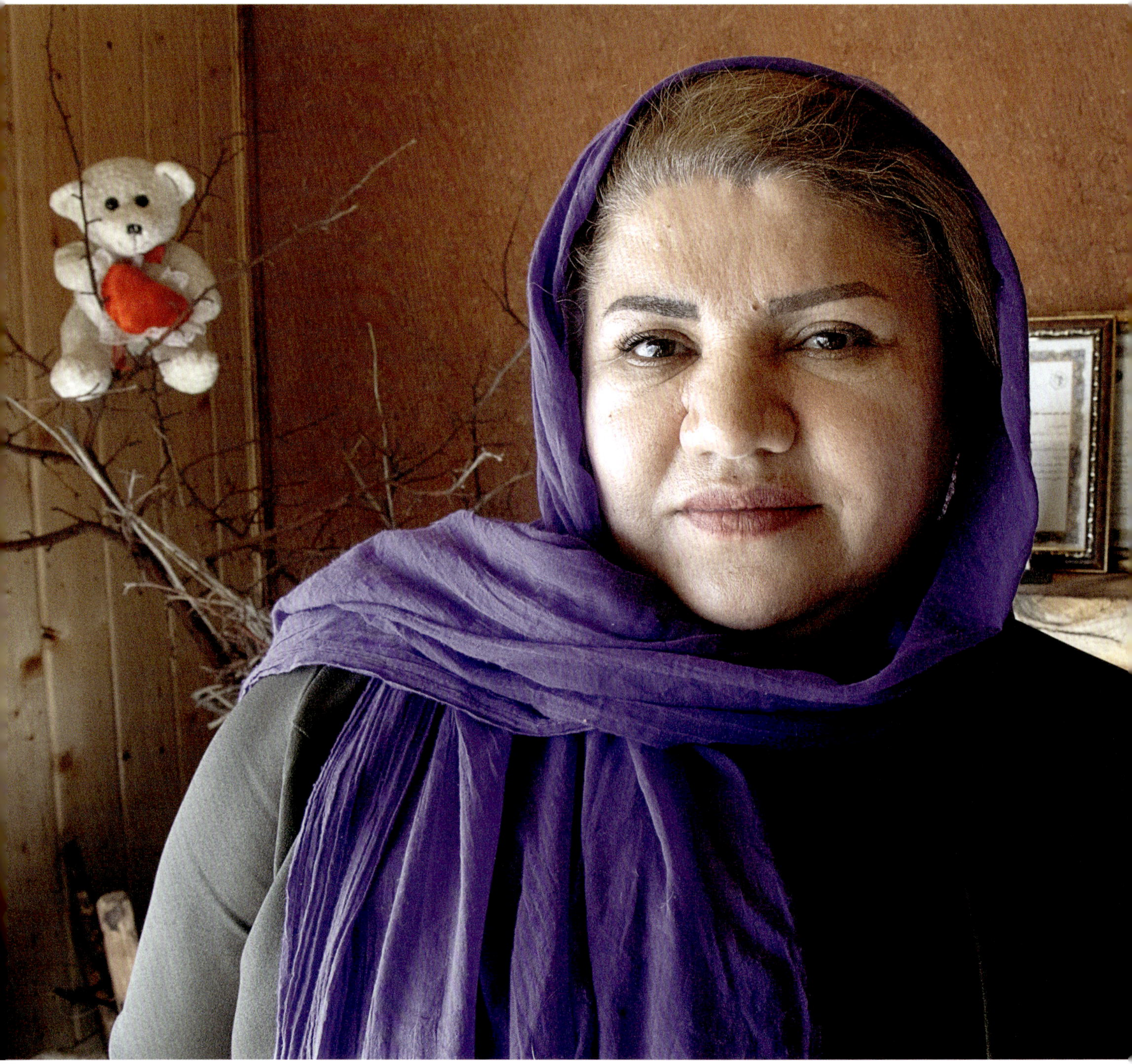

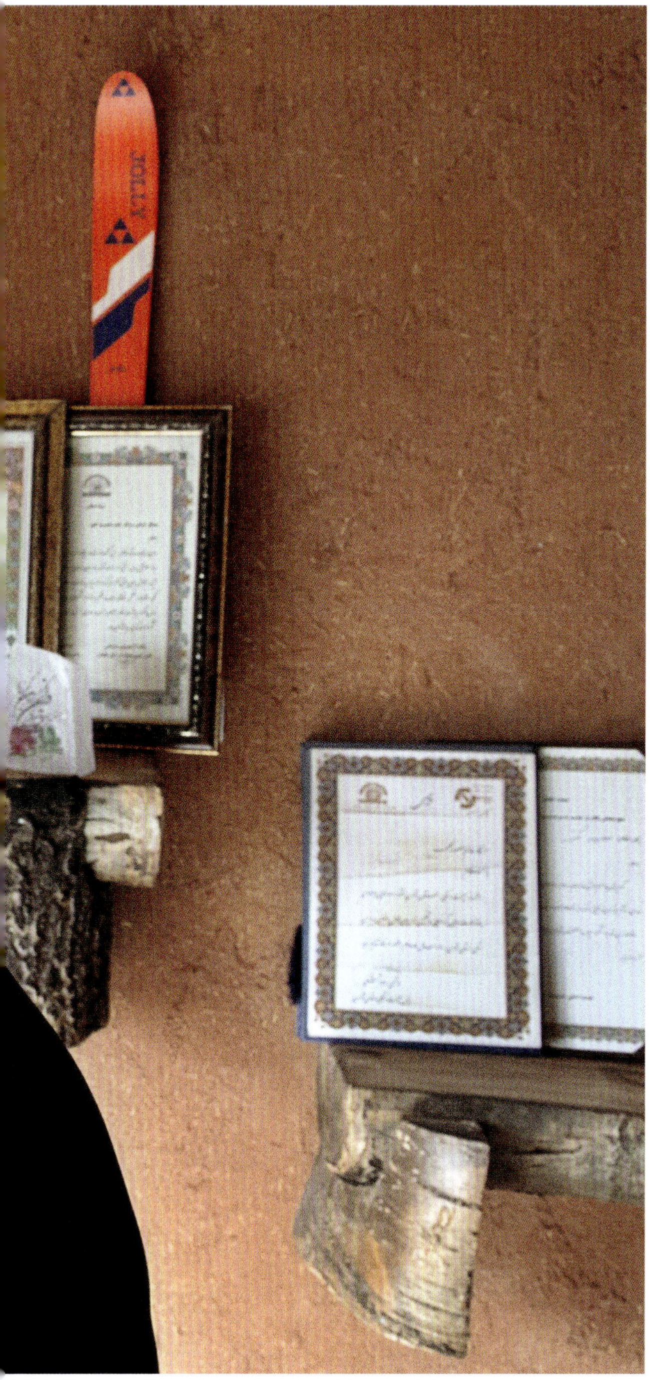

Masoumeh lives with her husband and son in their own house in Darbandsar, where her husband runs a traditional restaurant right next to the ski slope. The menu features typical Iranian dishes, mostly with rice, grilled meat, or chicken. *"Our restaurant is open all year round, but we have the most guests during the ski season. That's when my husband has the hardest time in the restaurant, because during the training season for the national team and my ski lessons, I can rarely help out."*
The Ski Sports Association has frequently recognized Masoumeh's work in recent years. She has hung her certificates in her living room next to her son's medal display case. By now, her twenty-three-year-old son shares the enthusiasm for skiing and regularly participates in national and international competitions. *"As a ski enthusiast, I'm naturally very pleased that my son shares the same interest with us. Therefore, I'm also very proud of his athletic achievements and the medals he has won."*

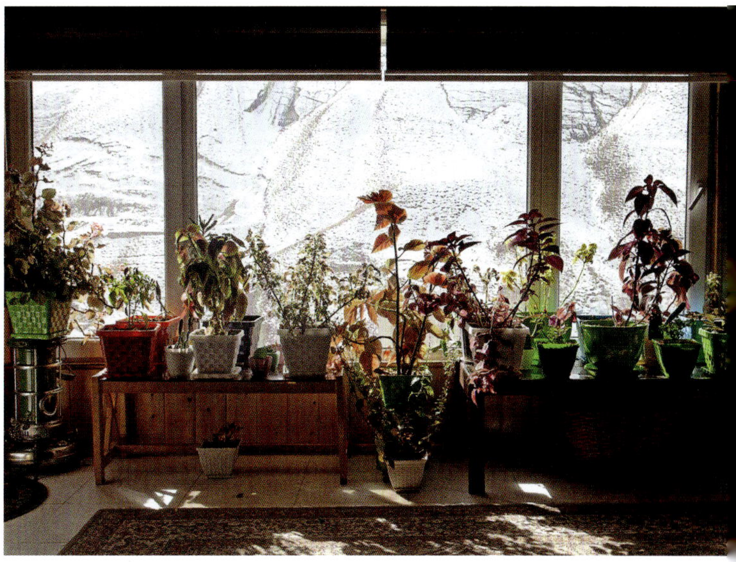

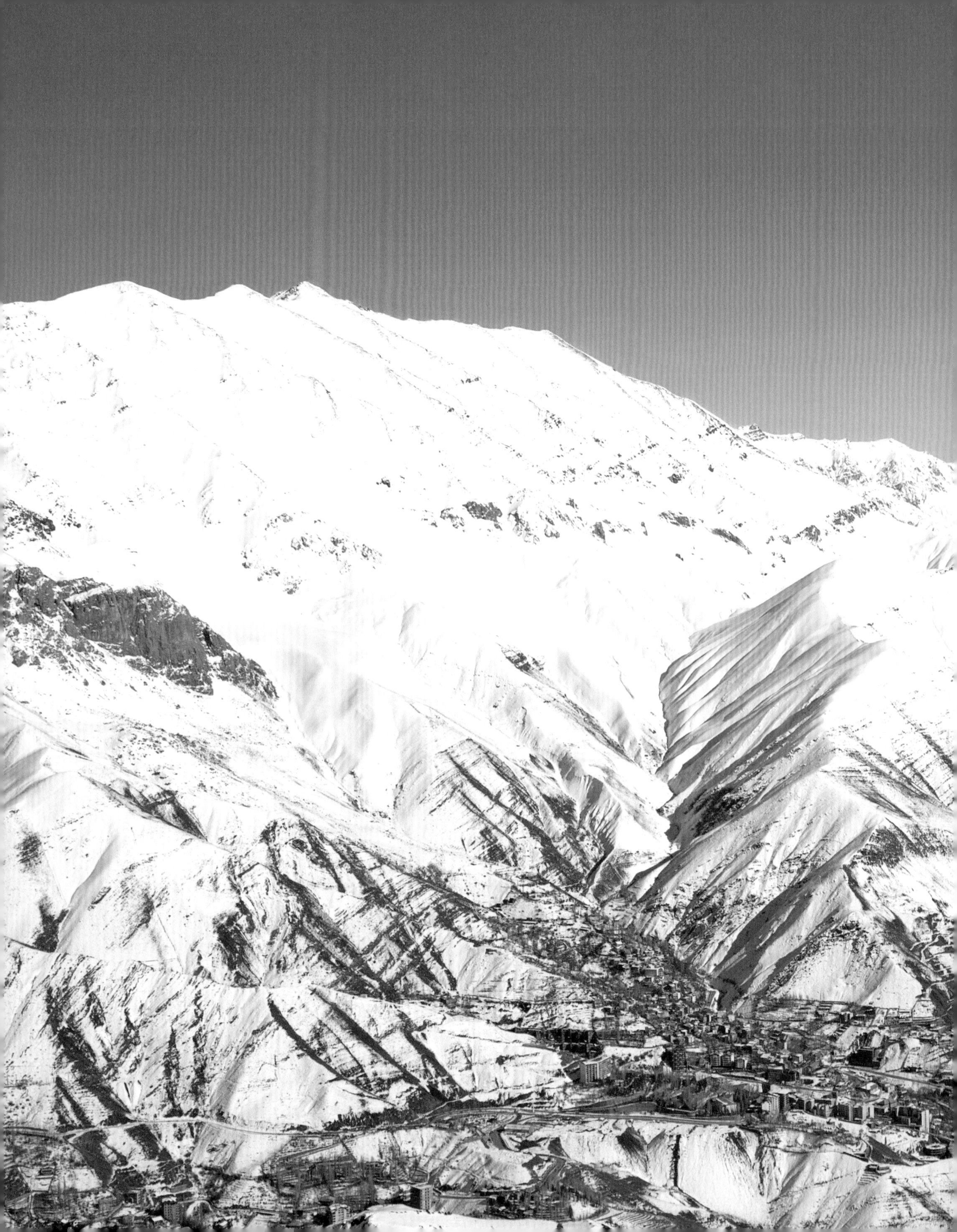

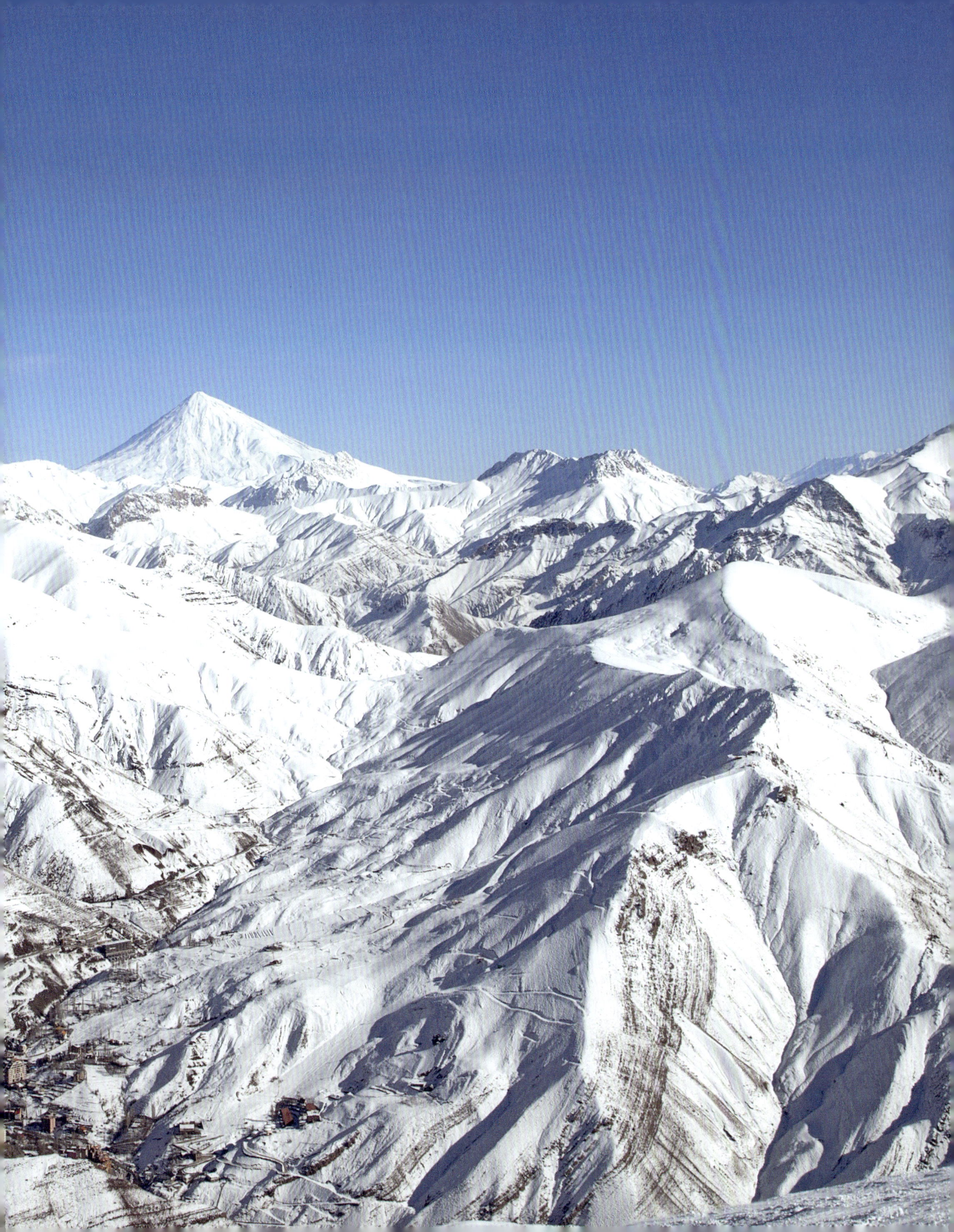

Maryam Khosravi

Golbou is a small village located 150 kilometers south-west of Mashhad in the Khorasan Razavi province and translates as *"Flower Scent."* As one of the saffron cultivation areas, the fragrance of saffron fills the village from late October to late November, which also inspired its name. Maryam and her husband Jafar have been married for thirty-five years and built their own house together fifteen years ago. Before that, they lived with their six-member family in a small adobe hut. Their three daughters pursued higher education, are now all married, and no longer live in the village. *"It was particularly important to me that my children receive a good education, to provide them with an opportunity to escape the routine of village life and the demanding fieldwork."* University education in Iran can be costly without a scholarship. Therefore, Maryam hopes that her sixteen-year-old son will perform well in next year's annual *concour*—the university entrance exam—and secure a spot in a state-funded university. The fifty-six-year-old herself only attended school until the sixth grade. In her hometown, there was only an elementary school up to the sixth grade. For higher education, one had to travel to the nearest cities, which was quite a journey. *"Although my father valued the education of his children, only my brothers were allowed to leave the family home at a young age to attend school in the city. This opportunity was denied to me and my sisters."*

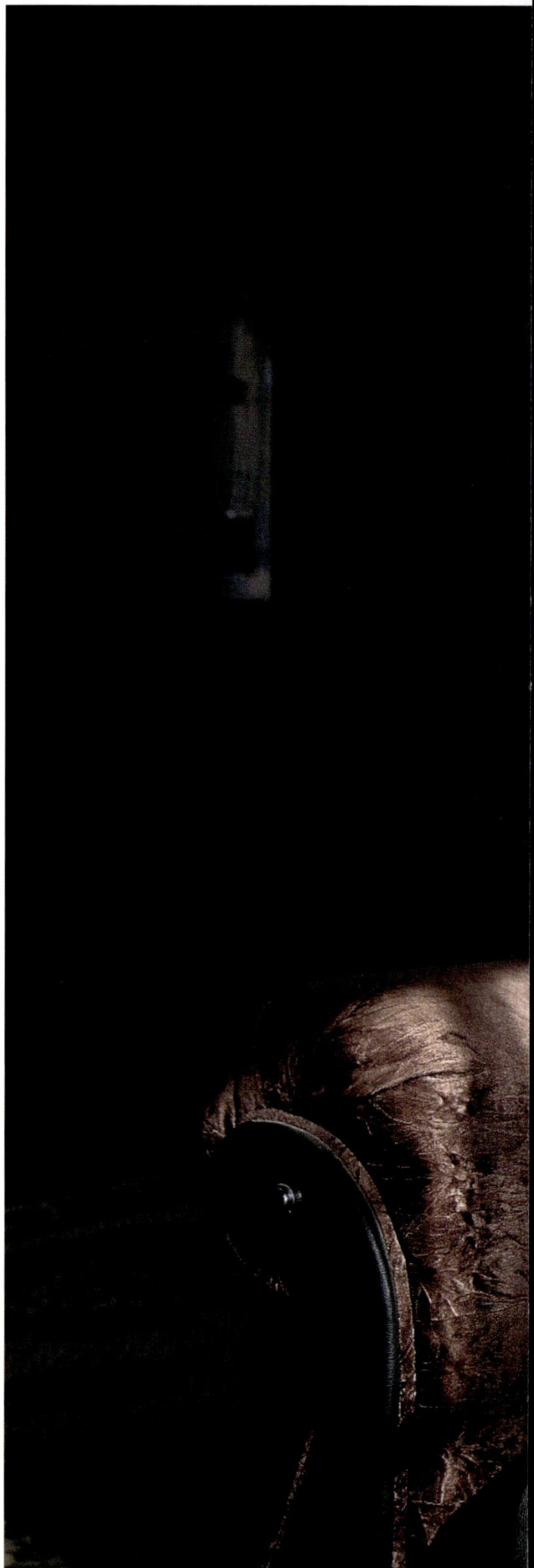

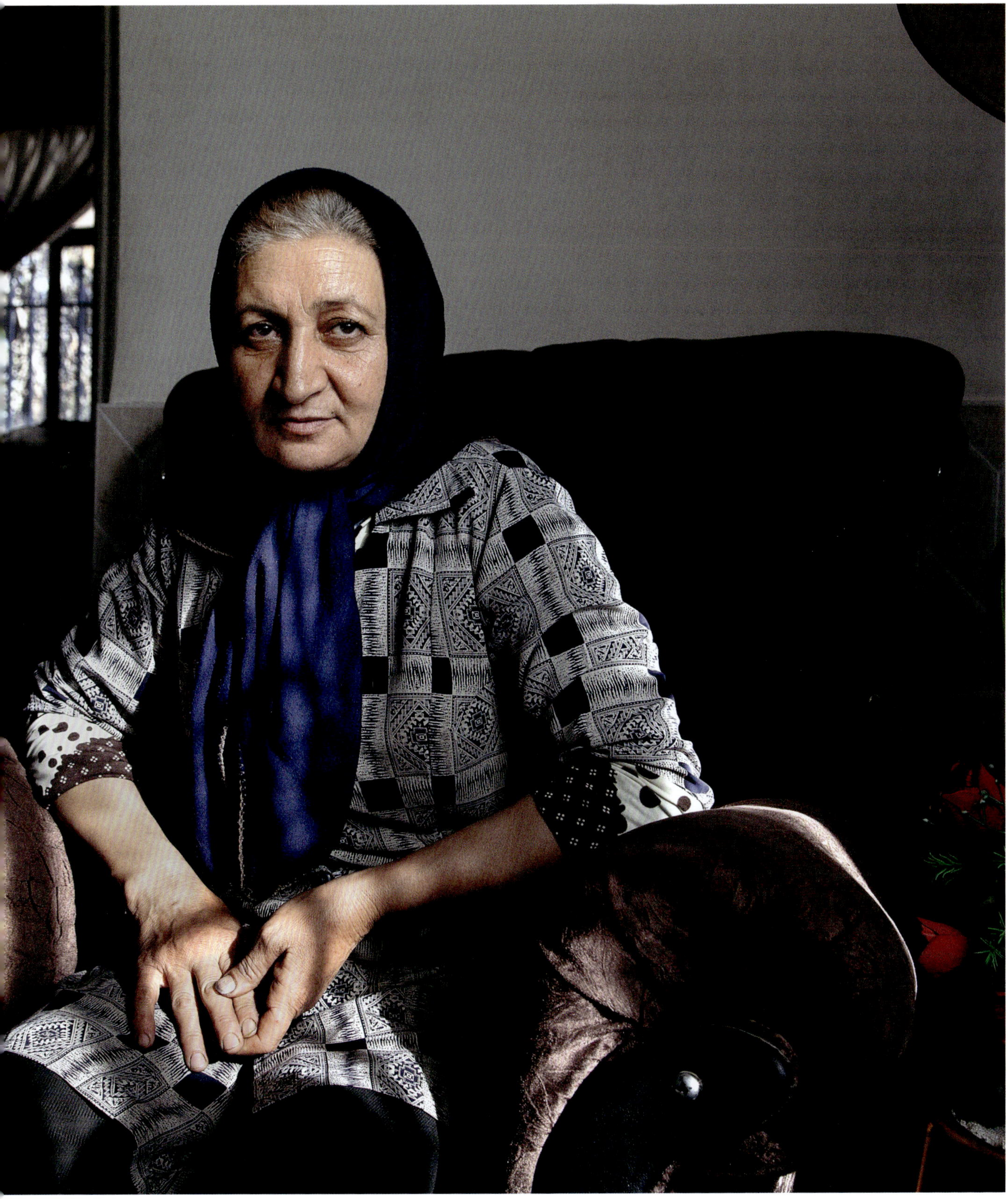

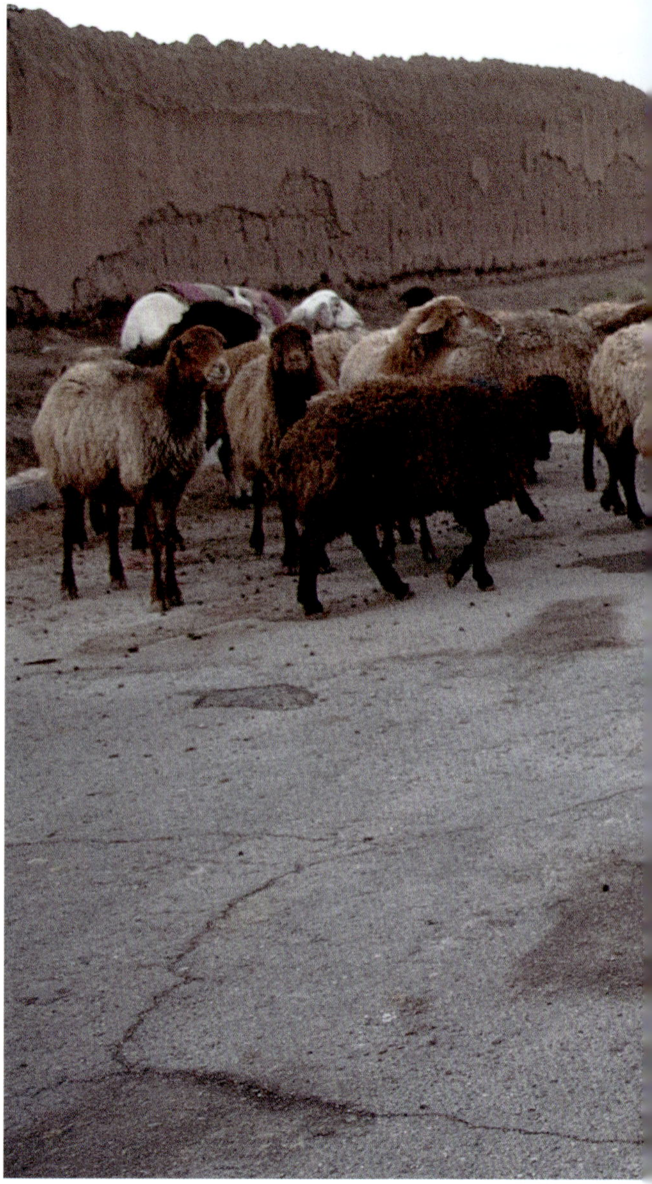

Every day, Maryam and her husband Jafar wake up at 5 o'clock and start their day with a cup of black tea together. Afterward, they head to the stable to let the sheep out. Maryam has already prepared Jafar's food for the day before breakfast. Her husband is usually out with the animals in the pasture from early morning until late at night. While Jafar is out, Maryam takes care of the other animals, prepares food for the chickens, collects the eggs, and cleans the chicken coop. *"I used to also take care of the children. But since they have become more independent, my workload has decreased. But I wouldn't have had the energy to take care of the children, the household, and the animals anymore."*

Maryam and Jafar own a 2,000-square-meter plantation, which, while requiring a lot of work, provides a good additional income for the family. During the saffron harvesting season, each morning after breakfast Maryam ties her chador around her waist and heads to the saffron plantation. The best quality saffron is obtained in November, but only if you gently pick the flowers every day at the first rays of sun, before the temperatures rise.

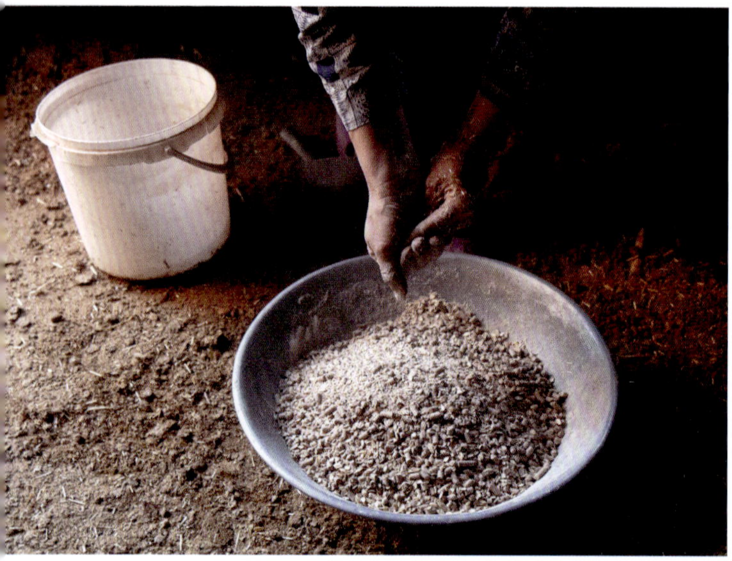

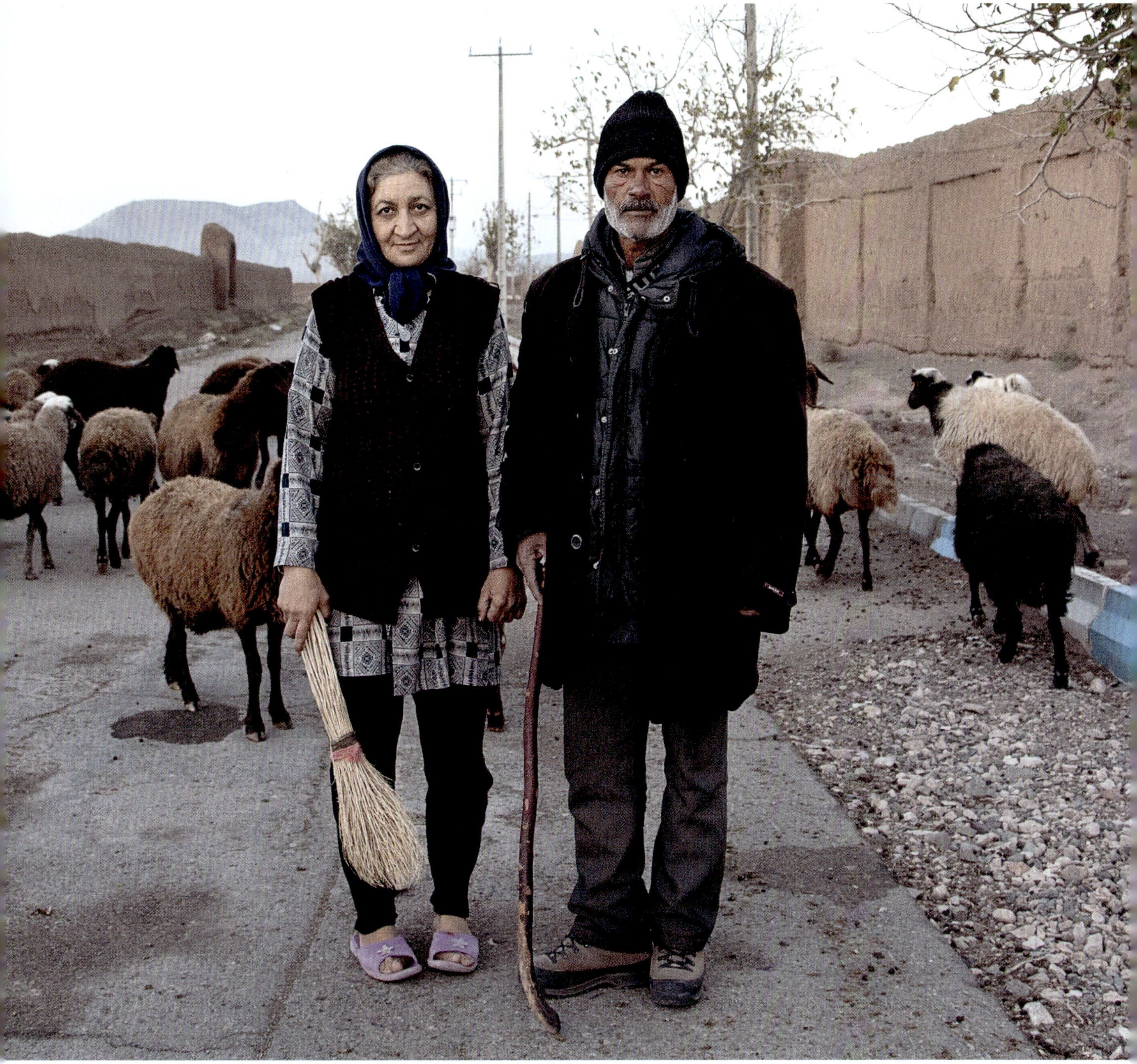

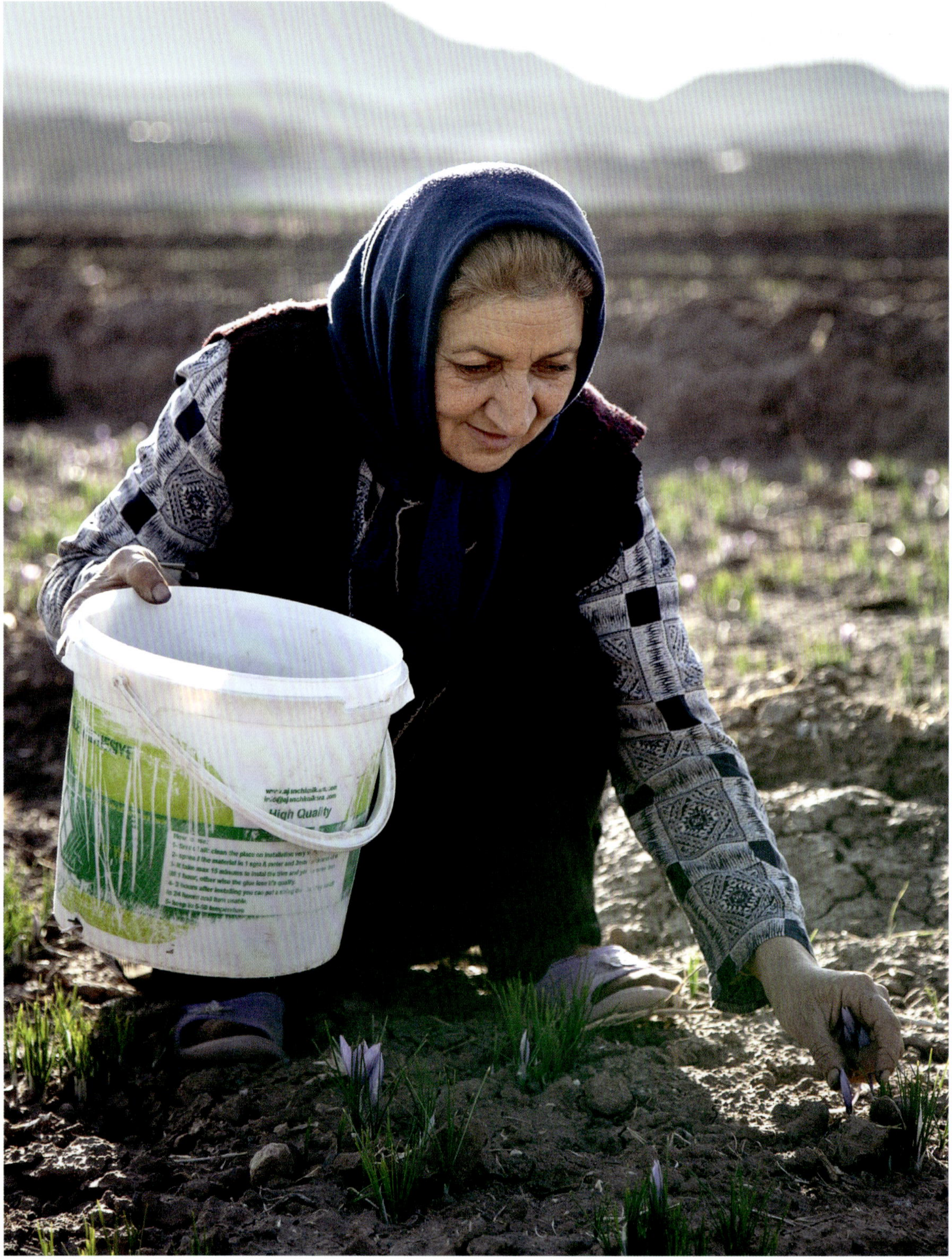
High Quality

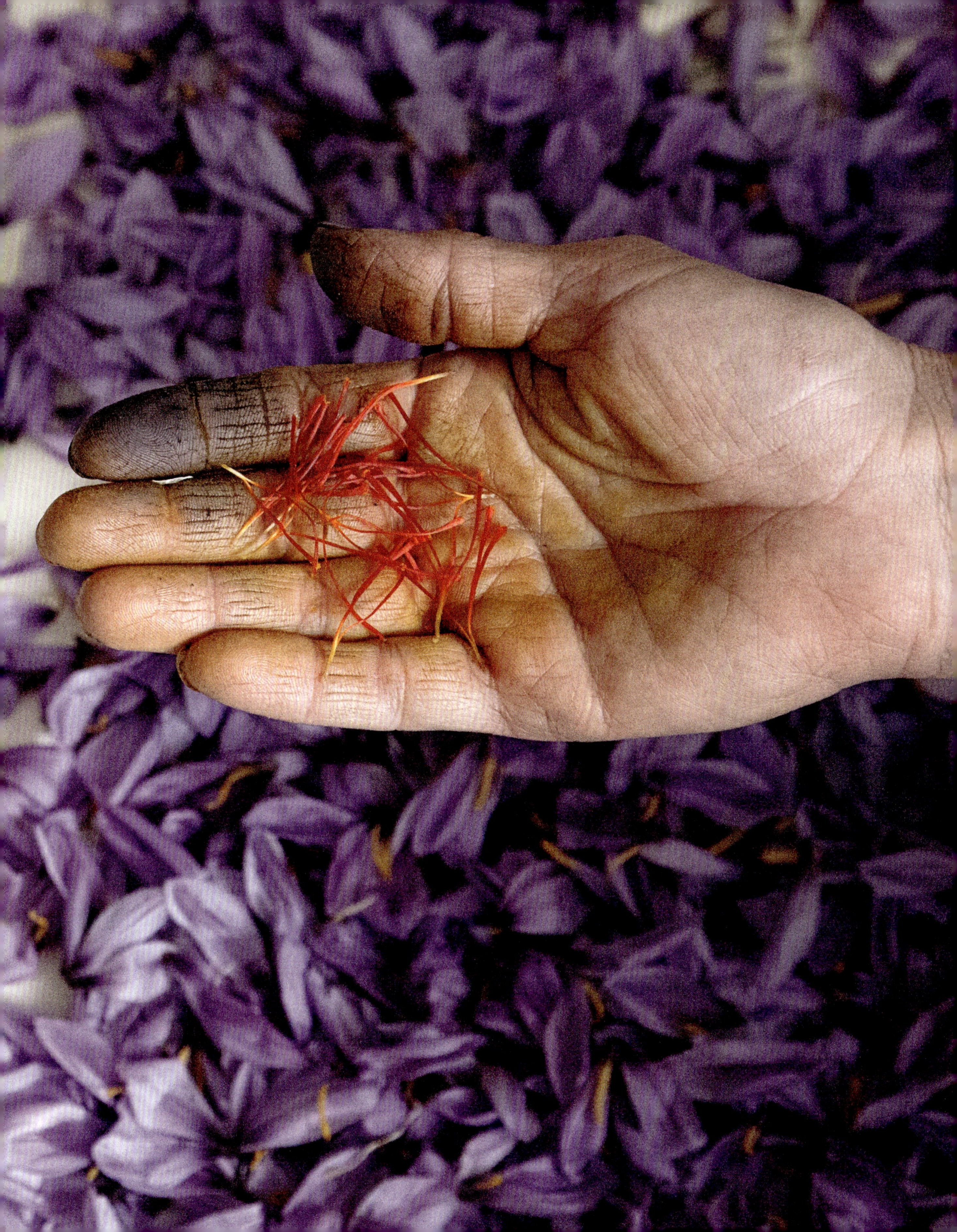

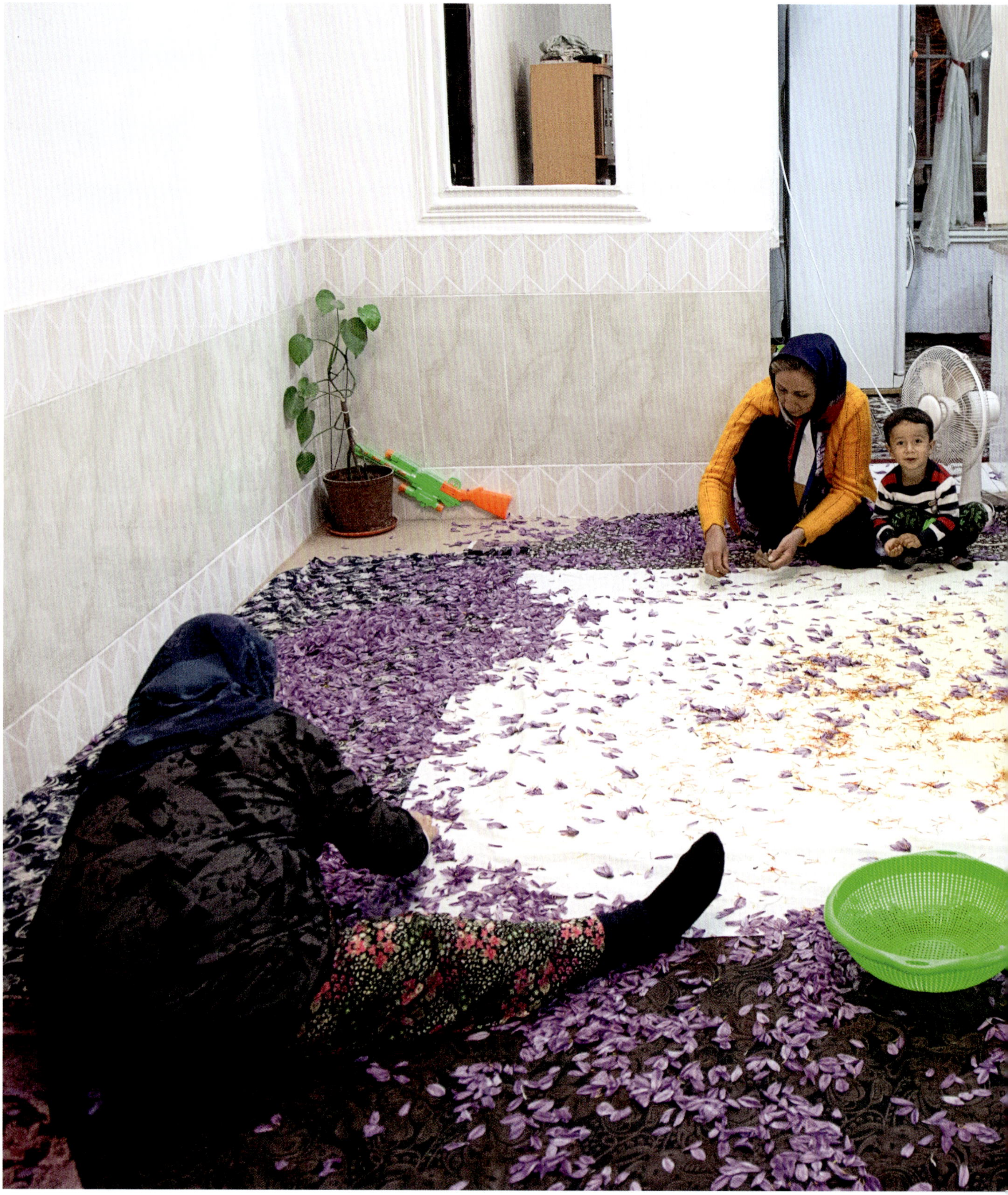

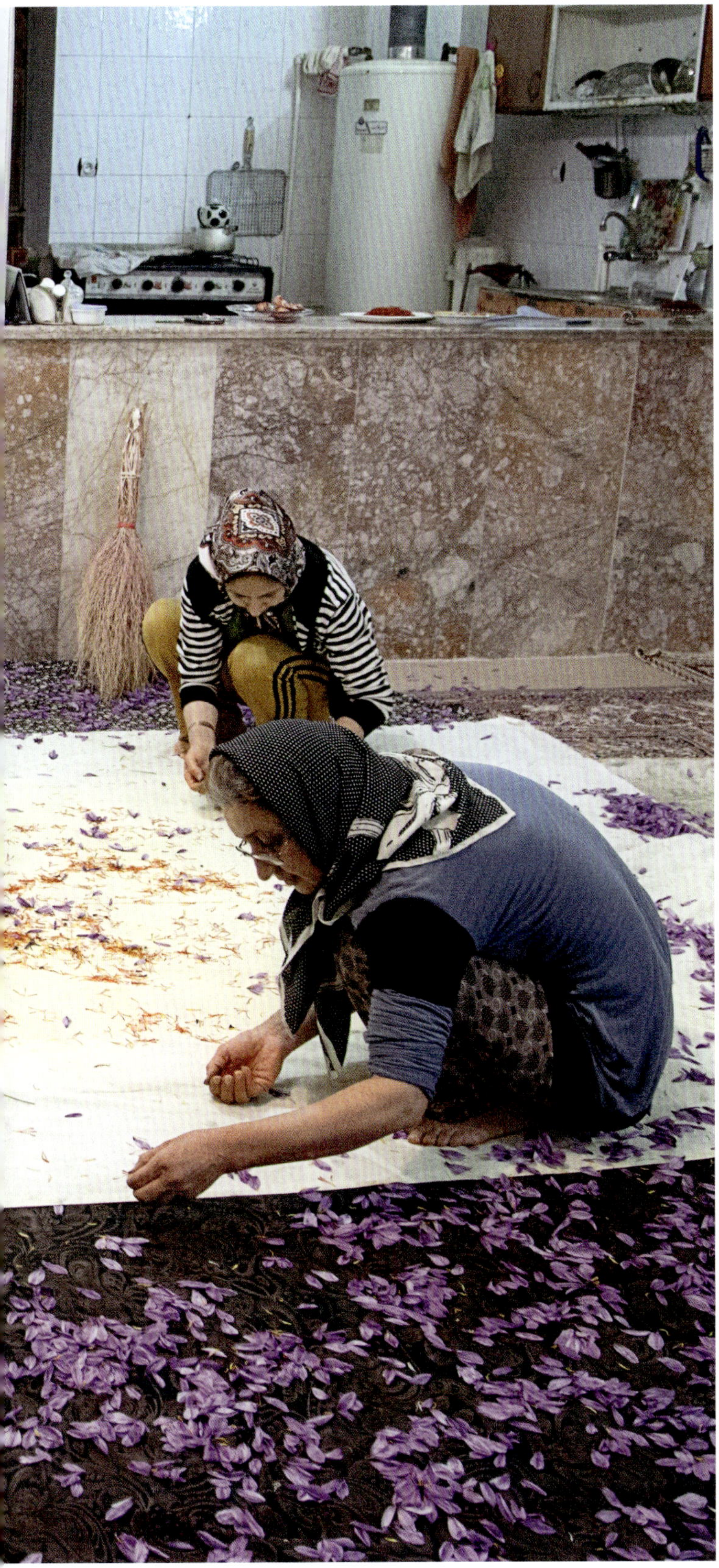

Maryam's two sisters and her daughter assist in plucking and collecting the delicate saffron threads. Usually, the flower stems are cut to separate the flowers from the saffron threads. In order to progress more quickly, Maryam and her sisters have optimized their method by first removing all the flowers from the stems and spreading them out on a white cloth. Then, they use a fan to generate a breeze, which helps separate the lighter flowers from the heavier saffron threads. This makes it much easier to collect the saffron threads, saving the women almost an hour of work each time.

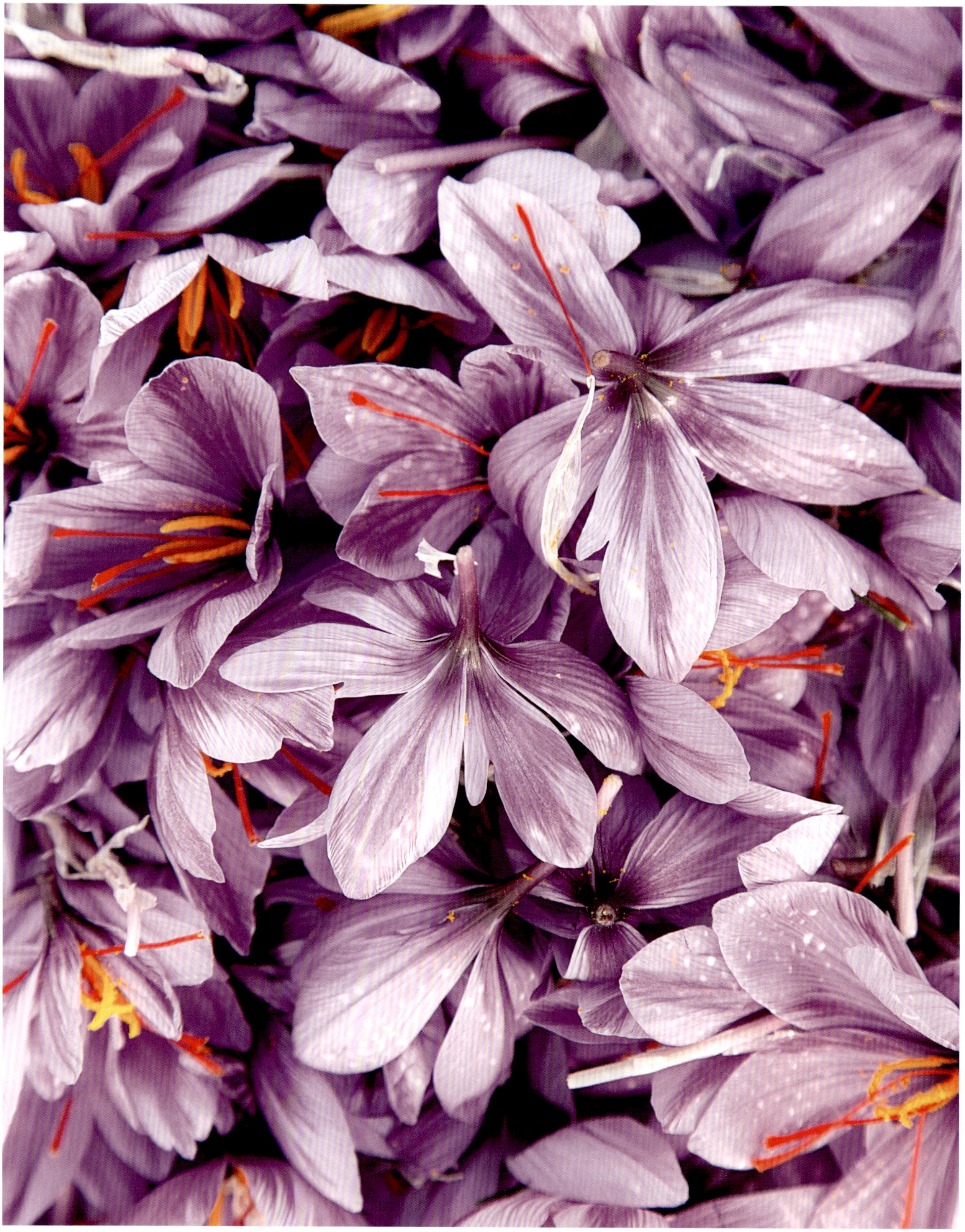

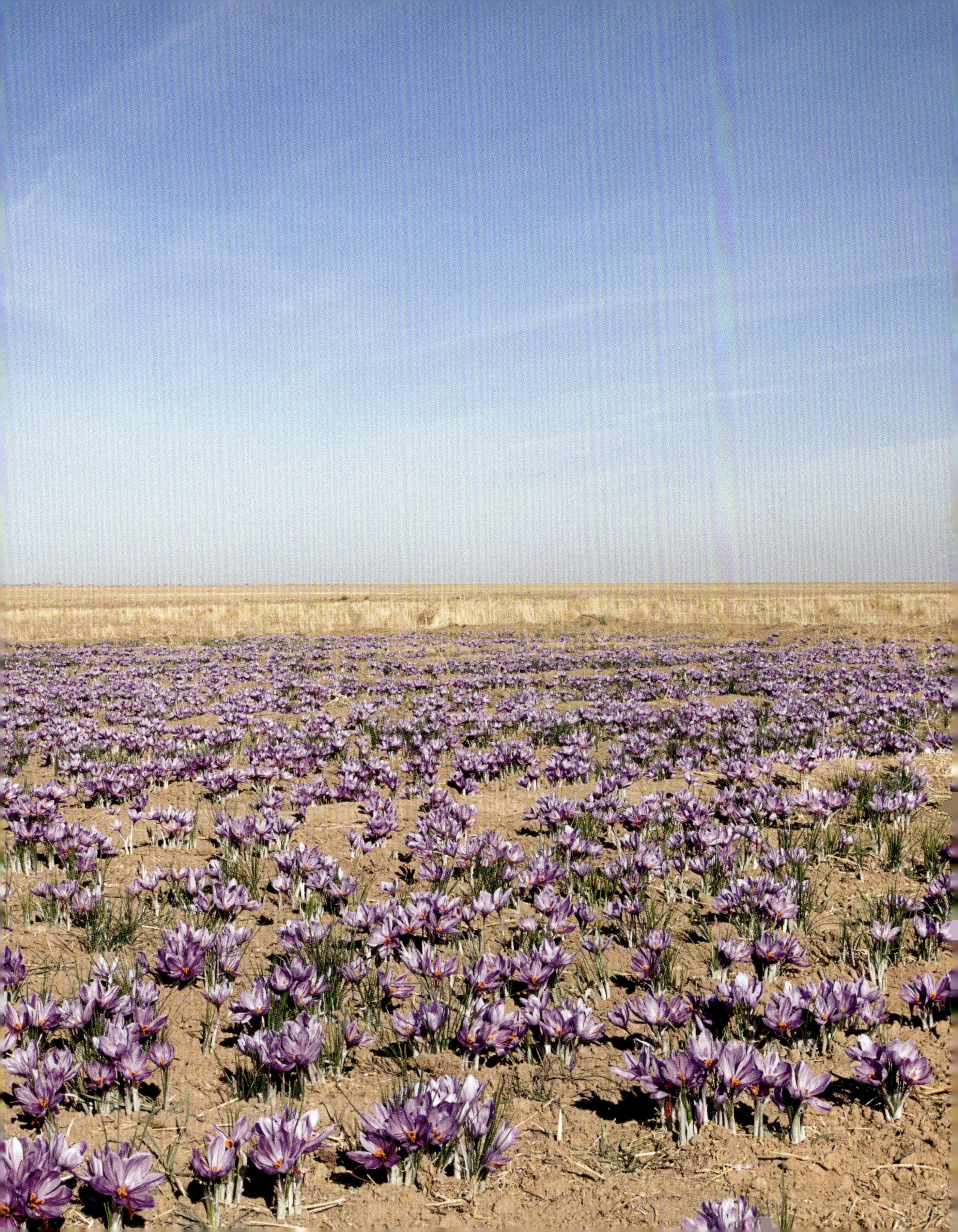

Bibi Zeinab Zendehbad

"I am thrilled when I can help young people find the right spouses," says Bibi Zeinab. Zeinab is actually her first name, but everyone calls her Bibi Zeinab. *Bibi* is an old-fashioned term for *Banoo*—which means lady. Many Iranian grandmothers are still affectionately called *Bibi* today. Bibi Zeinab lives in Mashhad, the second-largest city in Iran, which is the most important Shiite pilgrimage city, housing the tomb of the 8th Imam, Musa al Reza. Bibi Zeinab is a homemaker and has three children, all of whom are now married and no longer live at home. Her husband used to work in the military and is now retired. The fifty-seven-year-old explains that many religious families wish for their children to marry in a traditional manner. *"In the traditional wedding, there are many ceremonies: pre-marriage, marriage, and post-marriage ceremonies. It all begins with the marriage proposal—called 'Khastegari'—as soon as a suitable woman is found. The traditional search for a partner for the son is the most time-consuming task, for which the mothers and other women in the family are responsible. If the son cannot propose anyone himself, the women try to inquire about young, marriageable women at various occasions. Among women, it is common to discuss and exchange information about this at weddings, religious events, or when visiting friends and relatives. If the first impression aligns with the son's and mother's preferences, then the next step is to visit the girl's parents several times and introduce themselves. If there are multiple conversations, the two prospective spouses also get to know each other and spend several weeks getting acquainted. Once an agreement is reached between them, the parents are informed, and the traditional wedding ceremonies take place."*

After hearing repeatedly from families, friends, and neighbors about how difficult it had become to find the right spouse for their daughters and sons, Bibi Zeinab decided twenty years ago to become a volunteer matchmaker. Since then, she, along with women from the neighborhood, has been operating an office for traditional matchmaking. Bibi Zeinab and her team evaluate the forms filled out by parents, together with their daughters and sons, and conduct a matching process. When they find a couple that could be a good match, they provide the contact numbers of the prospective bride's family to the boy's family. This leads to initial meetings and encounters between the potential couple.

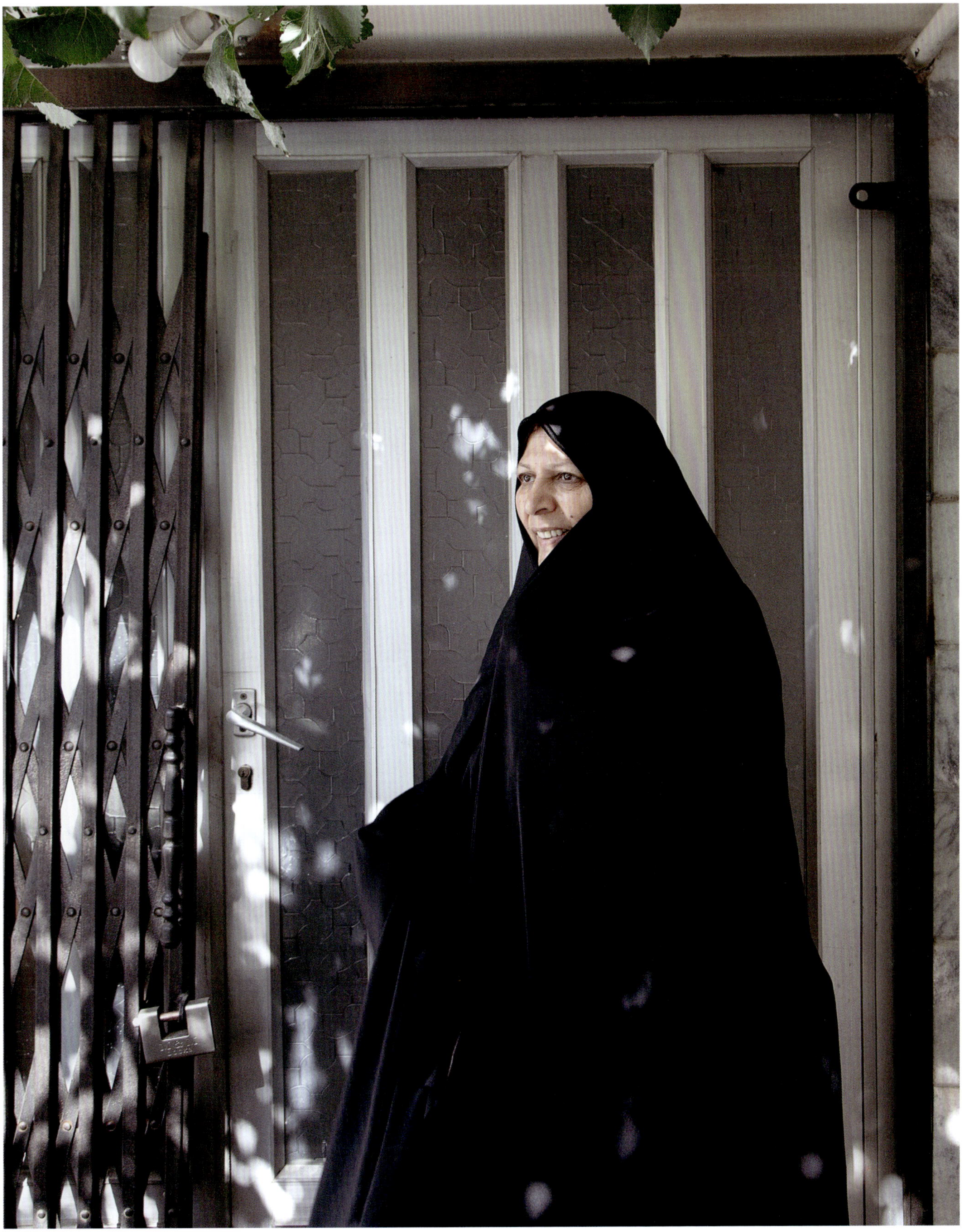

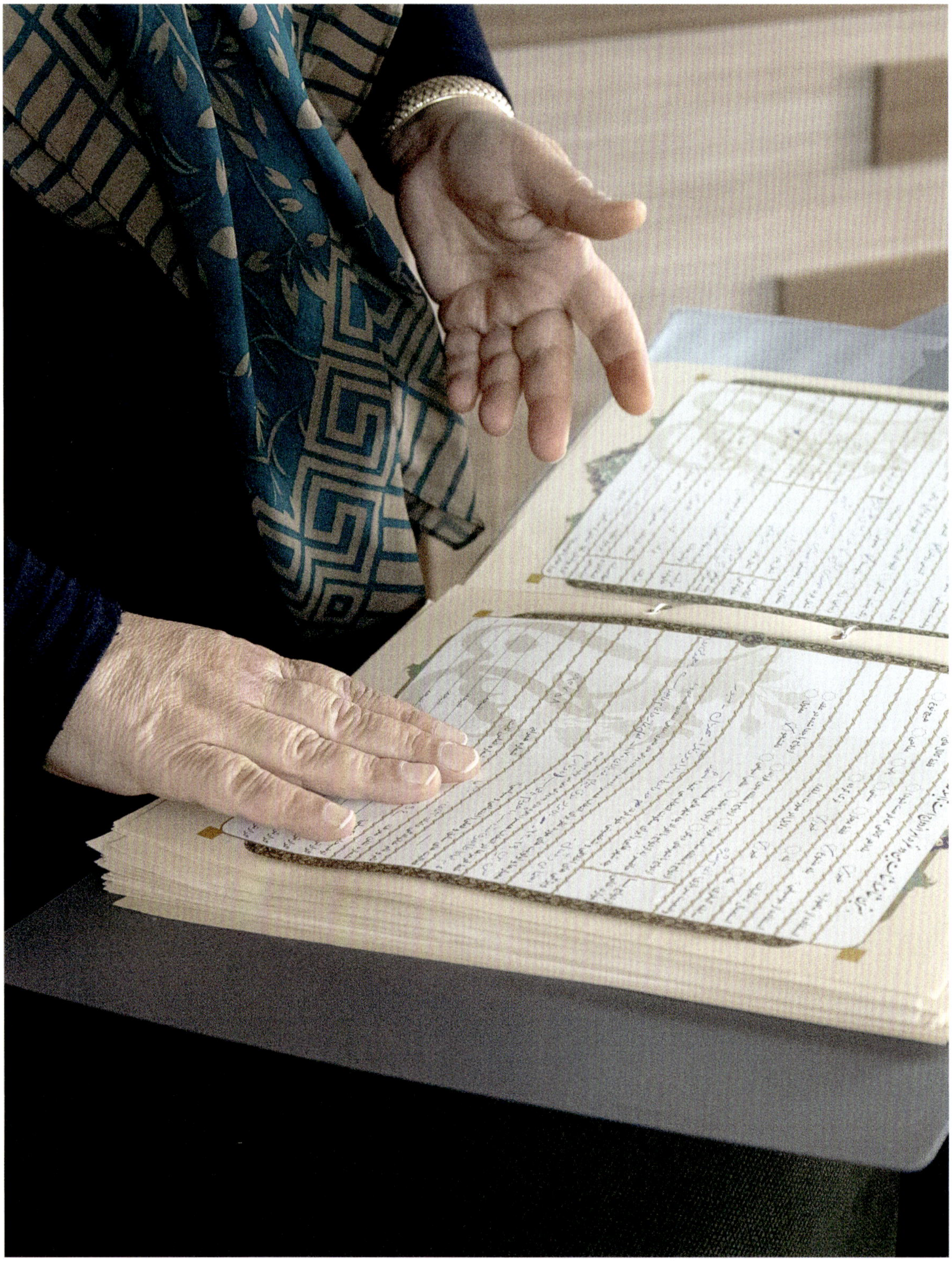

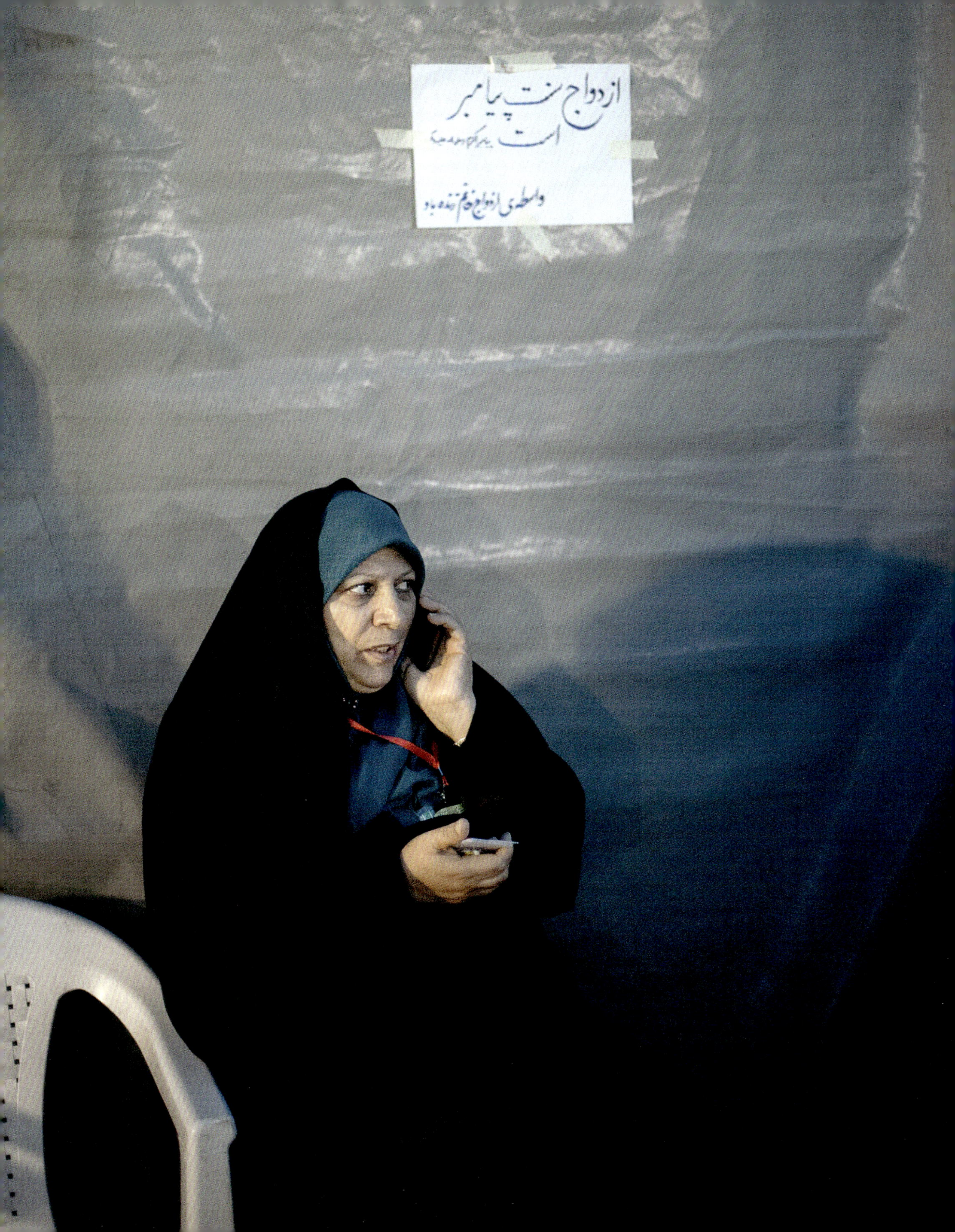
ازدواج سنت پیامبر
است

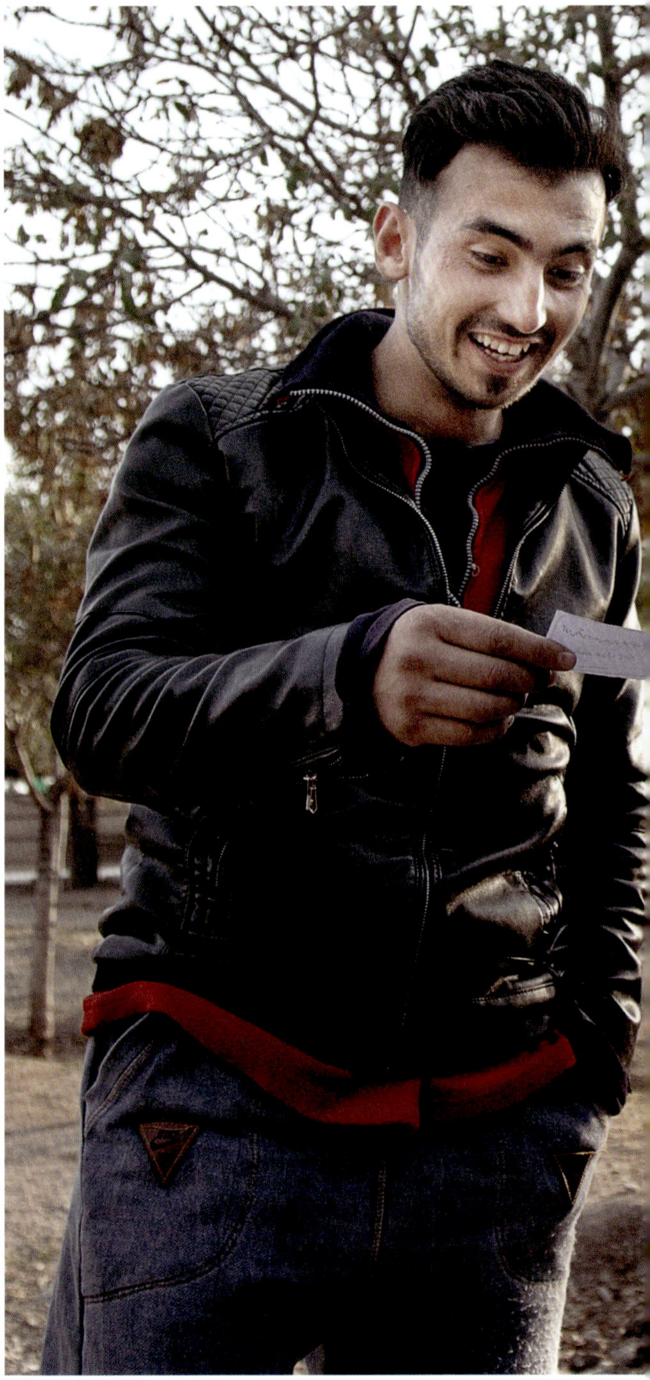

At a religious event in Mashhad, Bibi Zeinab hands out her business cards. The reactions from people vary: some are surprised, others are grateful—and some even show signs of embarrassment. Bibi's marketing strategy seems to be working: *"We have conducted thousands of successful matches so far, and many people have passed on my business card to others after receiving it at an event."*

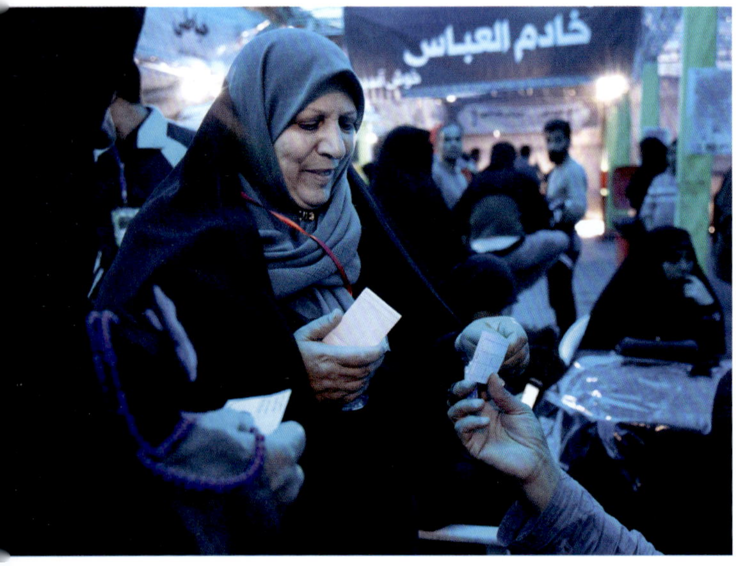

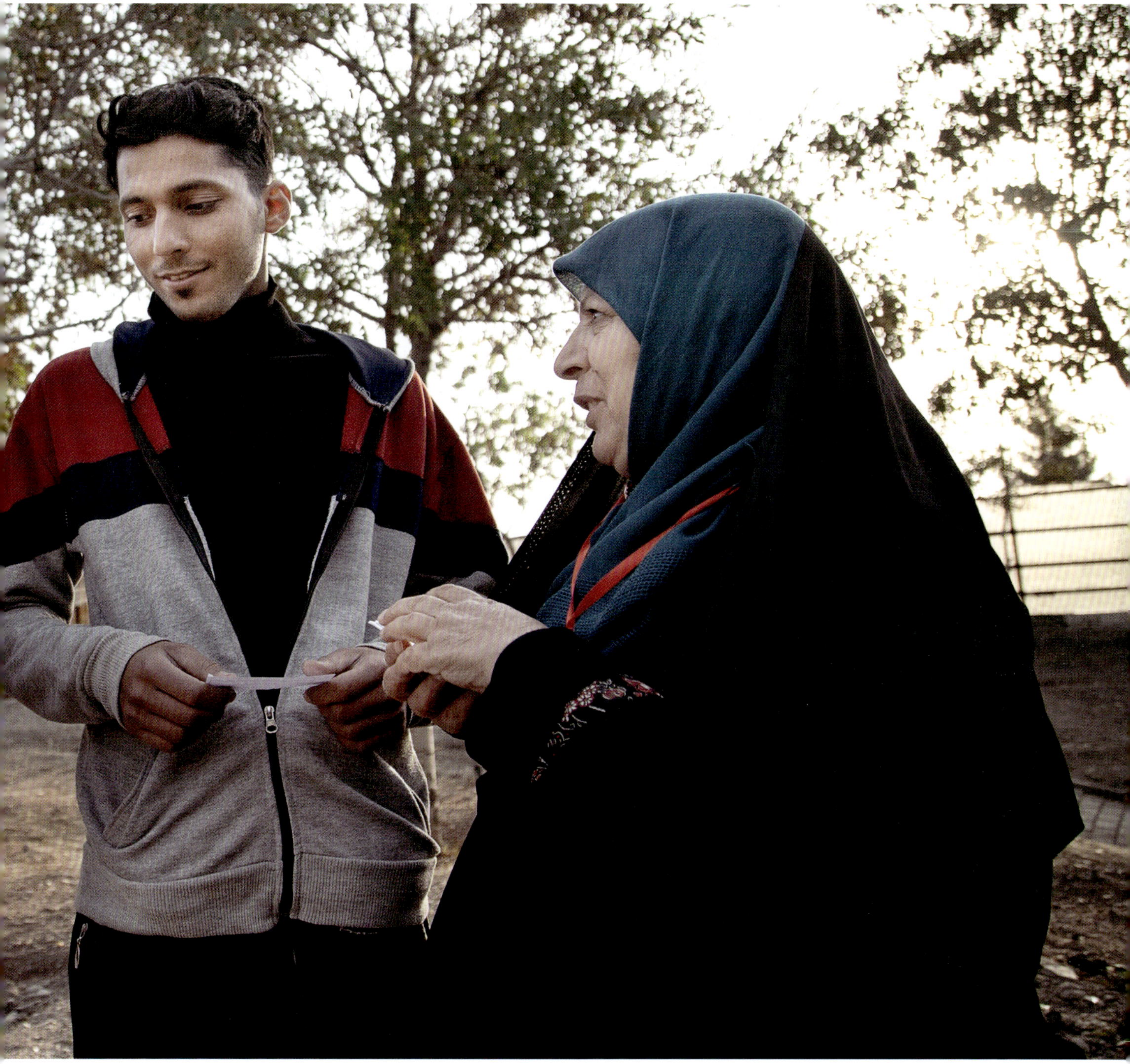

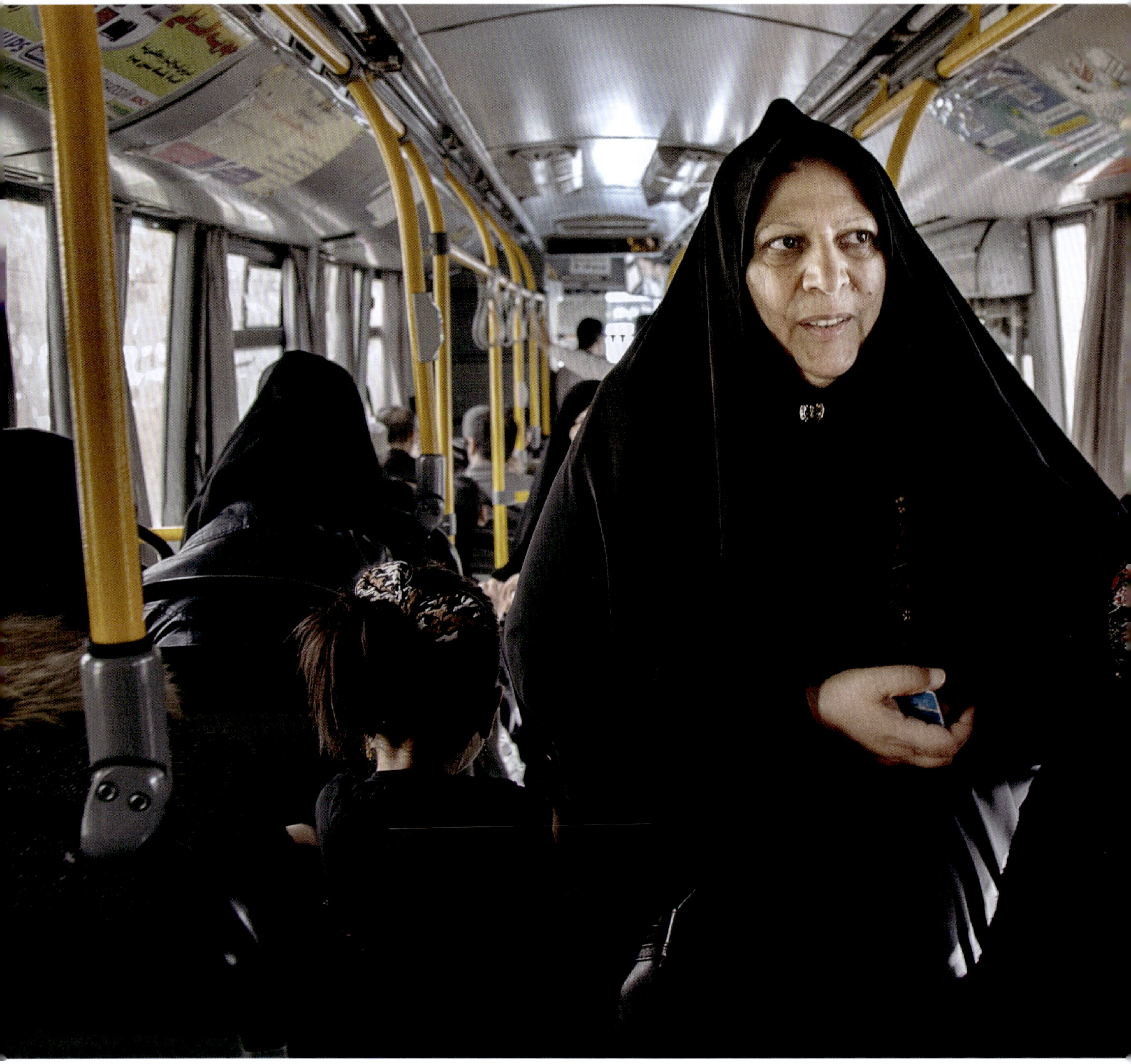

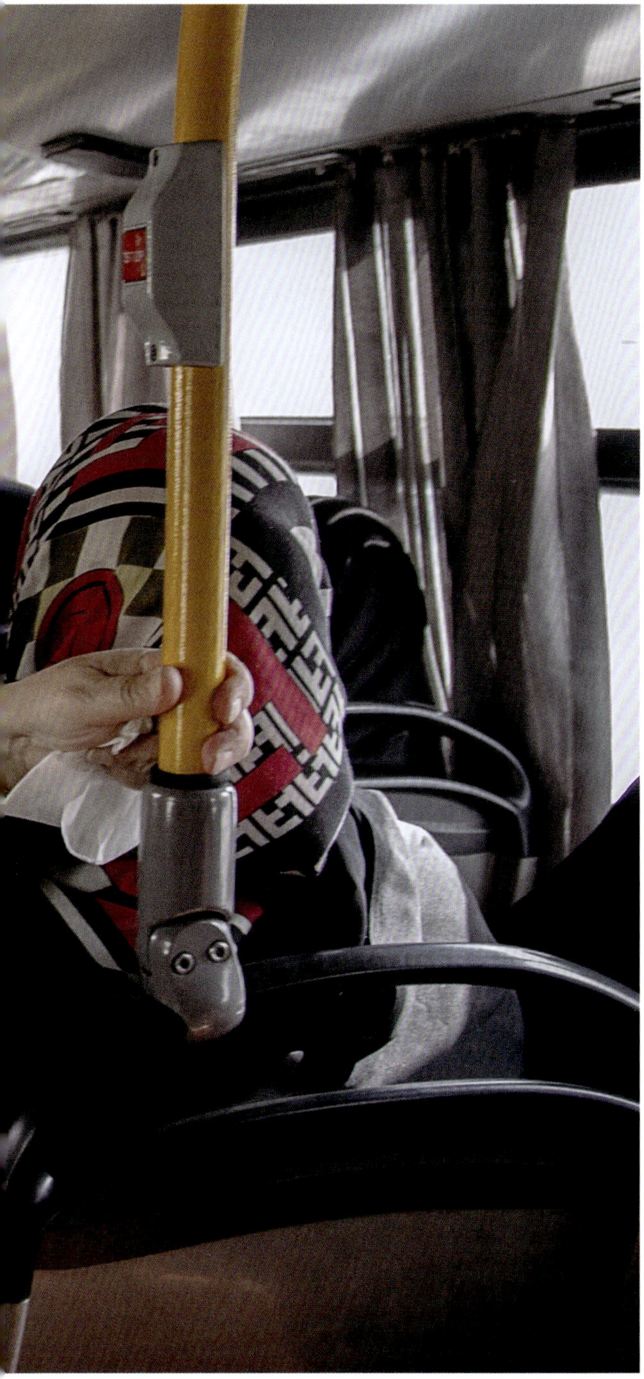

"The presence of women in society is very important, and they should not just stay at home. Even the smallest social activities are valuable and should be appreciated. But for me, the joy of the people I was able to help is enough," says Bibi Zeinab. She, along with ten other women from her neighborhood, volunteers once a week at the state health center to receive training from a doctor on personal hygiene and family health. Each of these women is responsible for educating forty families on these basics.

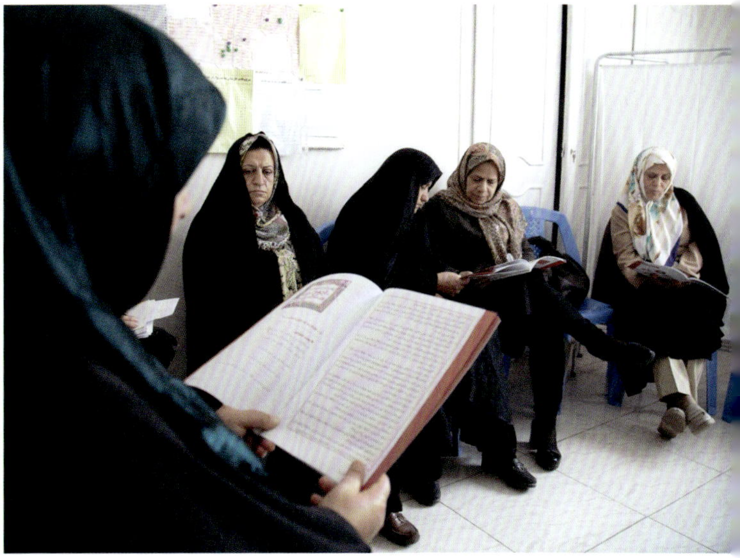

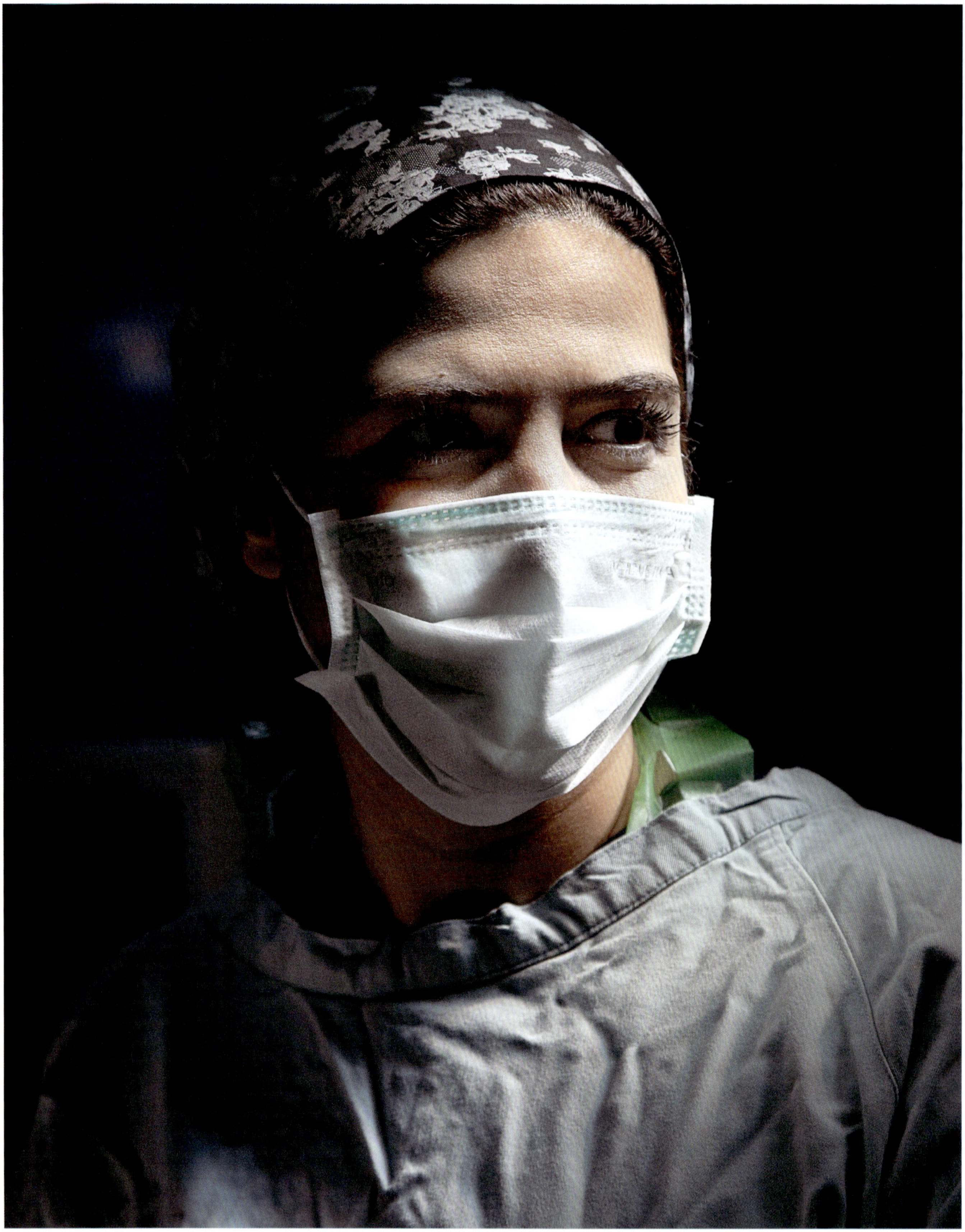

Fakhteh Khosroabadi

Fakhteh has been working as an operating room nurse specializing in plastic surgery for fifteen years at a private clinic in northern Tehran. *"I worked even during my university studies. There's no shame in work, even if it means washing other people's clothes. Unfortunately, some young women think differently. Anything you do to be independent from others is valuable. My mother taught me this attitude. She always told me that I should stand on my own two feet and achieve financial independence."* Fakhteh's mother passed away from cancer fourteen years ago. Fakhteh is thirty-eight years old, single, and lives with her younger sister and father in a four-bedroom condominium in Yousefabad, one of the oldest neighborhoods in Tehran.
"Since I broke up with my boyfriend, I've been trying to get to know myself better and continue to grow. What I still struggle with is dealing with sad events. That's why I've recently started taking self-awareness courses."

Her two dogs help her unwind and manage her racing thoughts. *"I love taking my dogs for walks in the park. They wait for me at the front door every day and greet me warmly."* For walks with her dogs, Fakhteh chooses less crowded places to avoid attracting attention. In Iran, it's unusual—although increasingly seen in urban areas—to keep dogs and other four-legged pets.
"After working for the same clinic for fifteen years, I will let my contract expire in the next two weeks. I had asked for a raise, which was not granted, and it hurt me deeply. I don't know why it affected me so much. Maybe because I expected them to recognize and appreciate my loyalty. Now I will take a short break and focus on things that have been neglected over the years: time for myself and my thoughts." Fakhteh is a passionate nature photographer and would love to take a road trip across Iran by car.

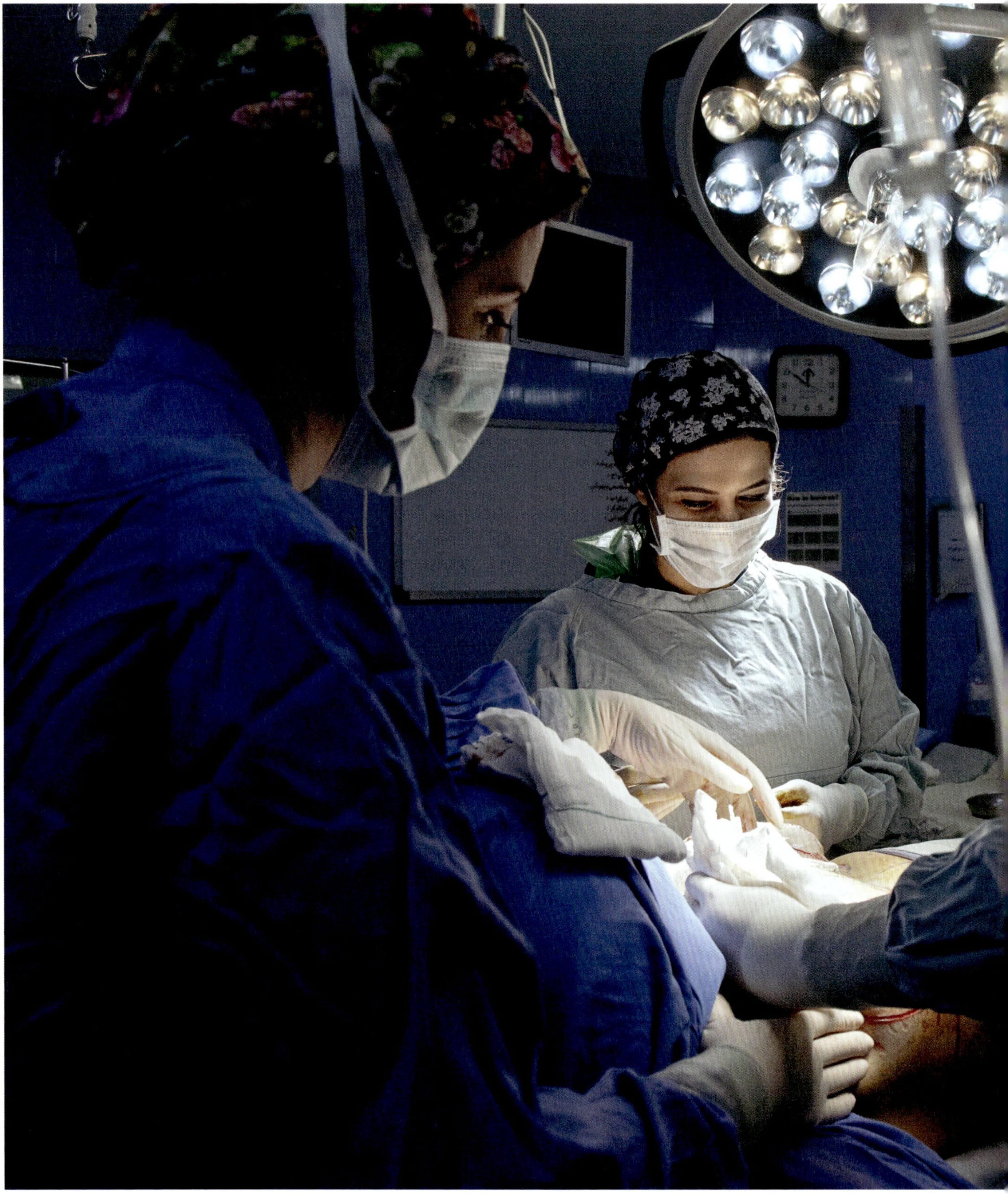

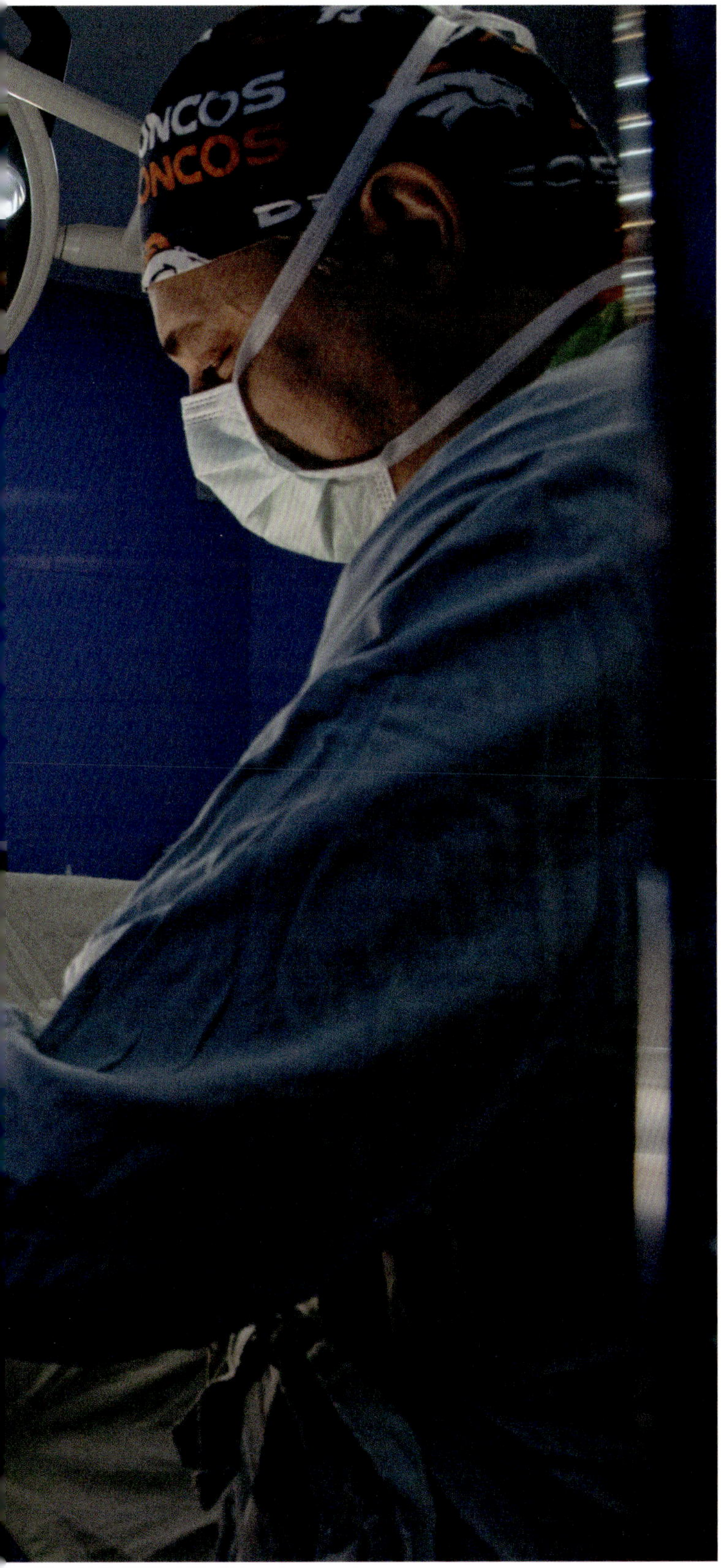

"Our patients come with anticipation and leave with joy. Most of the time, they are not sick or have any other physical complaints. Cosmetic surgeries in Iran have become a status symbol. Most women undergo cosmetic procedures due to beauty ideals and societal expectations," says Fakhteh. The upward trend in cosmetic nose surgeries has positioned Iran among the top ten countries with the highest rates of these operations. *"Many women choose to enhance their appearance to please their partner or husband. The balance has been lost in Iran: some women work hard and forget about their femininity, while others strive for a wealthy husband and focus primarily on their external appearance, often artificially enhanced. They forget about self-realization. The problem lies in our culture,"* says Fakhteh. *"We haven't taught our daughters to be the heroes of their own lives. Instead, they have often heard and seen that only a man can be the hero of their life."*

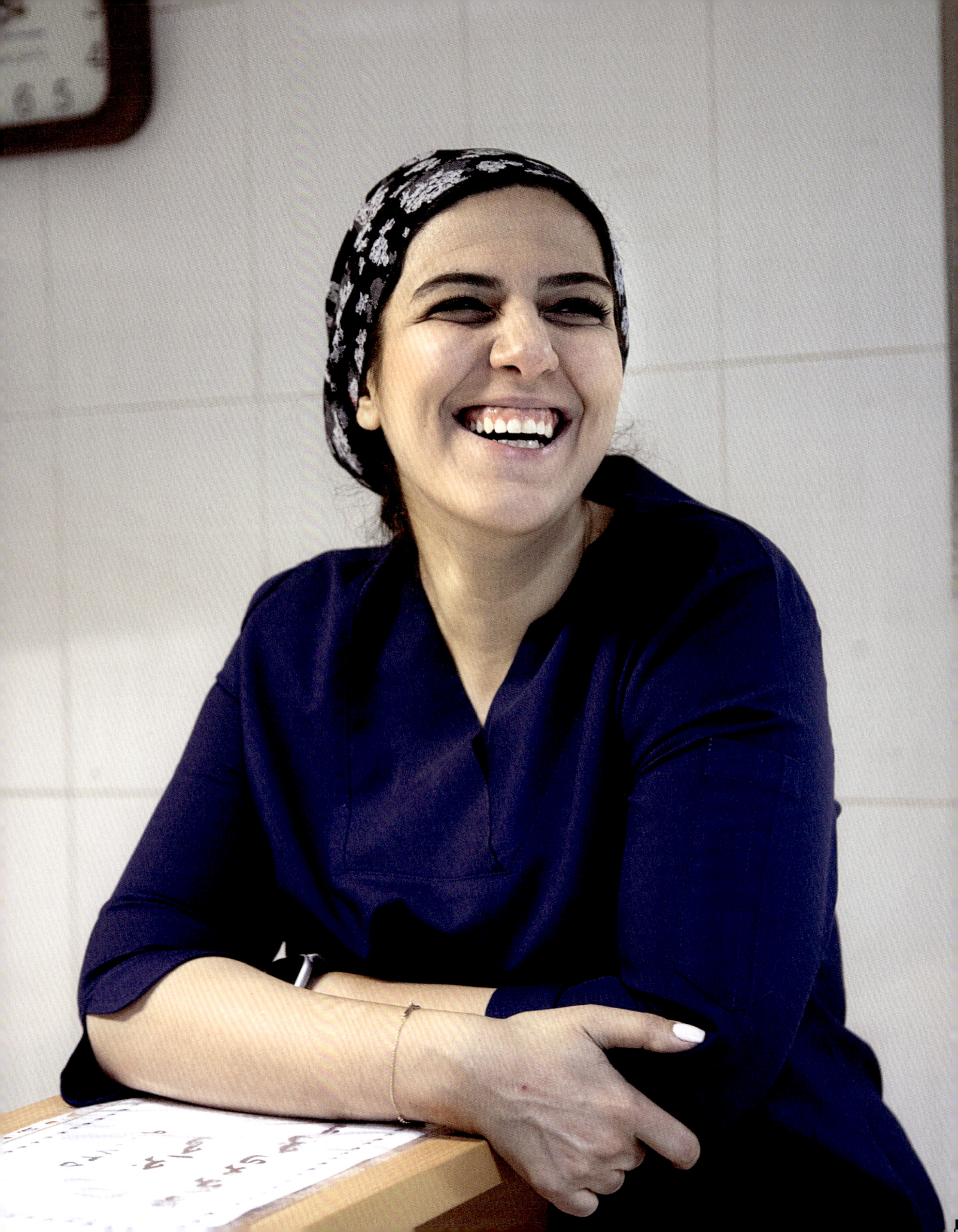

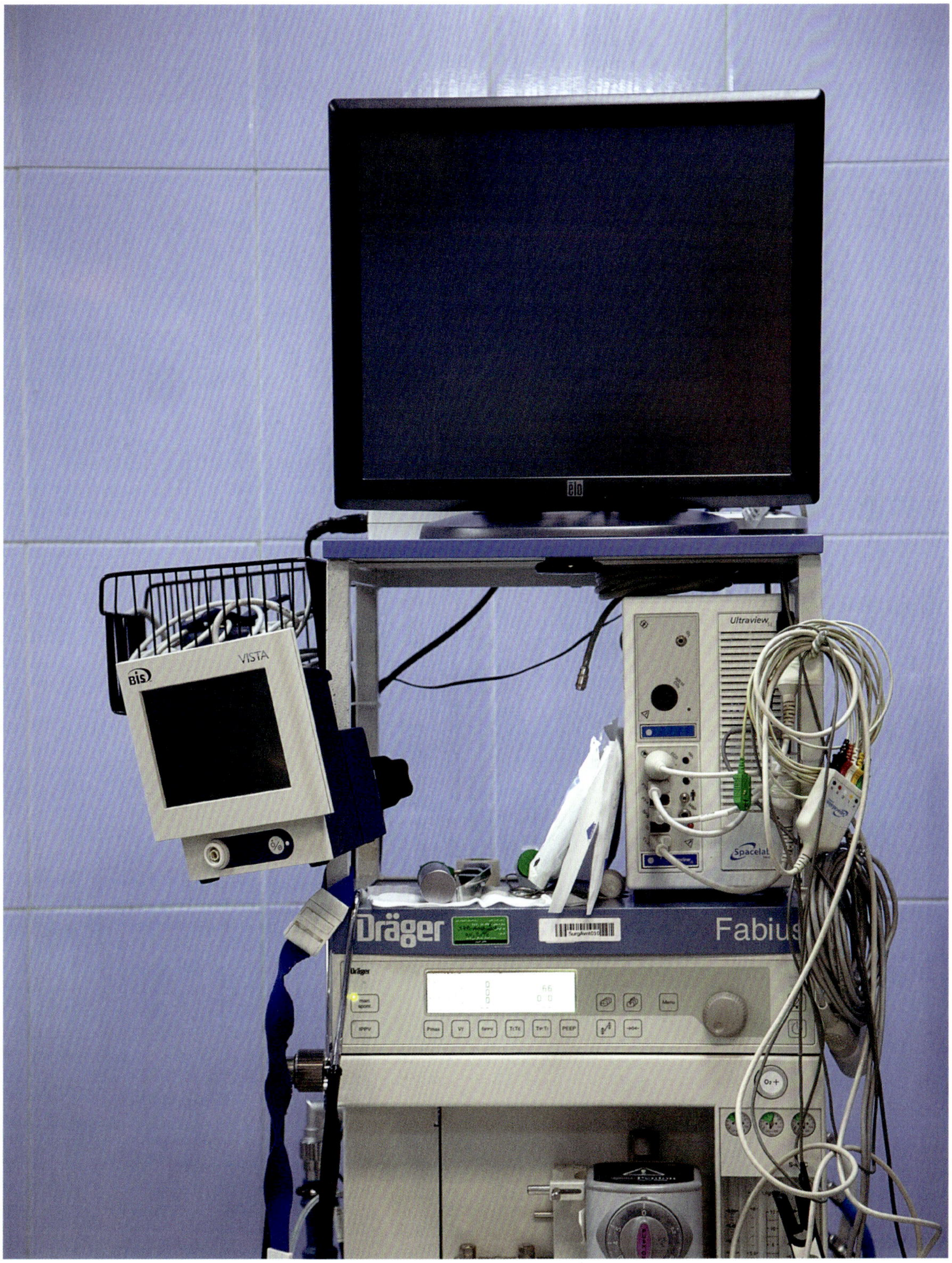
VISTA
Ultraview
Dräger
Fabius

"After working for the same clinic for fifteen years, I will let my contract expire in the next two weeks. I had asked for a raise, which was not granted, and it hurt me deeply."

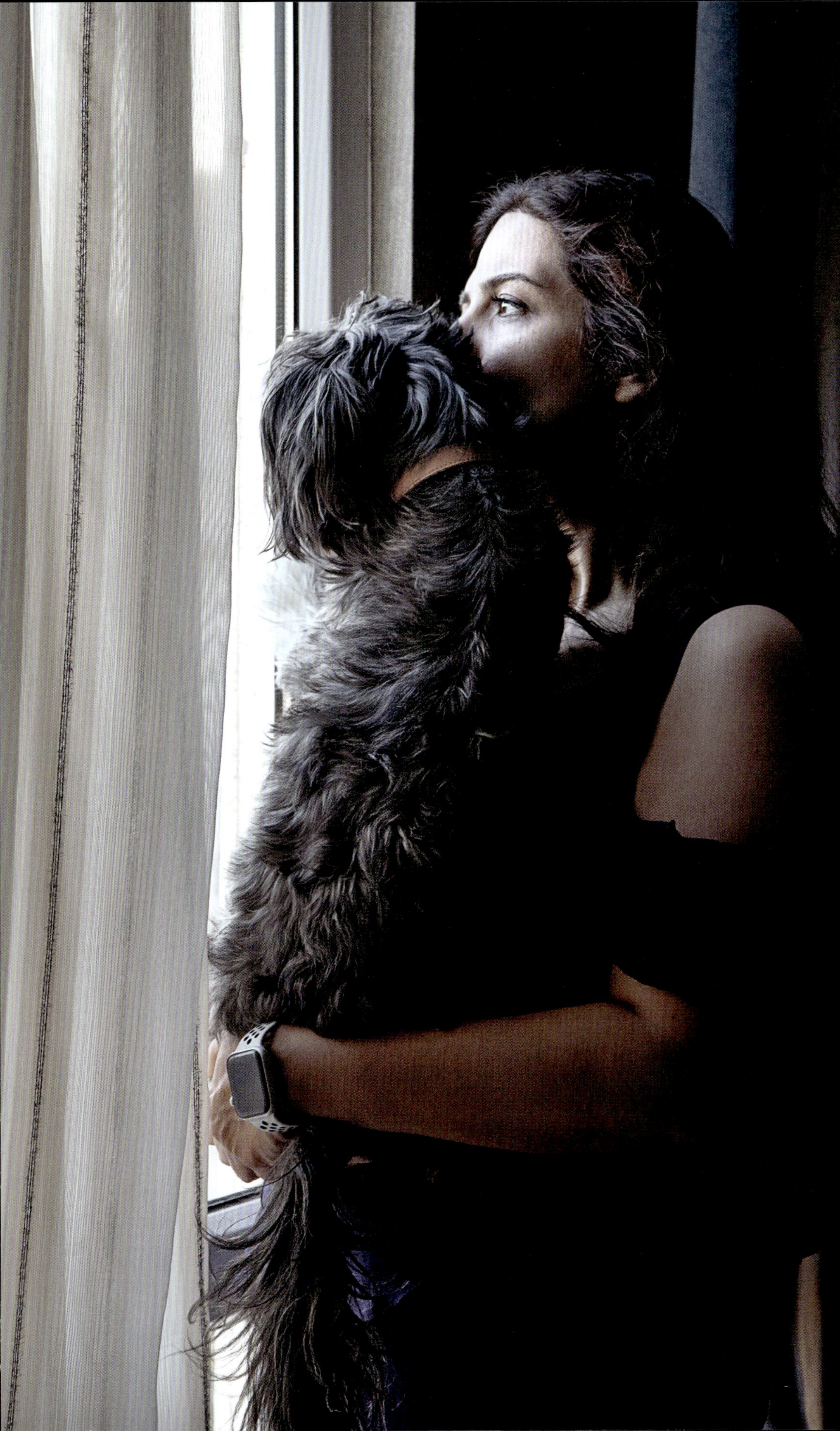

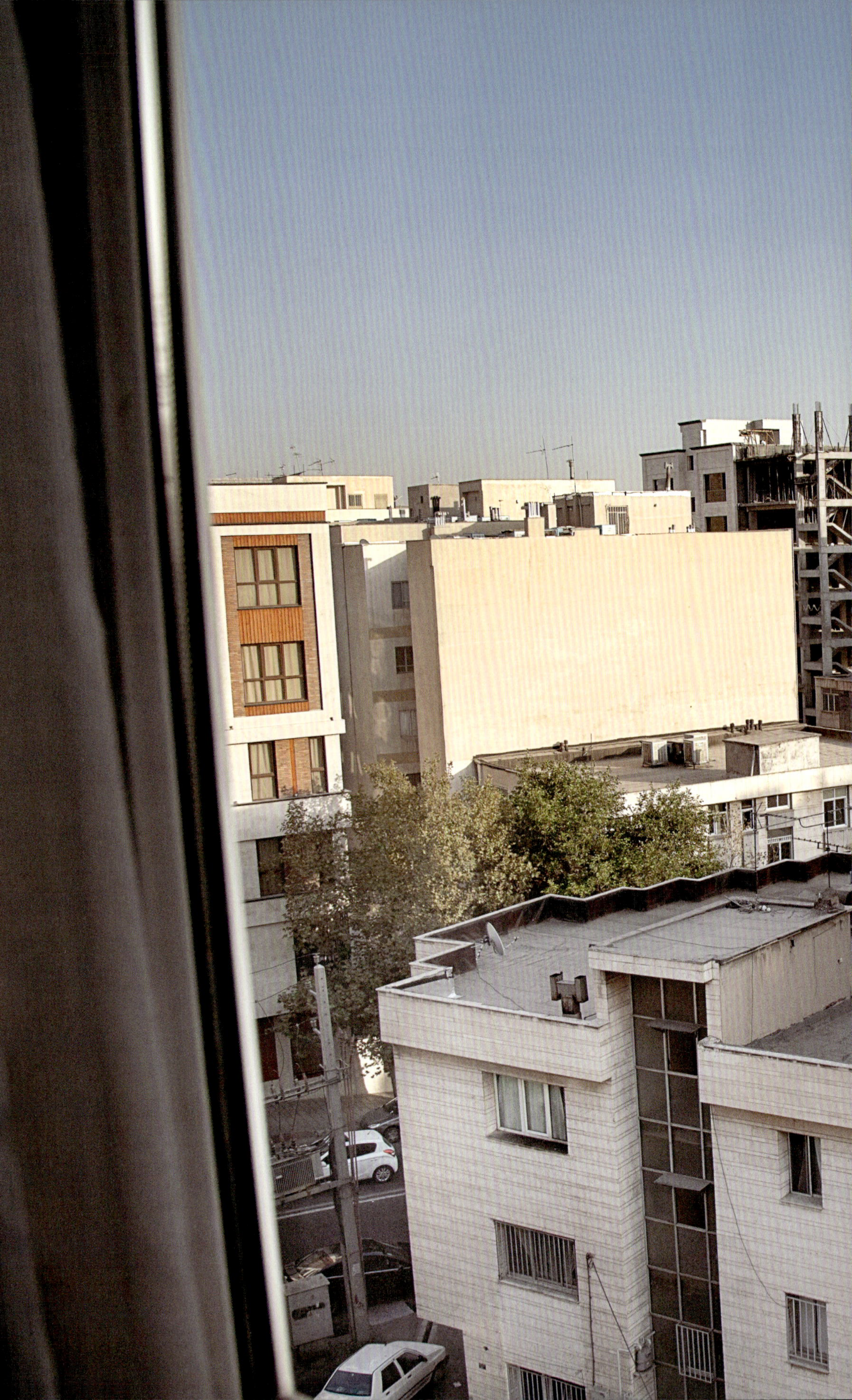

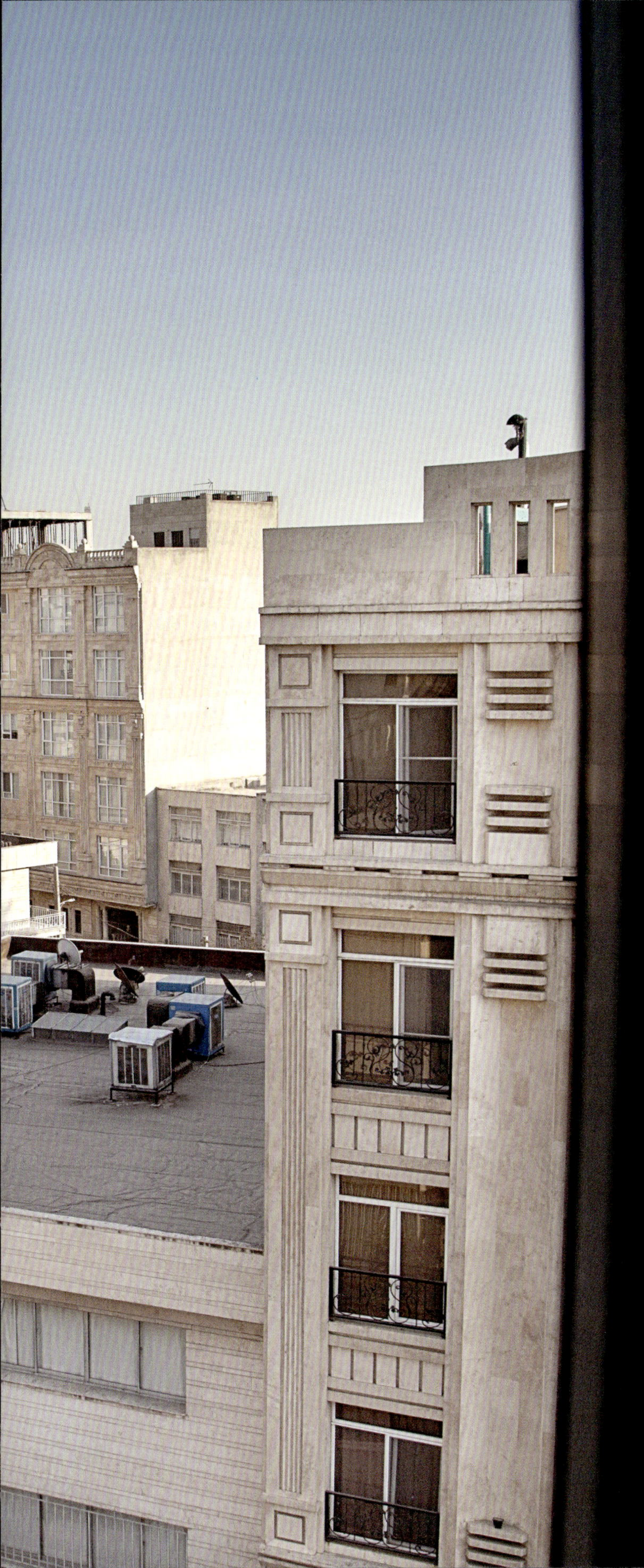

Shohreh Farokh Janali

Shohreh is a lawyer and worked in the legal field for five years after completing her studies. She started working in a law firm and had originally planned to take the bar exam. *"But I always had the desire to continue and promote the traditional handicrafts of my region,"* says Shohreh. She is single and lives with her parents in the village of Qasemabad in the Gilan province in northern Iran, near the Caspian Sea. They share a two-story house, with a garden and extensive farmland to the back, and a panoramic view of the hilly green landscape in front. *"My father is a farmer and livestock breeder. He produces animal and plant products like milk and cheese, kiwis and oranges, as well as ornamental plants. We also grow cucumbers, tomatoes, peas, beans, and corn for our own consumption,"* Shohreh happily explains. Shohreh's mother, Golafshan, is a housewife who helps her husband with the harvest and takes care of the animals—cows, goats, and chickens. She also taught Shohreh the art of weaving. Shohreh was allowed to sit at the loom as a child and quickly created her own patterns. The fabric woven by the women of Qasemabad is called *chadorshab*, which means "tent of the night." This is because, in addition to their household and fieldwork, women usually only had time to weave at night. Made from cotton and wool, the colorful fabrics are embellished with silk. They are then used to make handbags, tablecloths, or bedcovers. Often, the women use the fabrics to sew their traditional clothing. *Chadorshab* is also woven by women in other Iranian provinces, and only differs in the patterns and colors used.

"My father wanted me to receive a good education and he supported me in completing my university studies, but the desire to sit at the loom again grew stronger year by year. My father suggested that I finish my studies first, and if I still wanted to pursue the craft afterward, I could do so then." After earning her bachelor's degree and gaining a few years of professional experience, Shohreh decided to return to the loom. She modified her mother's loom to suit her needs and set up additional weaving spaces. She then offered women in her community who had also mastered the craft the opportunity to weave fabrics with her professionally. Shohreh established relationships with tour guides and vacation home operators, organizing visits to Qasemabad with tours of her weaving studio. Today, Shohreh employs several women who earn income from selling their fabrics to tourists. Shohreh believes it's important for visitors to see not only the end product, but also the work and tradition that goes into it. *"This is the only way people can truly appreciate the value of a product. Additionally, it's an exciting journey into the history of my village and my culture,"* explains the thirty-one-year-old proudly, as she sits at the loom. Qasemabad has since been registered by the World Crafts Council and awarded the title of World Craft Village.

"I am very grateful and happy to have received the necessary support from my parents to showcase our craft to the world. While many girls in our village marry early, my parents never pressured me into it." Shohreh is a pioneer in her craft in Qasemabad, serving as a role model for many young girls. She is aware of this role and, on every occasion, is happy to help the girls and boys in her village become more independent. On weekends, she takes the youth on hikes and teaches them skills like building a campfire.

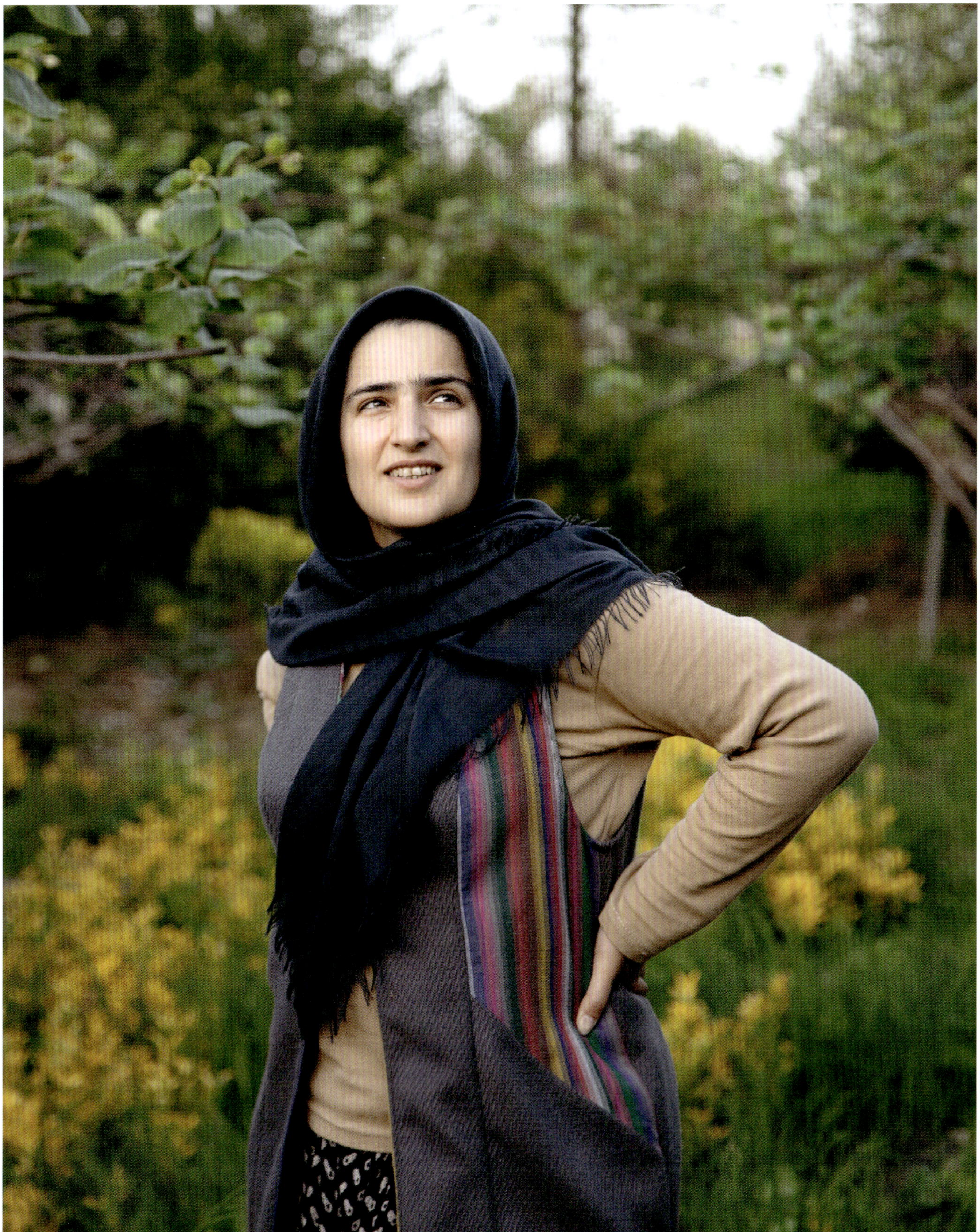

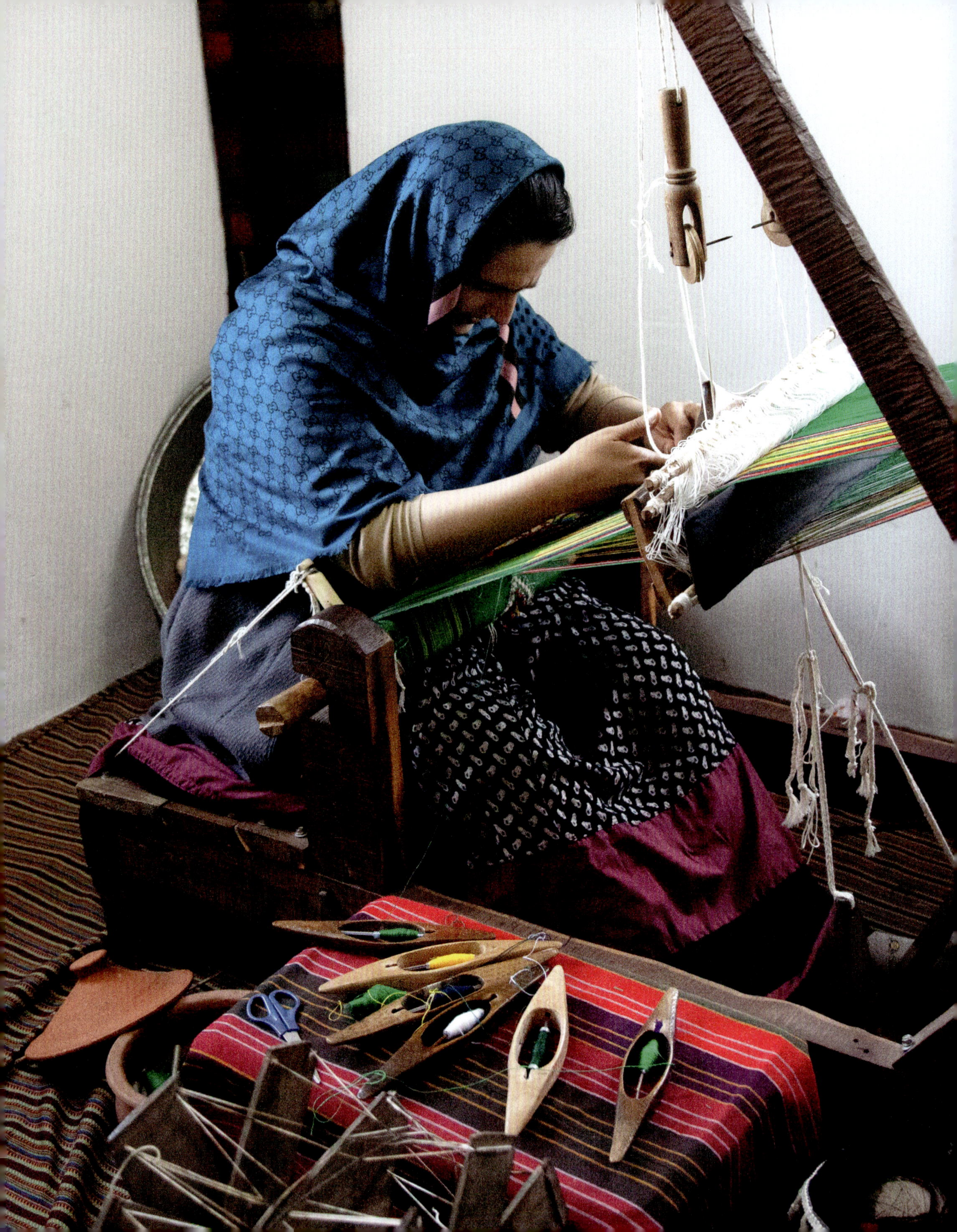

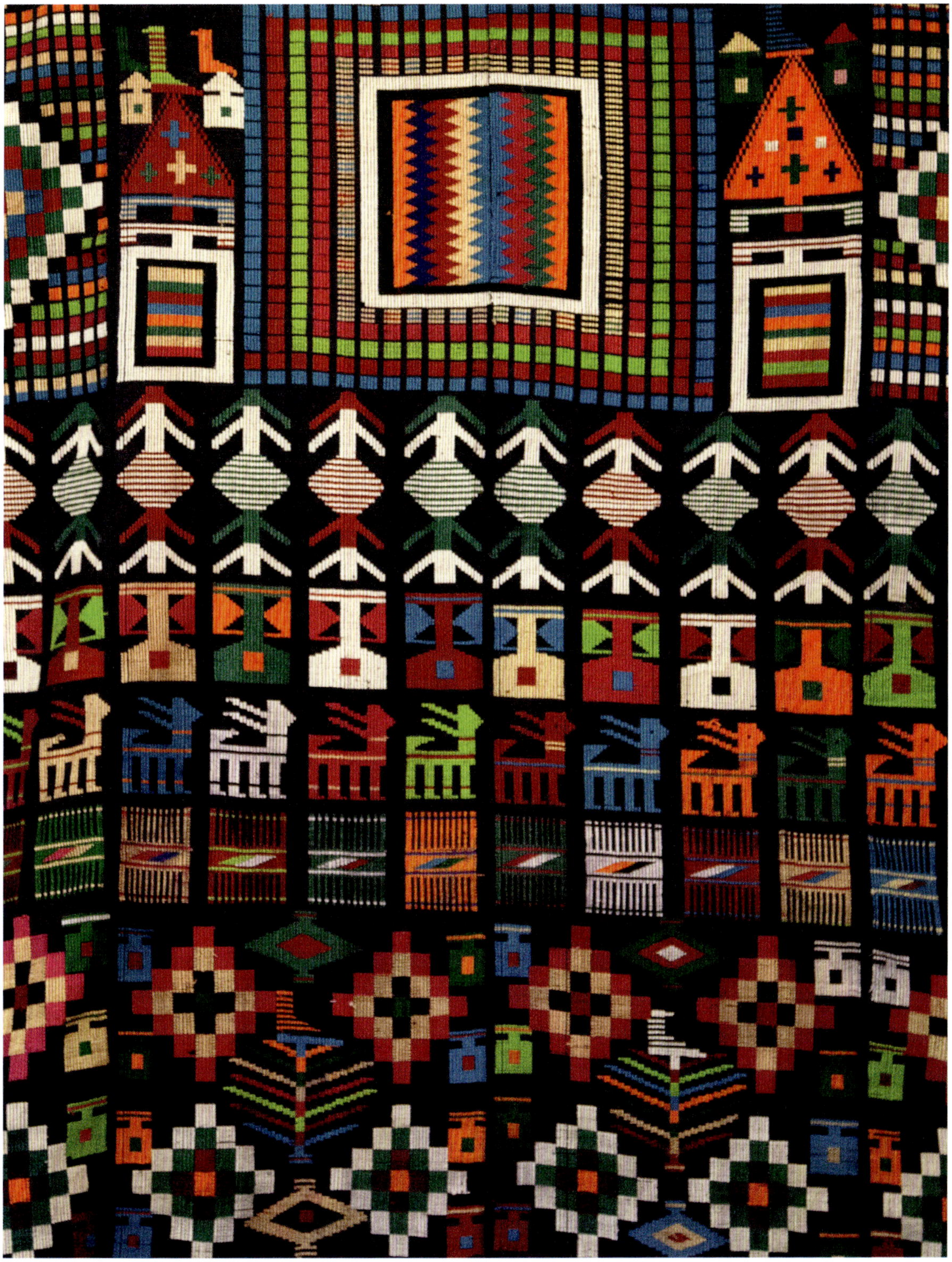

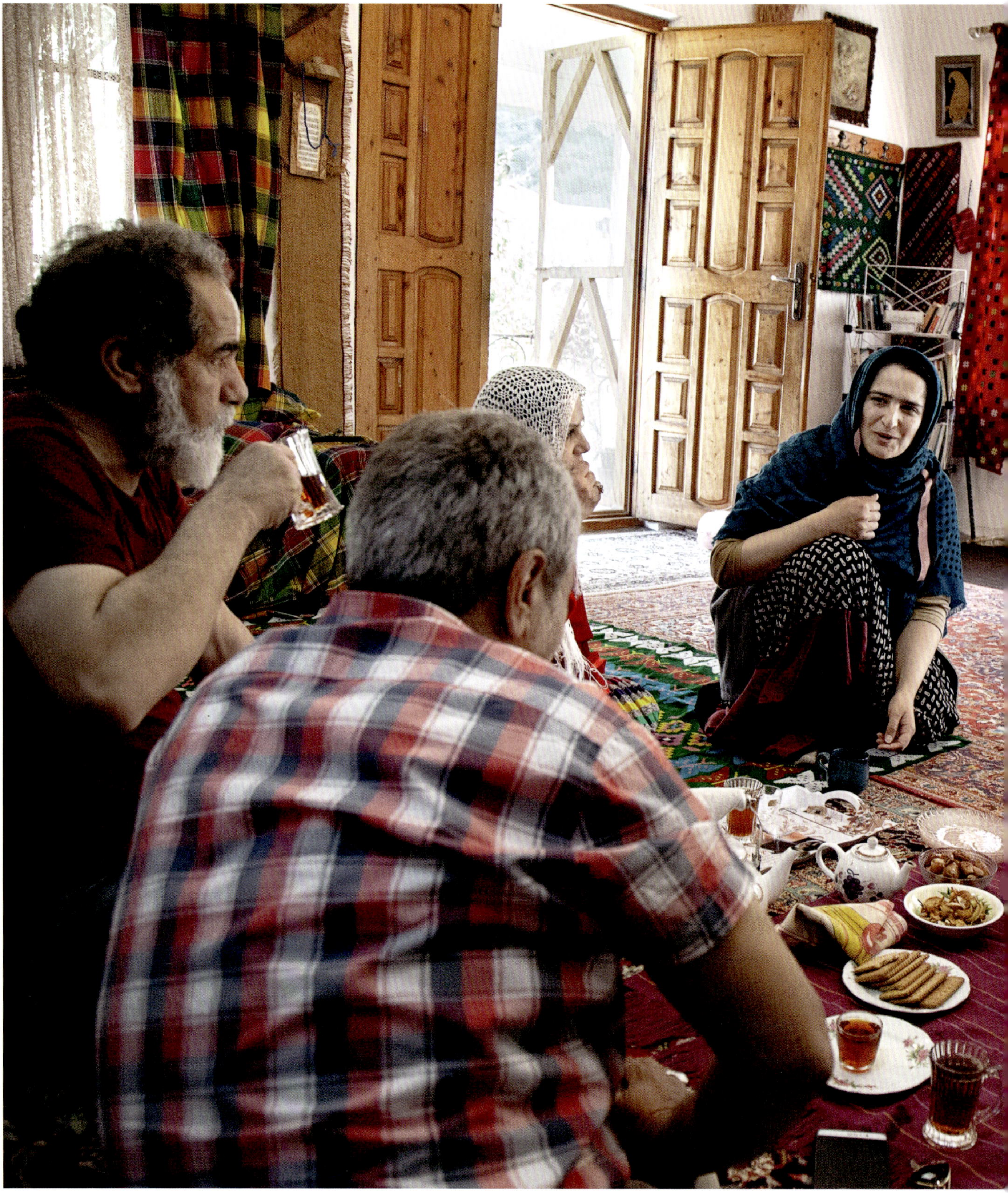

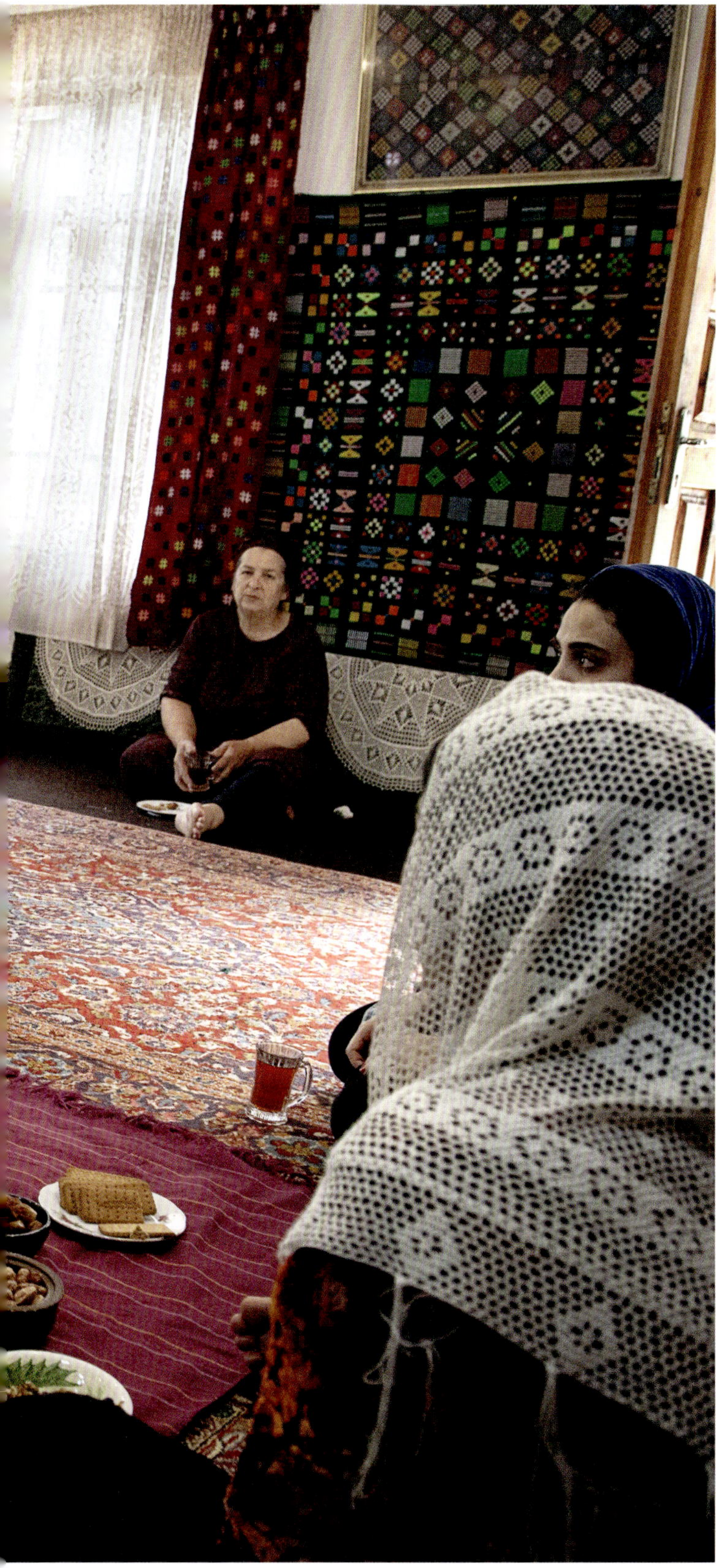

The couple Mahin and Khosrow own an old, picturesque house called Gileboom and offer accommodations for tourists in Qasemabad. Many Iranian and foreign tourists visit Qasemabad throughout the year—for relaxation, hiking, or swimming in the Caspian Sea—and stay for several nights with Mahin and Khosrow. Shohreh collaborates with the couple, offering guests a guided tour of the village and a visit to her weaving studio, where intricately patterned pieces can also be purchased directly. Shohreh takes the time to engage with her guests. They are served local black tea along with traditional pastries, while she explains the craft and the significance of the patterns on the fabrics. Guests are also invited to try their hand at weaving a few knots in a *chadorshab*, and to try on the traditional attire of the region, which typically consists of a colorful skirt and blouse. Additionally, they wear a white headscarf, crocheted from silk.

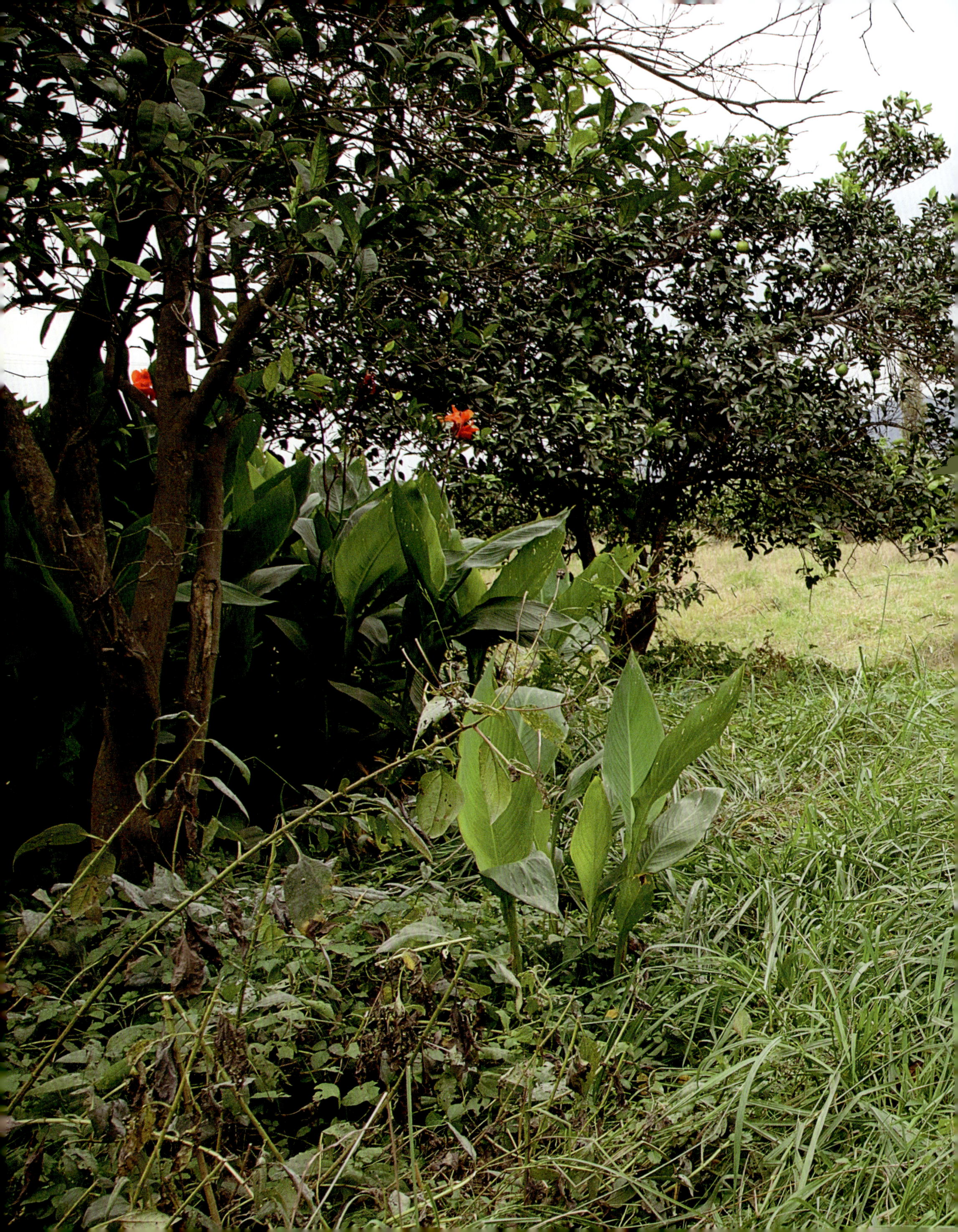

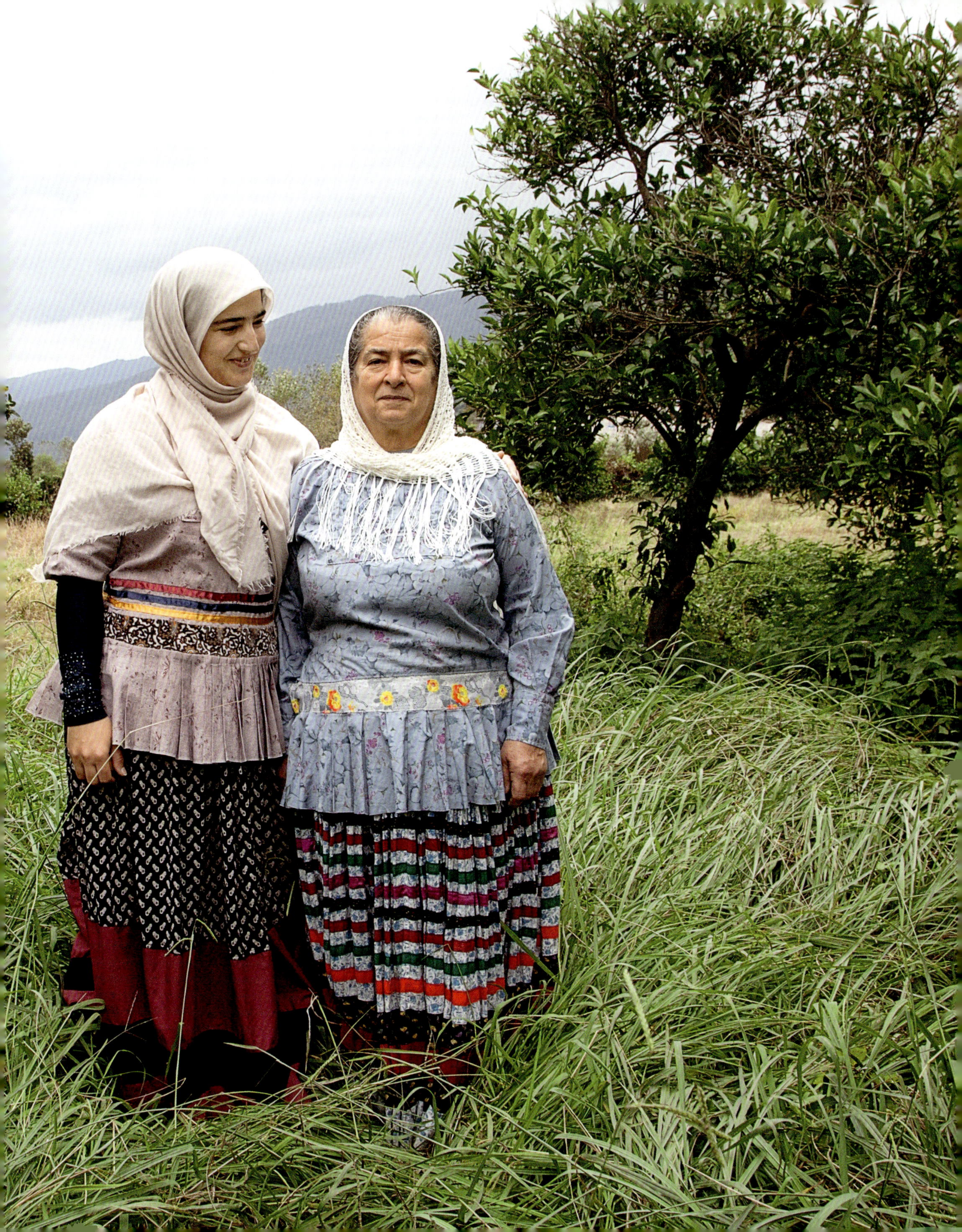

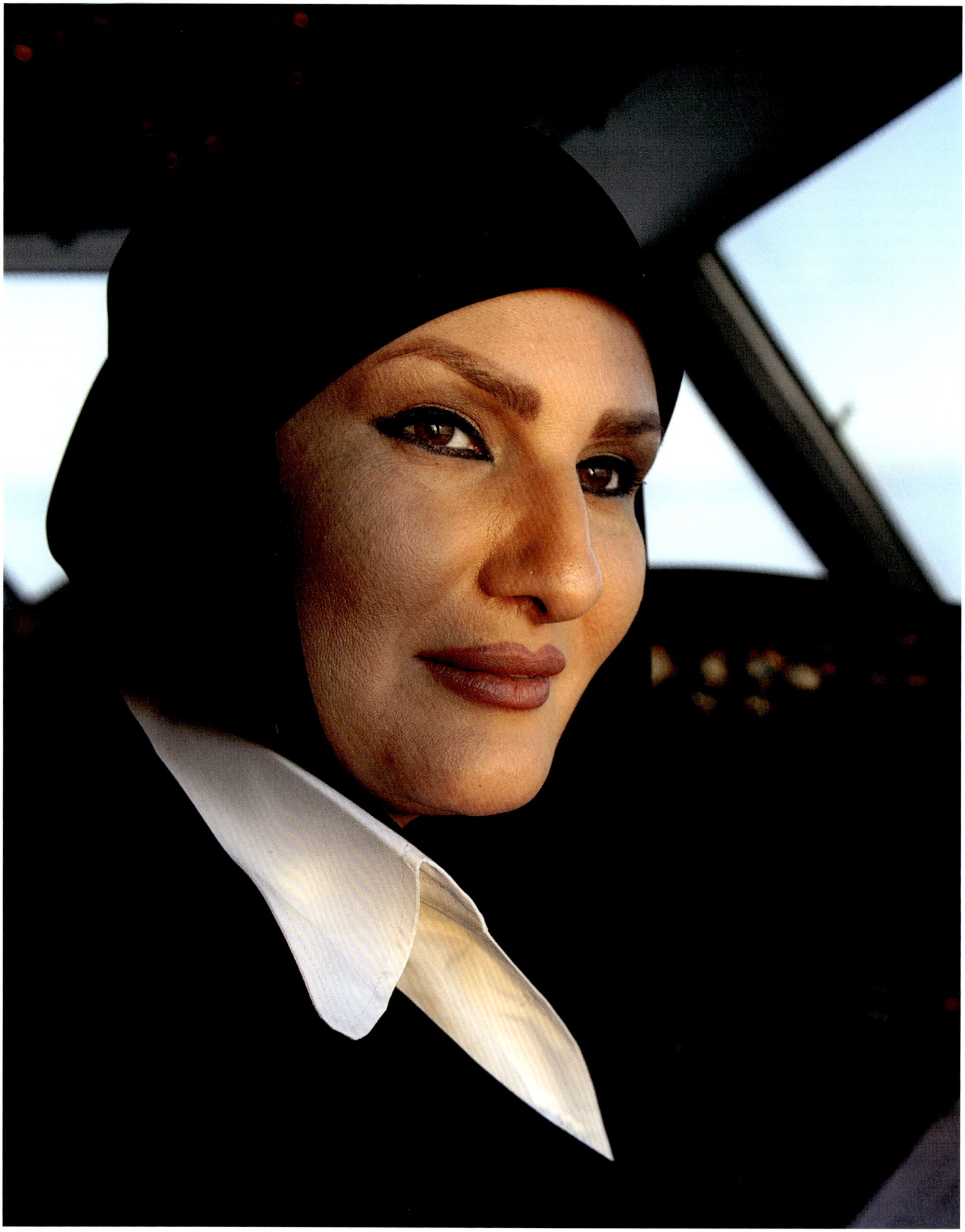

Fahimeh Ahmadi Dastjerdi

"Although women are making more and more progress in society, this new understanding of roles is noticed by many men but not necessarily accepted—even some women do not accept this new role. Especially when a woman works in male-dominated professions," says Fahimeh, Iran's first female flight engineer. Employed as a copilot by an airline for fourteen years, Fahimeh shares that men are consistently preferred when it comes to hiring in the aviation industry. *"At a certain time, there was a high demand for flight engineers in Iran. Although the admission criteria were strict, and a very good result was expected in the final exams, I successfully applied to an airline and was accepted."*

The predominant view of women held by Iranian men is still that of a caring housewife and mother, explains the thirty-eight-year-old Fahimeh. *"Unfortunately, many still don't trust us with more. This is especially true in the aviation industry. Gender has nothing to do with acquiring new skills; it's all about hard work. Female pioneers who venture into male-dominated domains face the toughest challenges. For subsequent female beginners, the start will gradually become easier as society gets accustomed to the new situation, and acceptance increases."*

Fahimeh hopes for future gender equality where employers evaluate a person's competencies rather than their gender. As the first female pilot in Iran, she shares: *"When passengers notice that their flight captain is a woman, some are positively surprised, while others find it uncomfortable. It's not uncommon for passengers, after a flight, to want to peek into the cockpit to ensure that there really is a female pilot. That motivates me to continue and work toward a day when a glimpse into the cockpit won't be necessary because it has become the norm."* She is currently a captain and is the first and only woman to fly Airbus A320 aircraft in Iran.

“Female pioneers who venture into male-dominated domains face the toughest challenges.”

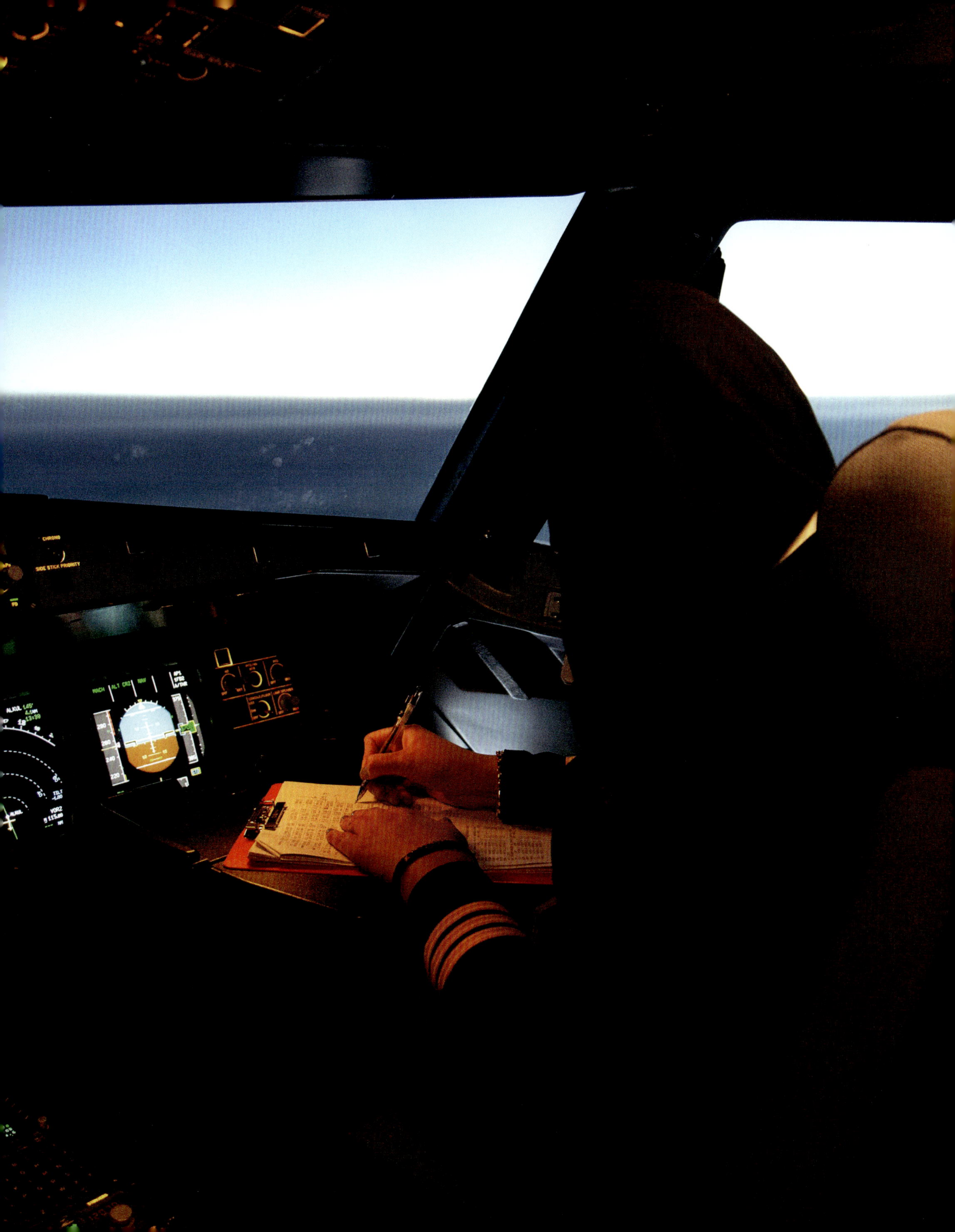
SIDE STICK PRIORITY

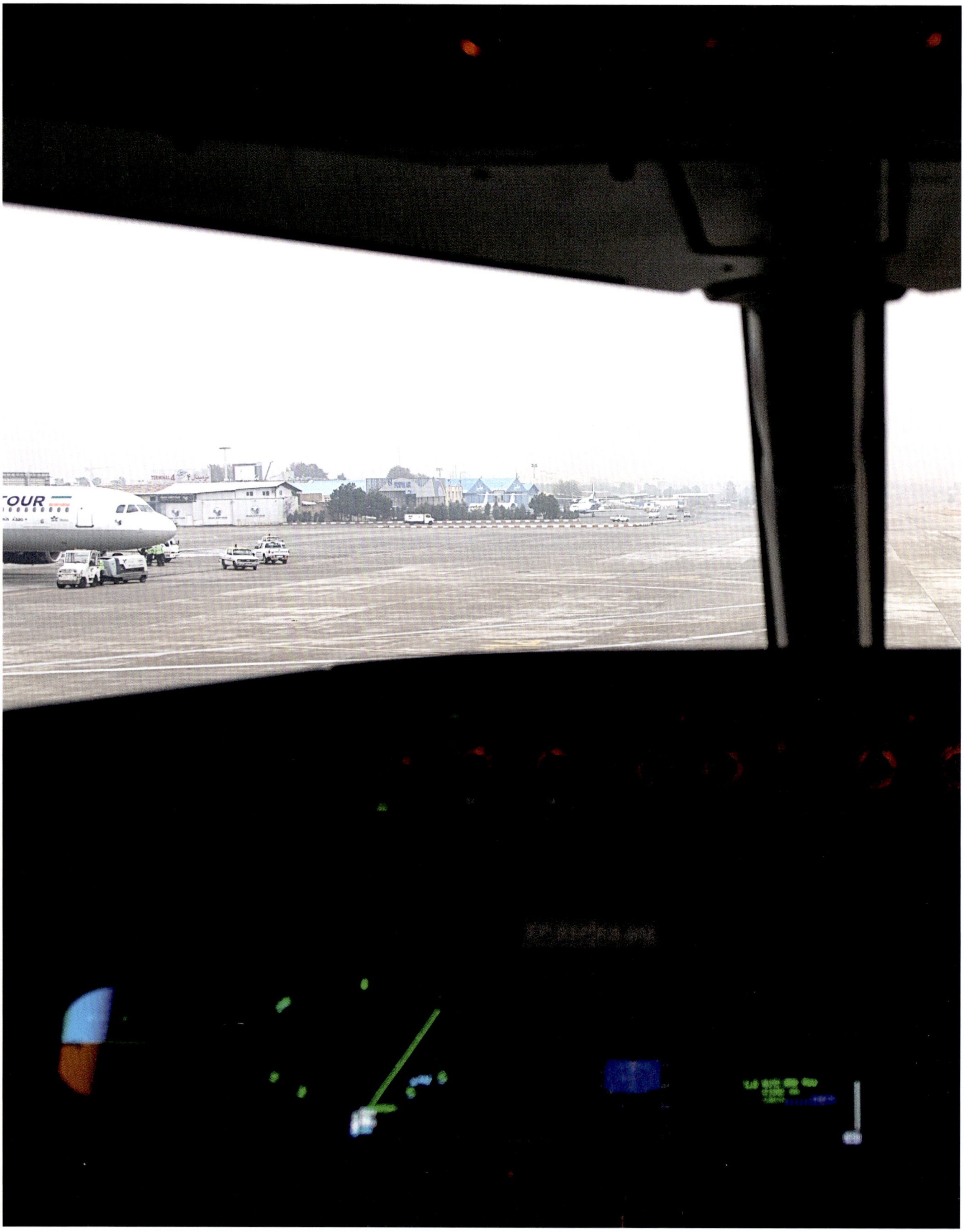

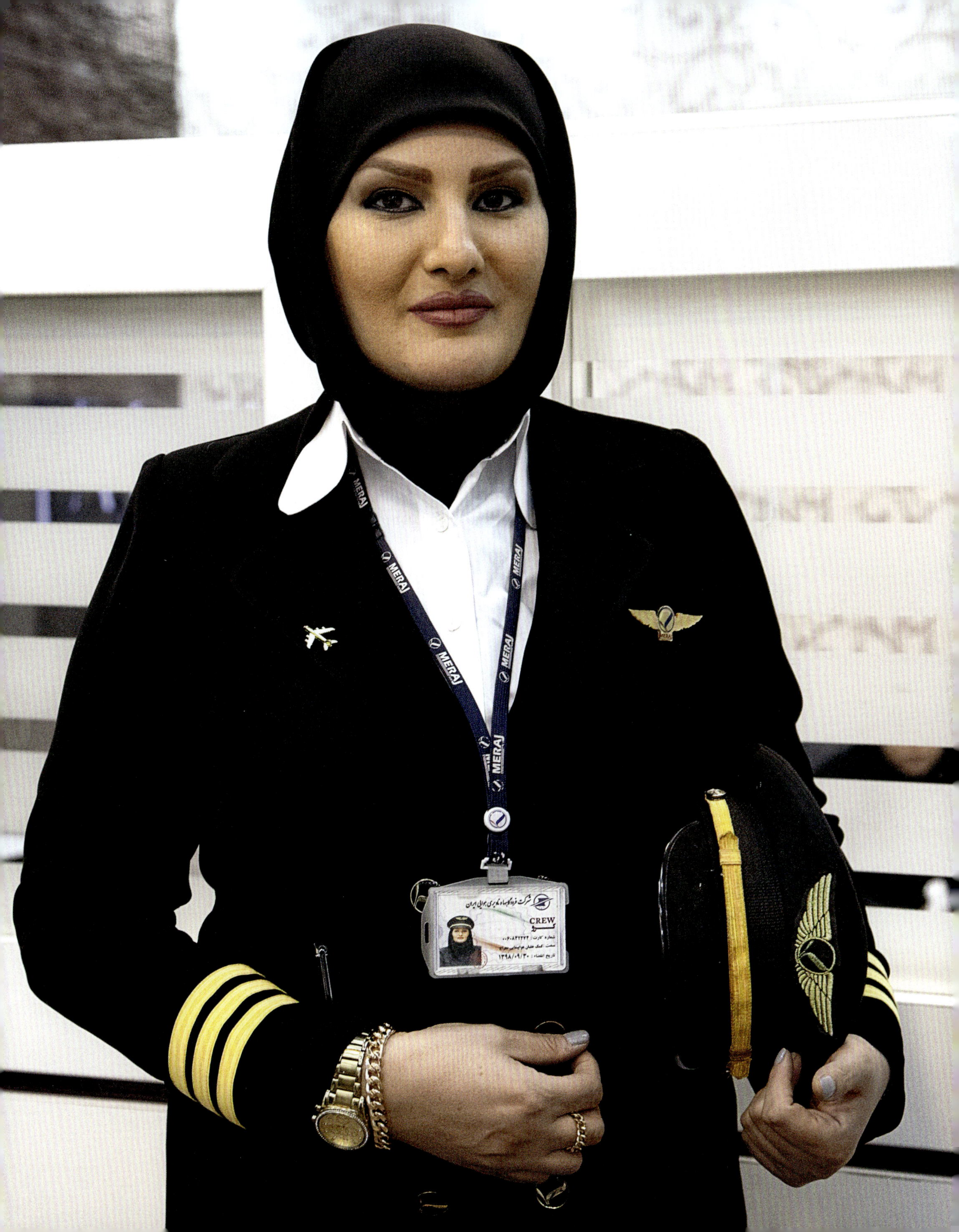
MERAJ
CREW

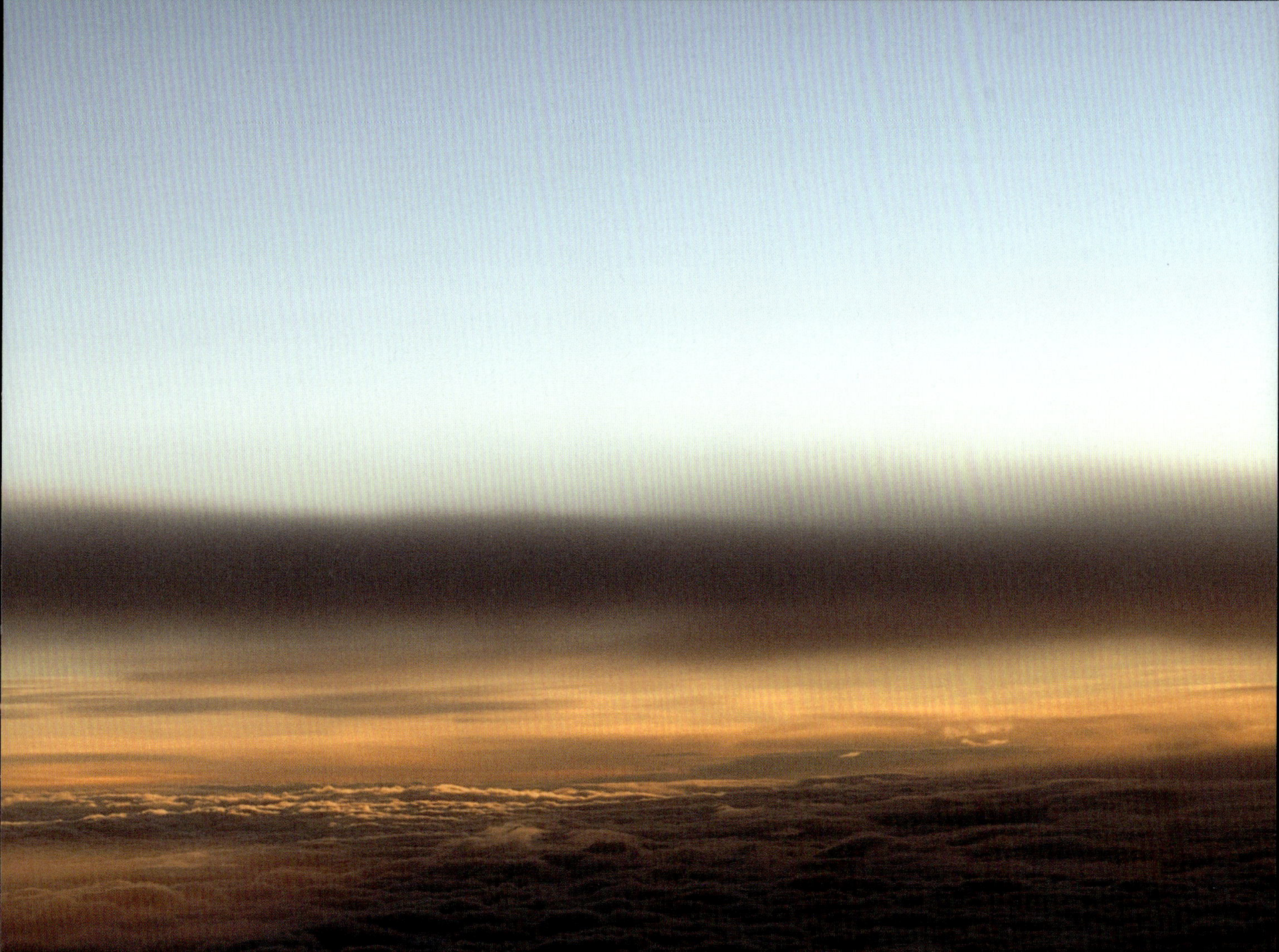

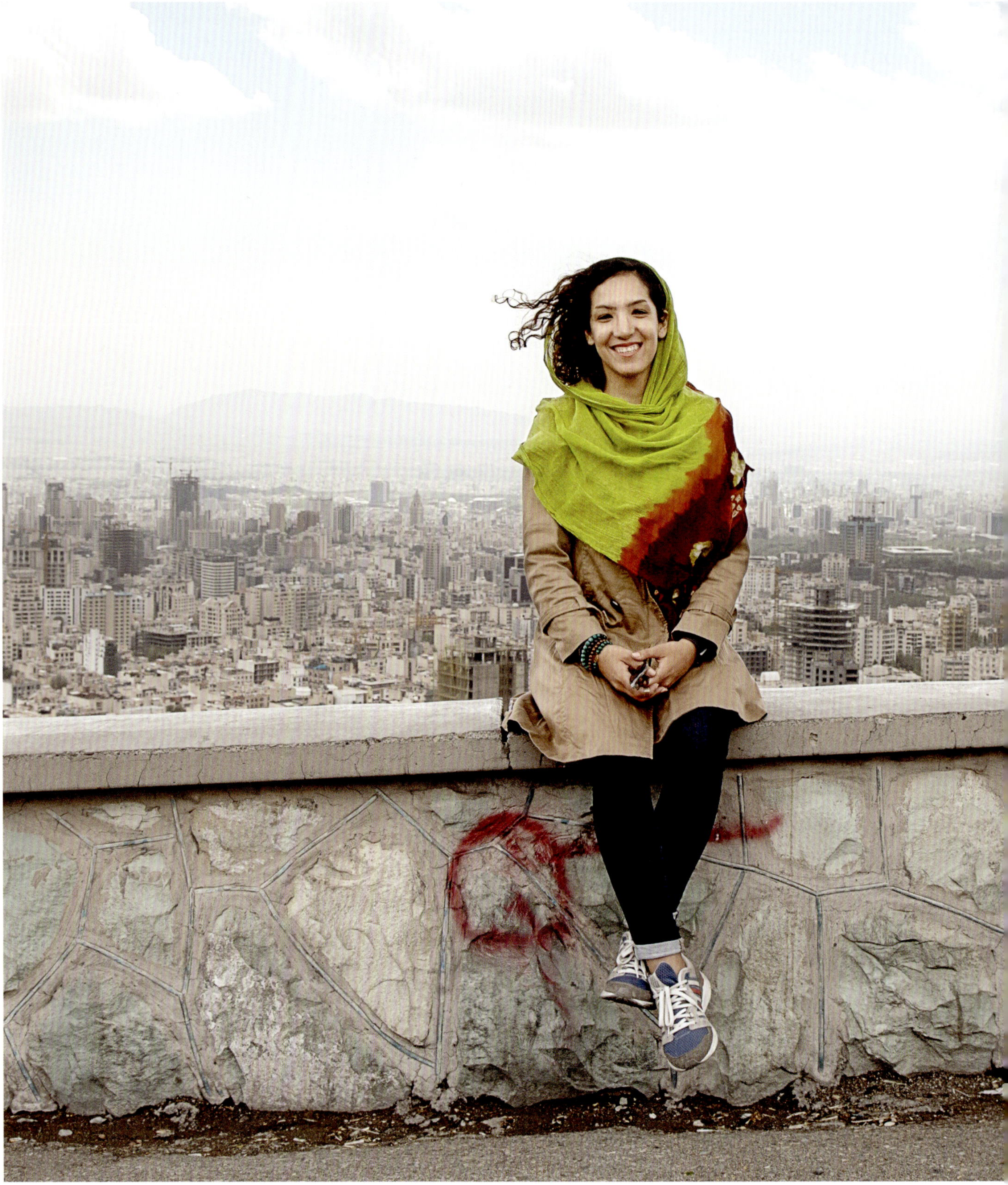

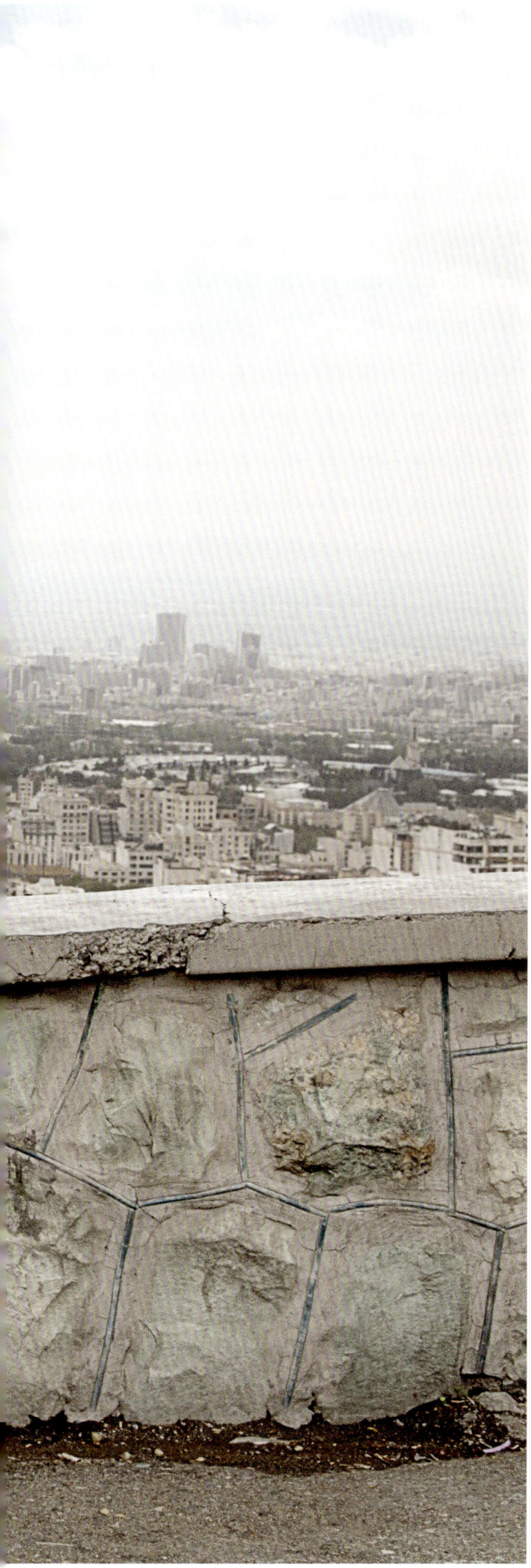

Fatemeh Akrami

"As a child, I was very active and interested in exciting and varied sports. With the support of my parents, I found my way to gymnastics and artistic gymnastics at an early age." For over ten years, Fatemeh trained in the club and participated in national and international competitions. Countless medals are stacked in her room. *"I even gave away many of my medals,"* says the then twenty-six-year-old.

In Iran, participation in gymnastics and artistic gymnastics in clubs and official competitions is only possible for girls and young women until the age of eighteen.

Therefore, Fatemeh looked for an alternative. *"Through my classmate Dariush, I got to know the sport of parkour. On the way home from university, he suggested trying parkour in the park. Although I had heard of it, I didn't know you could do it anywhere. We went to the park and ran through some smaller obstacles. On the first day, I learned different techniques, and it started to become more and more interesting. That motivated me to continue with this sport."* Since then, Dariush and Fatemeh not only share their common interest in parkour training but are also a couple now.

In addition to parkour, Fatemeh has also taken a liking to extreme sports. She is even called the "bird girl" for being the first woman to try skydiving in Iran. *"At first, I wanted to learn skydiving, but I realized that there are no skydiving schools for women in Iran. The nearest school was in Dubai, so I signed up there."* Fatemeh now earns her own money as a gymnastics and fitness trainer for young girls. In her athletic activities, she is also financially supported by her parents, whose only condition was that Fatemeh's academic education not suffer.

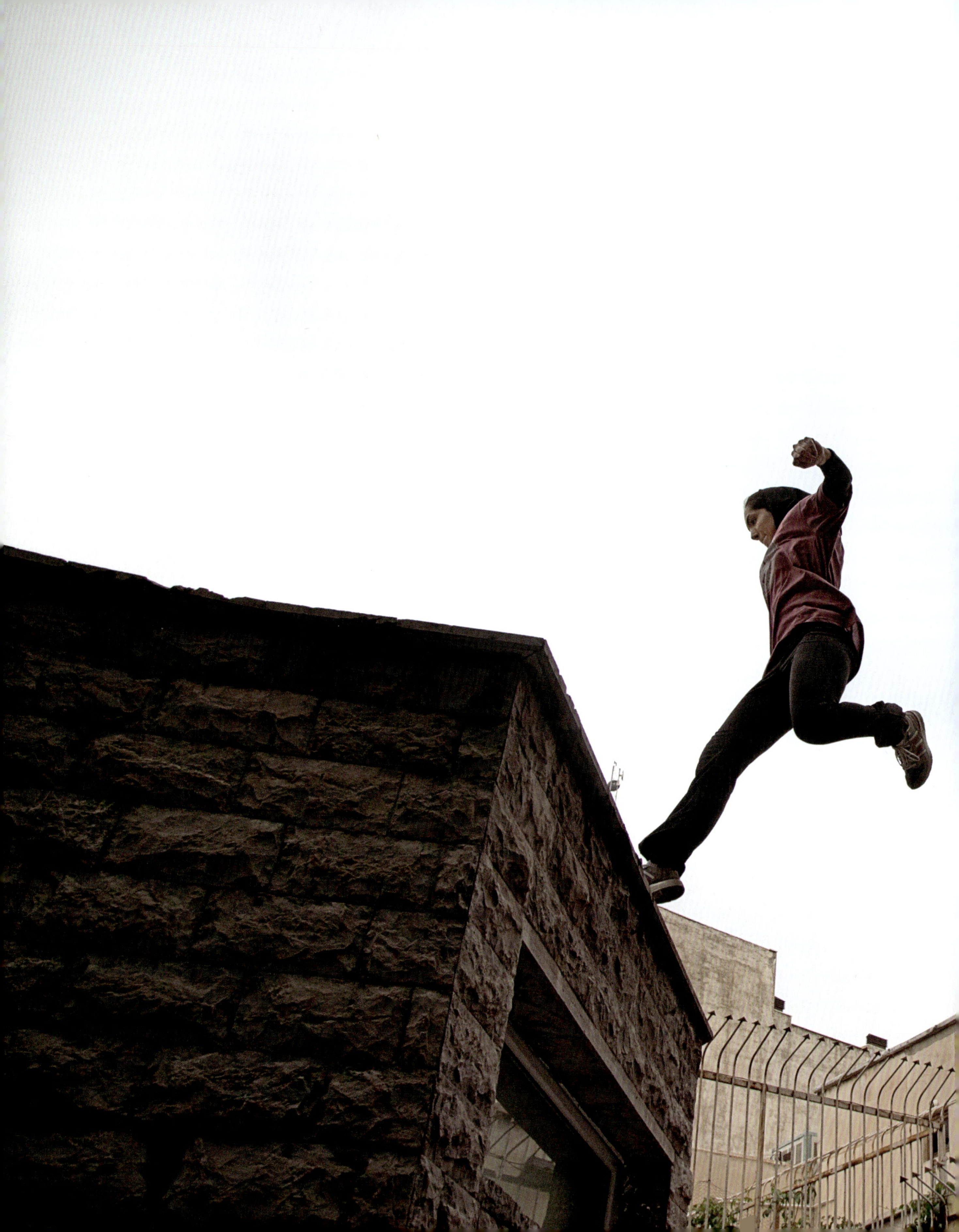

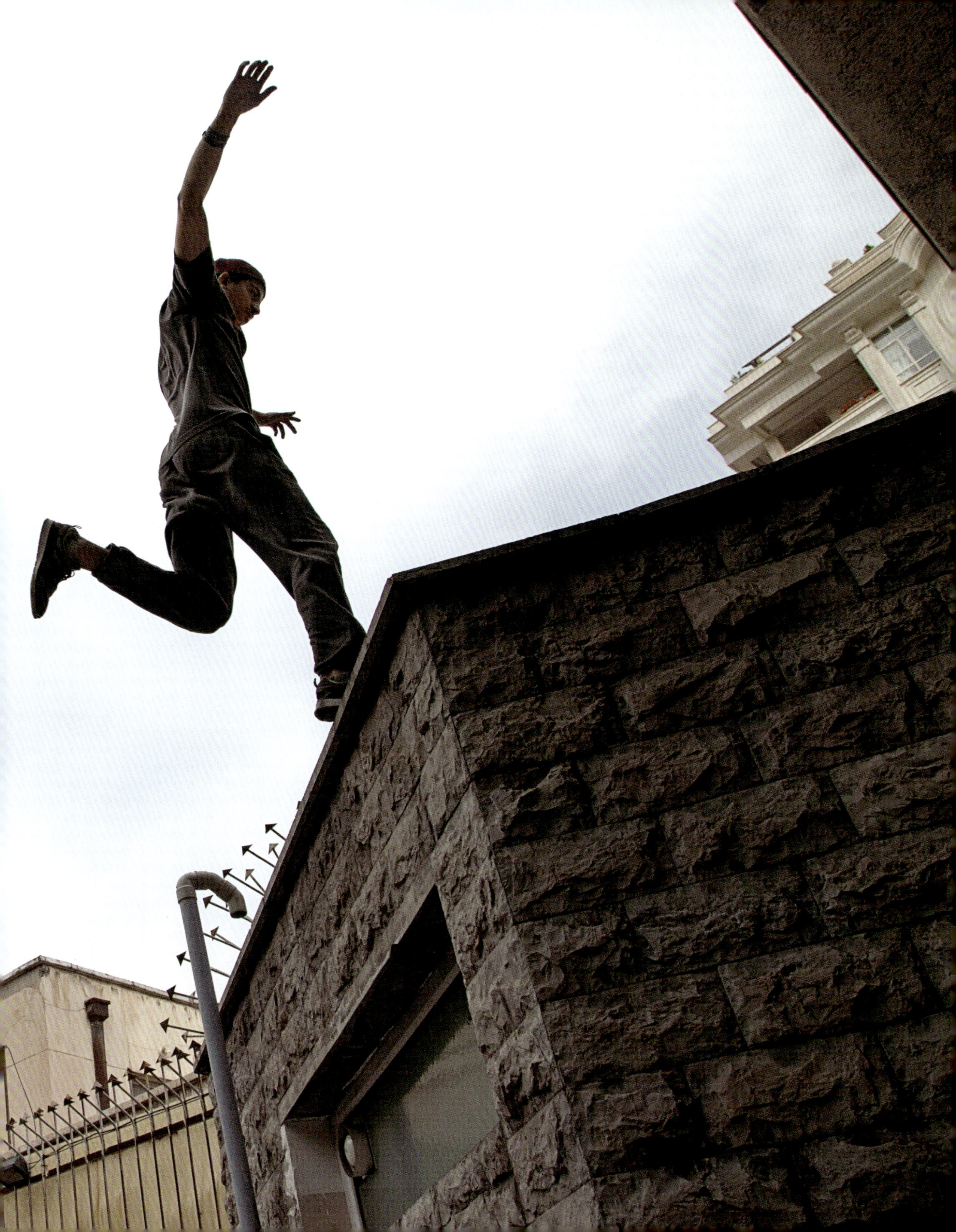

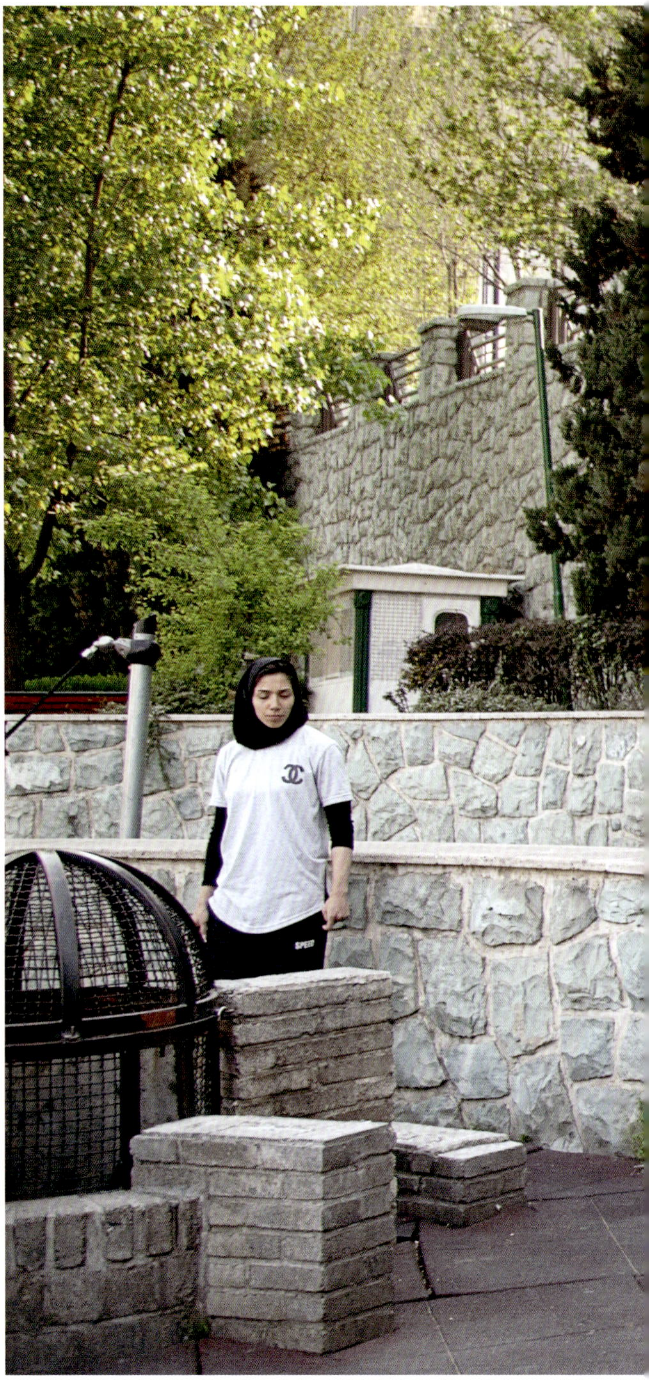

During the week, Fatemeh meets up with her friends to learn and practice specific parkour techniques. They have chosen a playground in Tavalod Park in northern Tehran for their training sessions. Initially, the women in the group put on T-shirts to secure their headscarves. Before jumping, Fatemeh shares: *"It is really challenging to move and train in the summer heat with a coat, a headscarf, and sports clothing, but I have no problem with it because I love the sport."*

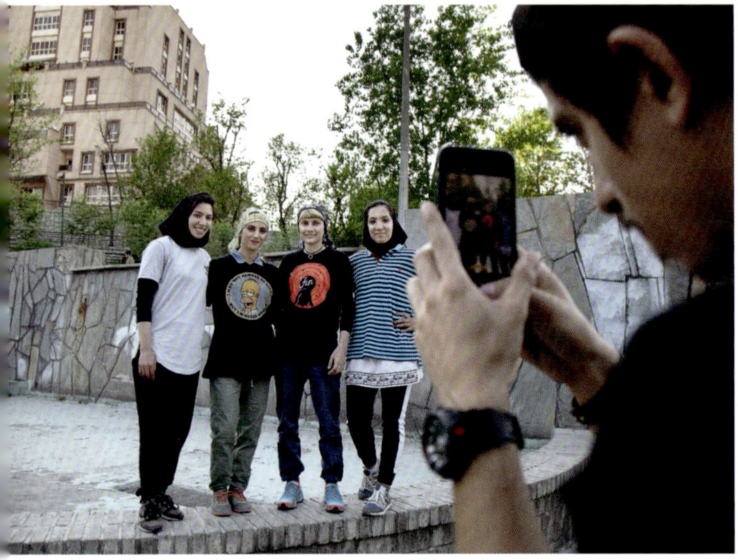

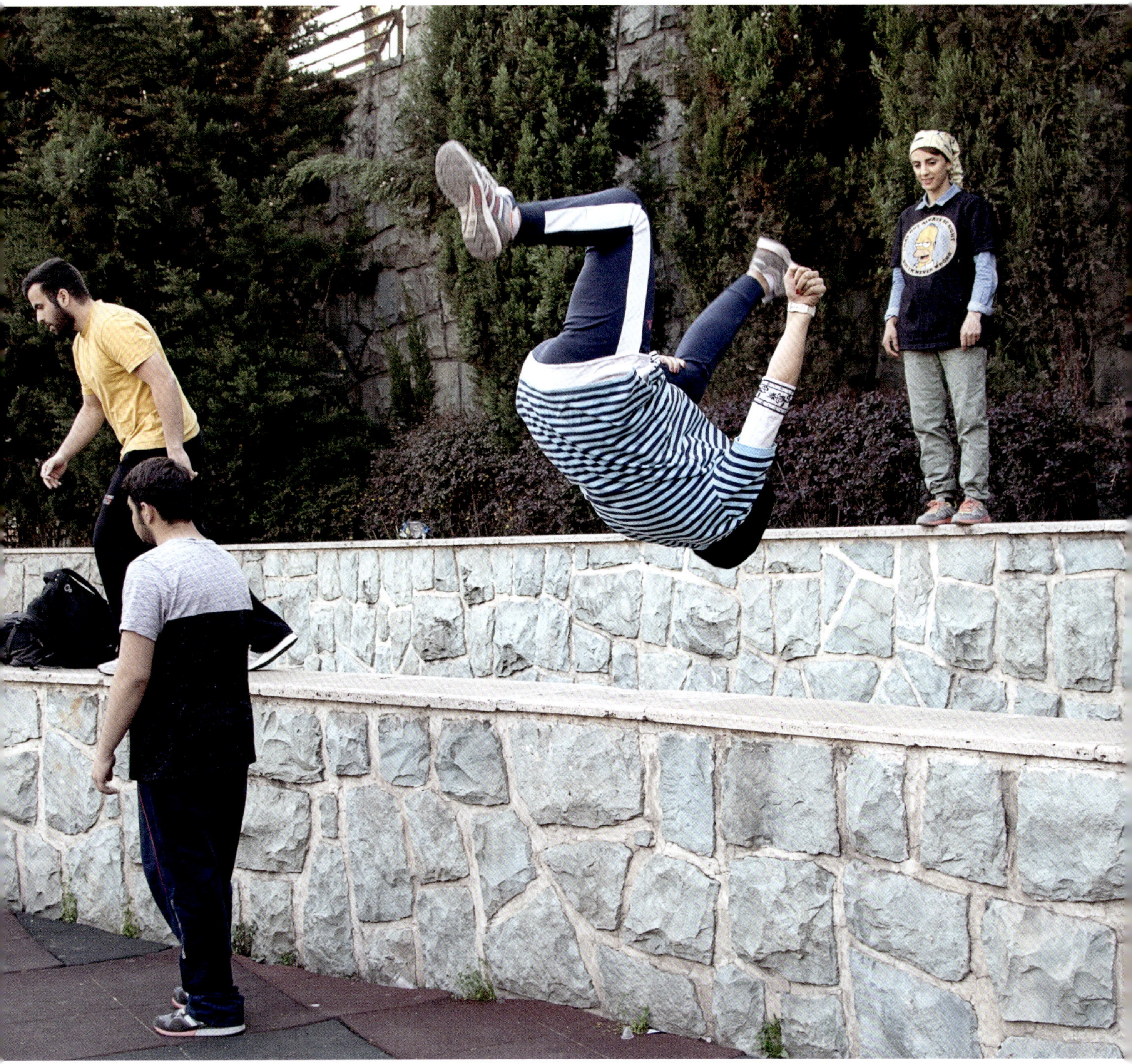

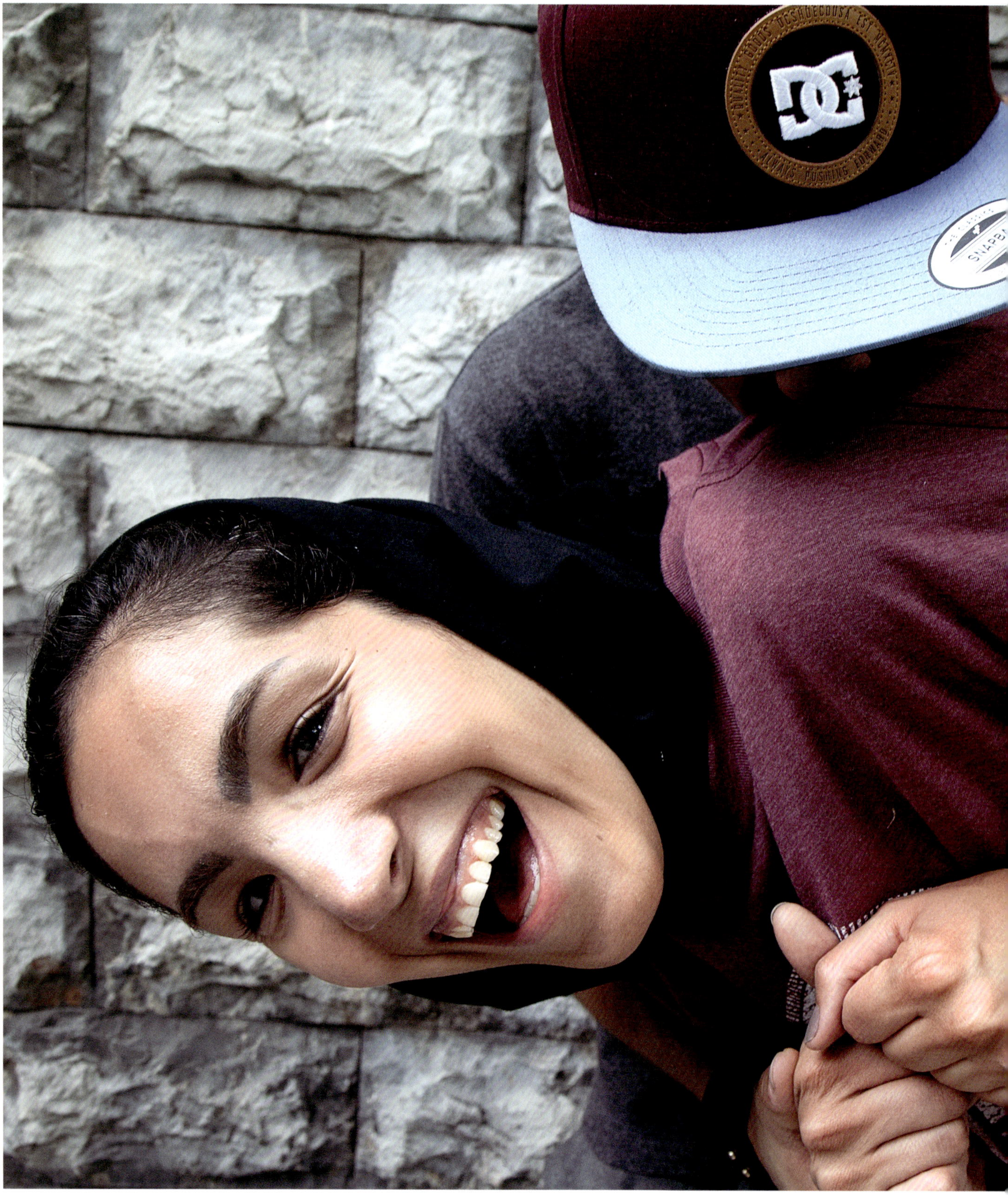

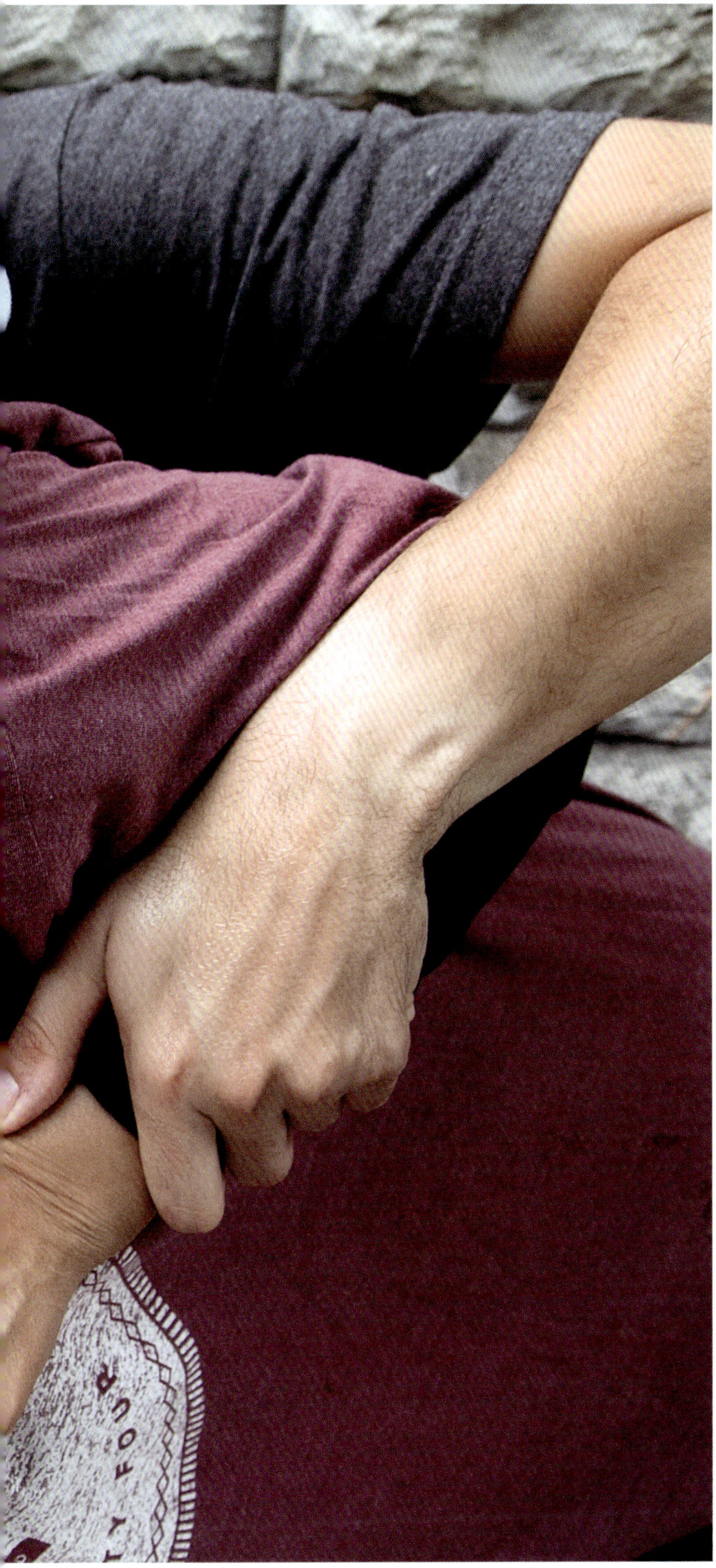

Fatemeh's boyfriend Dariush is a parkour trainer in Tehran. In 2017, both participated in the World Freerunning Parkour Federation (WFPF) Level 1 and 2 coaching certification in Thailand, and they can now be called "certified parkour trainers." Fatemeh is the only woman in Iran with an international parkour certificate. She currently works as a trainer for the Iranian gymnastics youth in Tehran. Sports halls and fitness studios in Iran are gender-segregated, with men and women attending at different times.

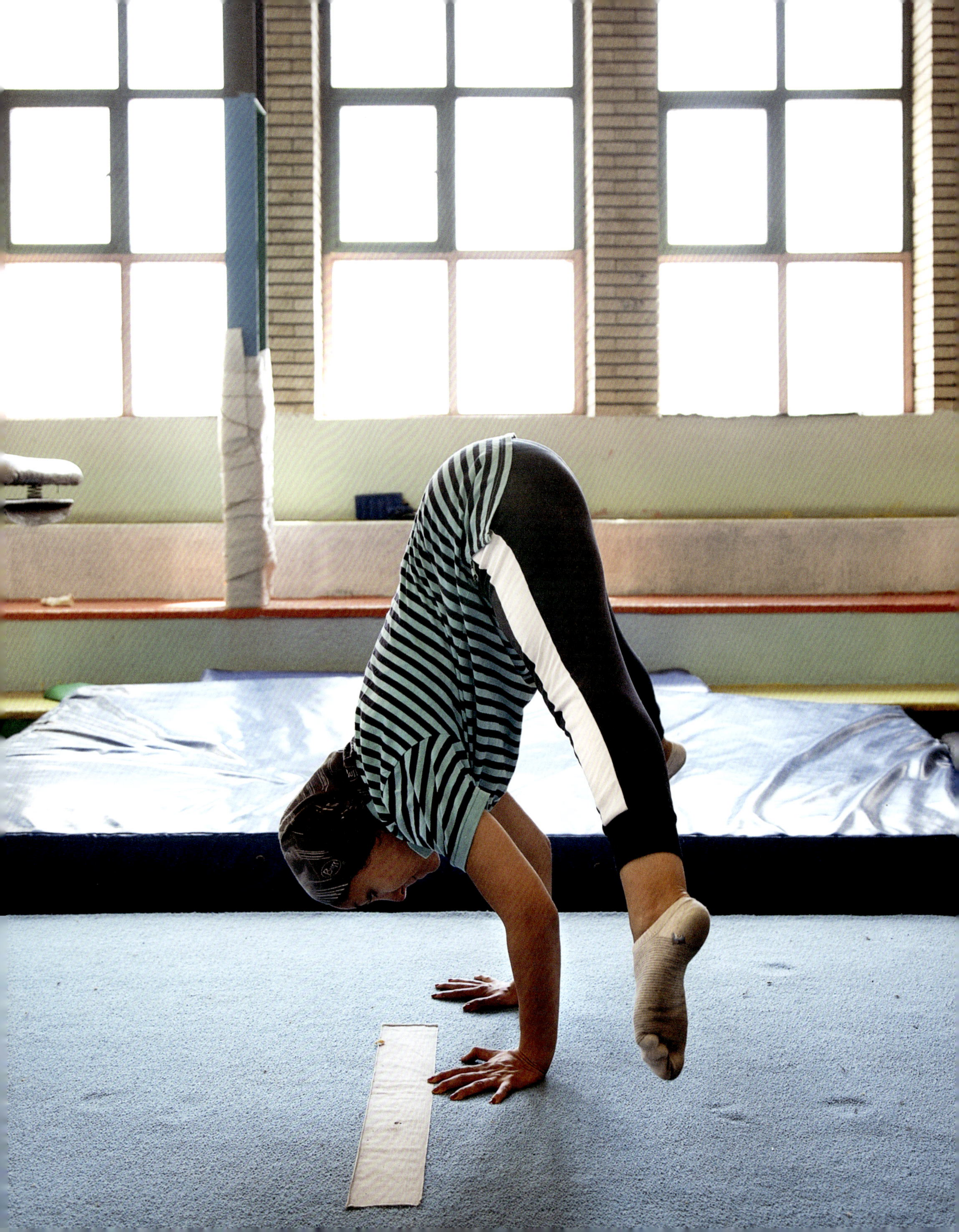

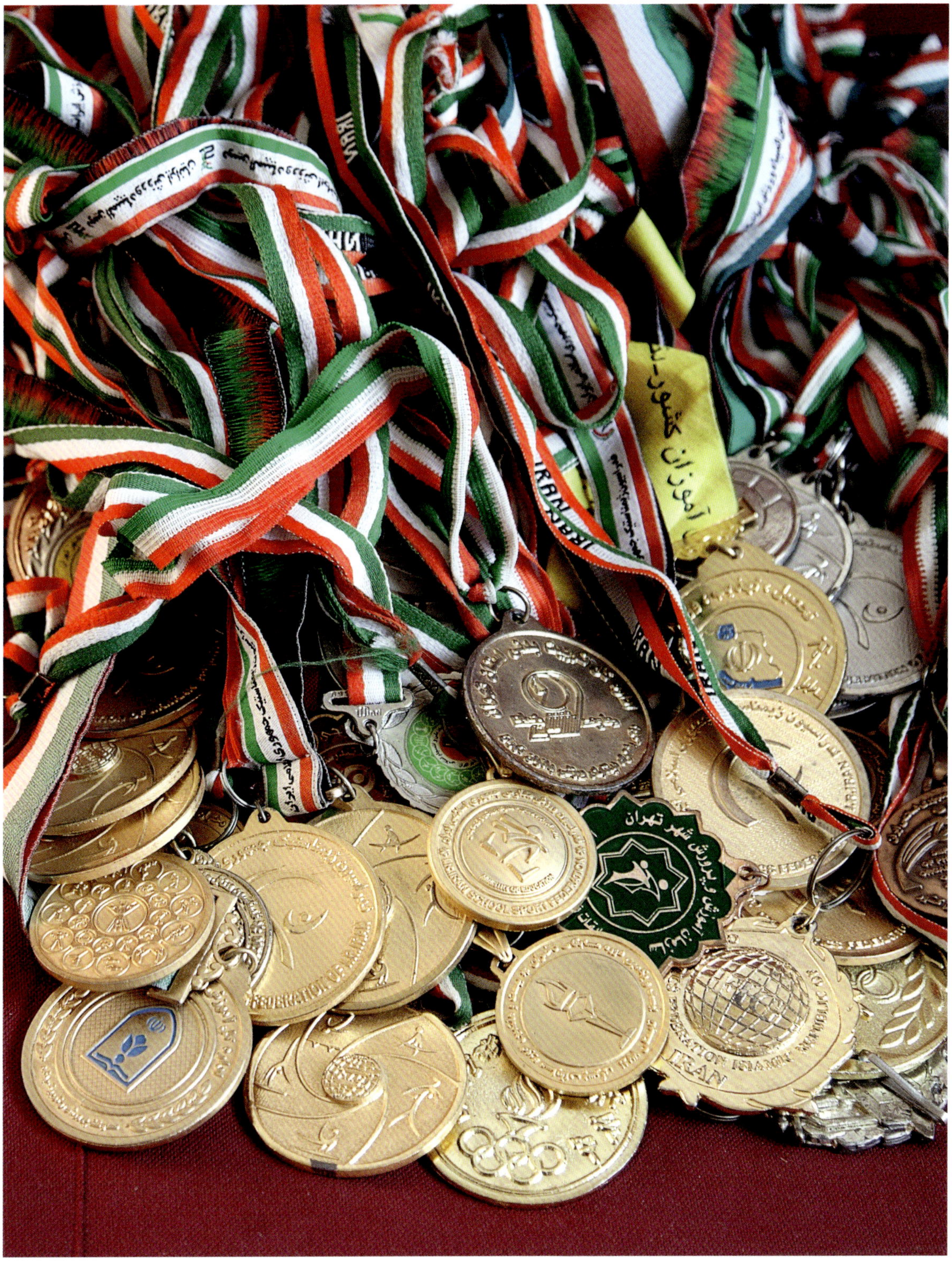
SCHOOL SPORT FEDERATION
IRAN

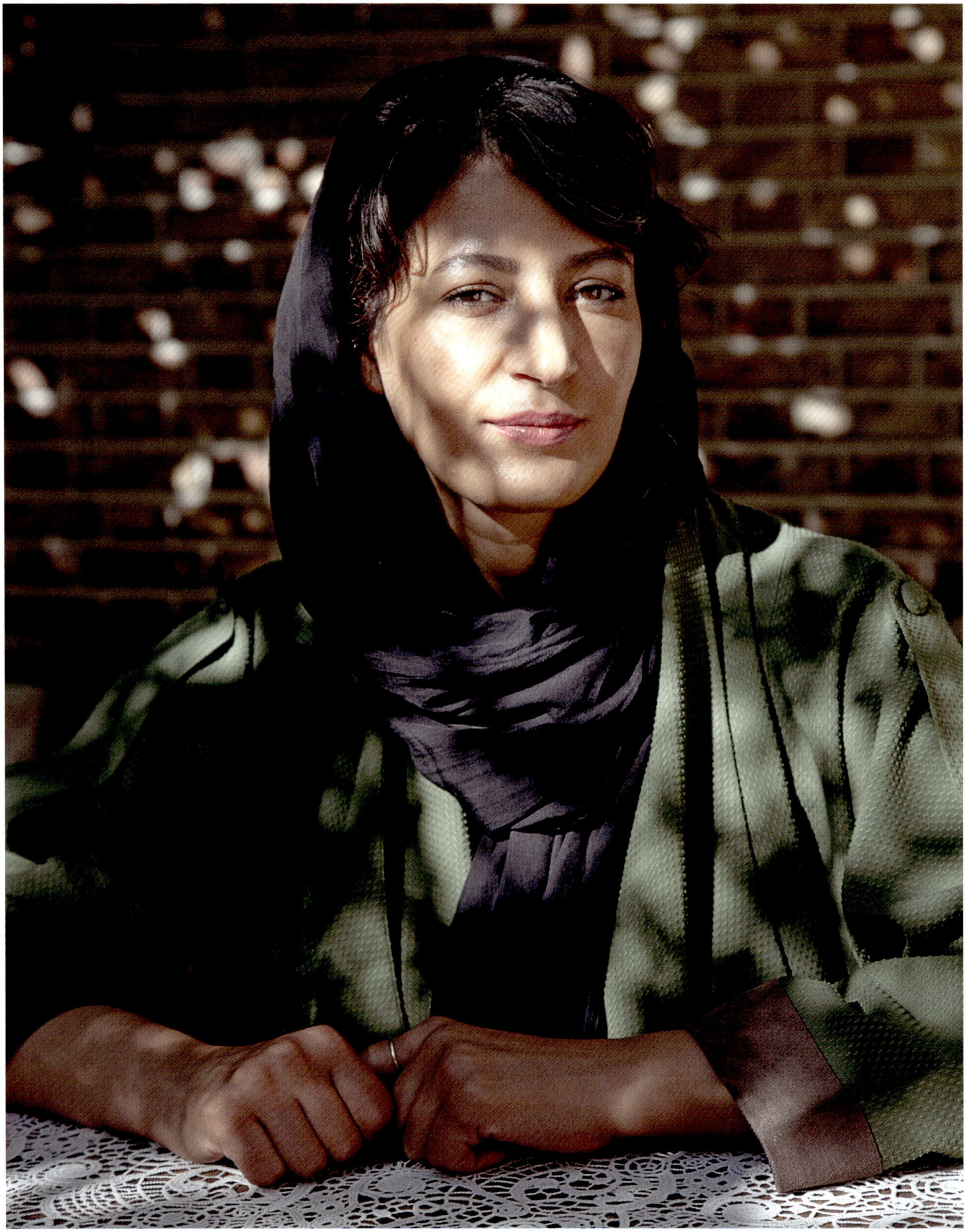

Safoura Mirzaeian

Safoura is one of the managers of Café Tehroon. She studied software engineering and worked for five years at an energy company in Tehran. However, she didn't want to spend her entire life in an office. Therefore, she decided to open a café in the Negarestan Museum garden with her husband Alireza, located in one of Tehran's oldest buildings from the nineteenth century. *"I believe I am a hardworking person and not afraid of physical work. But when the café finally started doing well after three years of hard work, suddenly our lease with the museum was not renewed, and I briefly thought about giving up. It hit us hard, and I think I took it personally,"* describes the forty-one-year-old Safoura about her early days as a café owner. *"Fortunately, we encouraged each other and, along with our friends, embarked on a fresh start."* Shortly afterward, they reopened Café Tehroon, this time in an old house from the 1950s, right on Villa Street in the center of Tehran. *"It lifts my spirits to see different people linger in our café. That gives me a good feeling. Most Iranian women have to fight to assert their new role in society. I have a seven-year-old daughter and, in addition to my work, I must fulfill my traditional role as a good mother and housewife. Even if we women pursue a job, we must not neglect our traditional role so that our new role in society continues to be accepted. In the minds of many men, there is still a distinction between women's and men's work. And even when it is widely accepted that women can have a profession, many men still cannot or do not want to accept helping with household chores or parenting. My husband also finds it difficult at times to take on household tasks,"* says Safoura with a smile on her face.

Through a greenhouse directly behind the entrance gate, one enters the courtyard of the café. In the middle of the courtyard is a small fountain, surrounded by colorful ornamental plants, as is typical in most old Iranian houses. The café walls are adorned with pictures from old Tehran and its people. Accompanied by classical Iranian music, one experiences a nostalgic journey into the 1950s of Iran. Safoura describes the concept of her café as follows: *"We wanted to create a homely living-room atmosphere in the style of the 1950s. This is why we serve an Iranian daily dish every lunchtime in our café, which we've usually only had in our grandmother's kitchen at home. We want to evoke a feeling of comfort."* To refine her concept, Safoura regularly talks to both her staff and her guests. Often, new ideas for the daily menu emerge from these conversations. The kitchen now also offers *ashe reshte*, a vegetarian stew with legumes and various herbs, topped with dissolved yogurt and mint powder mixed with butter. It is a traditional dish that many Iranians enjoy taking on a family picnic.

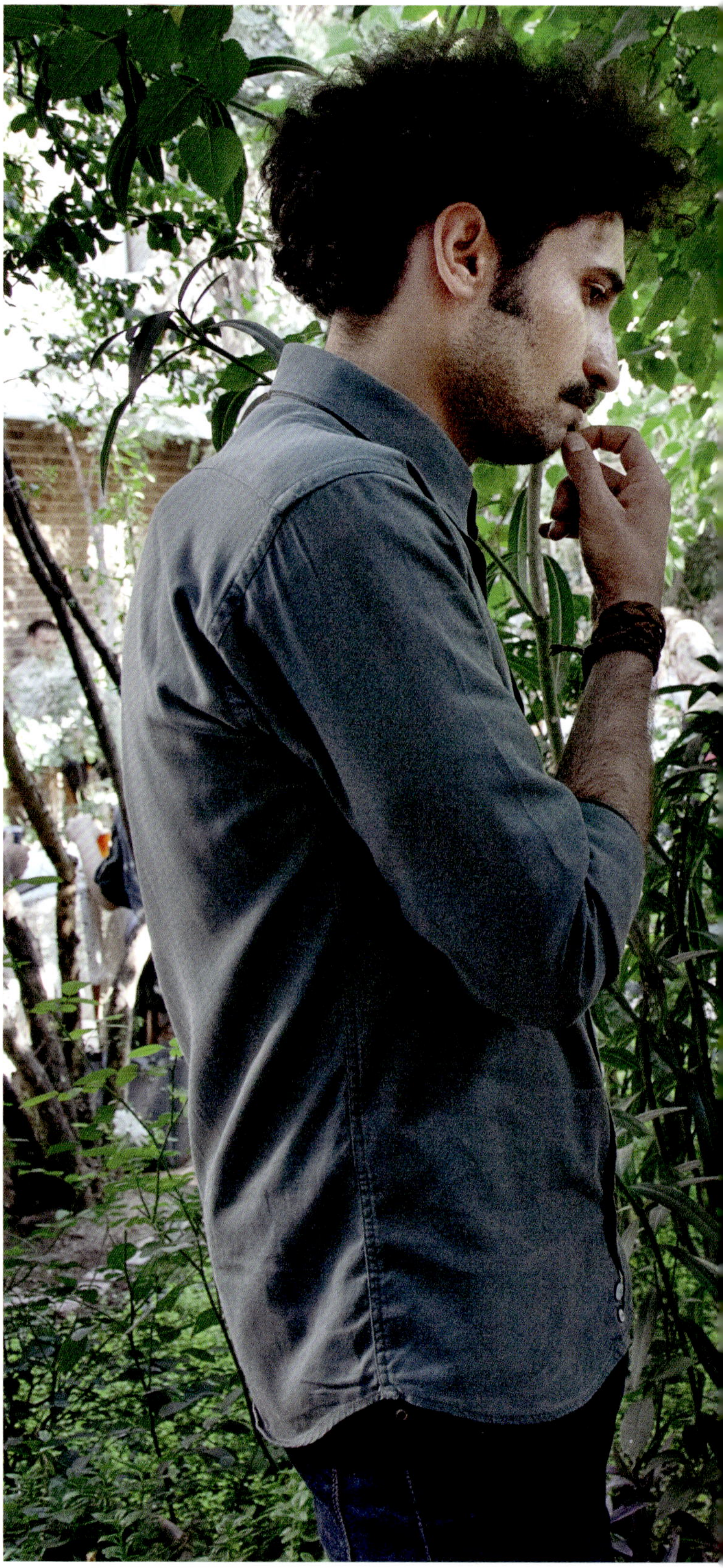

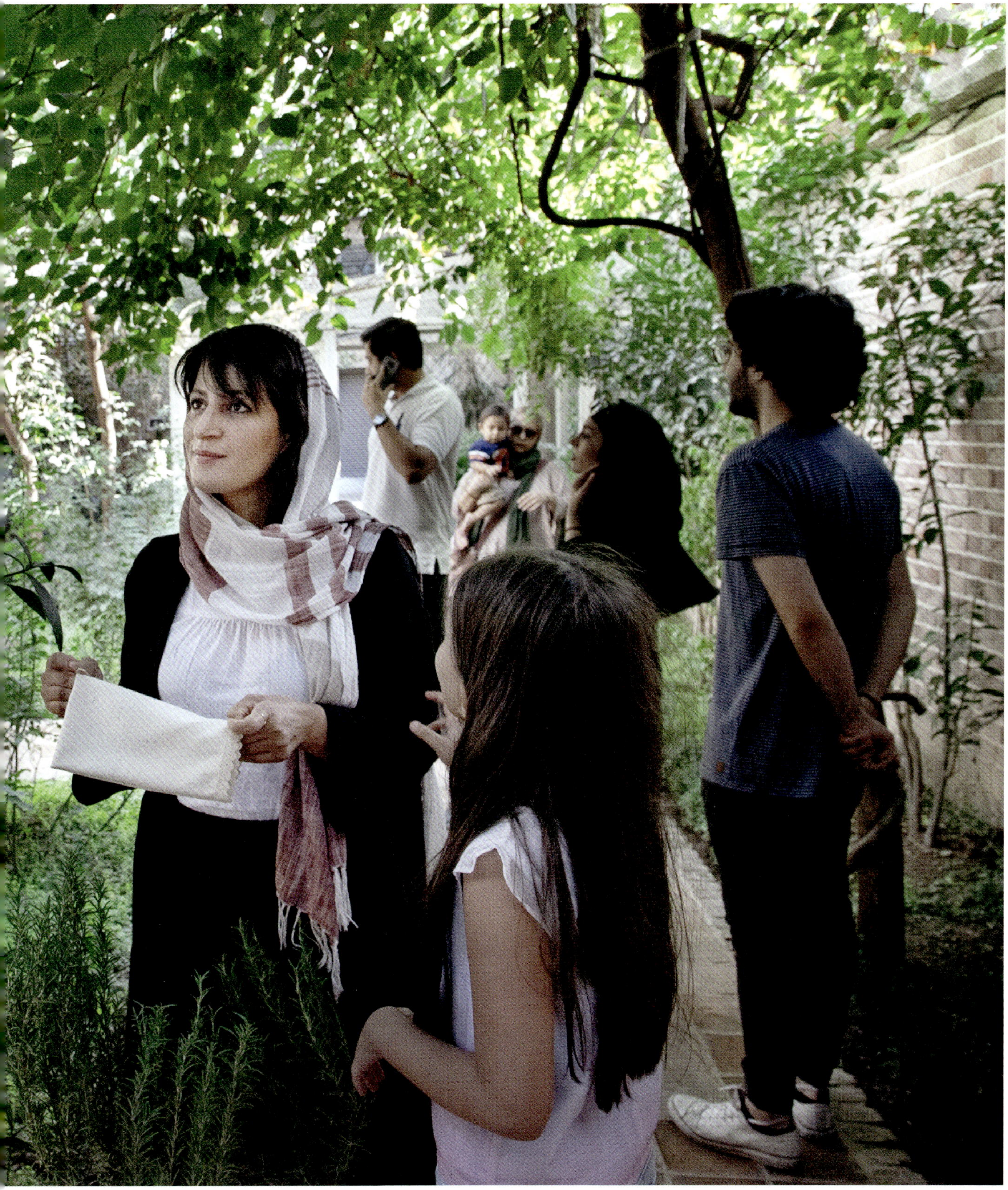

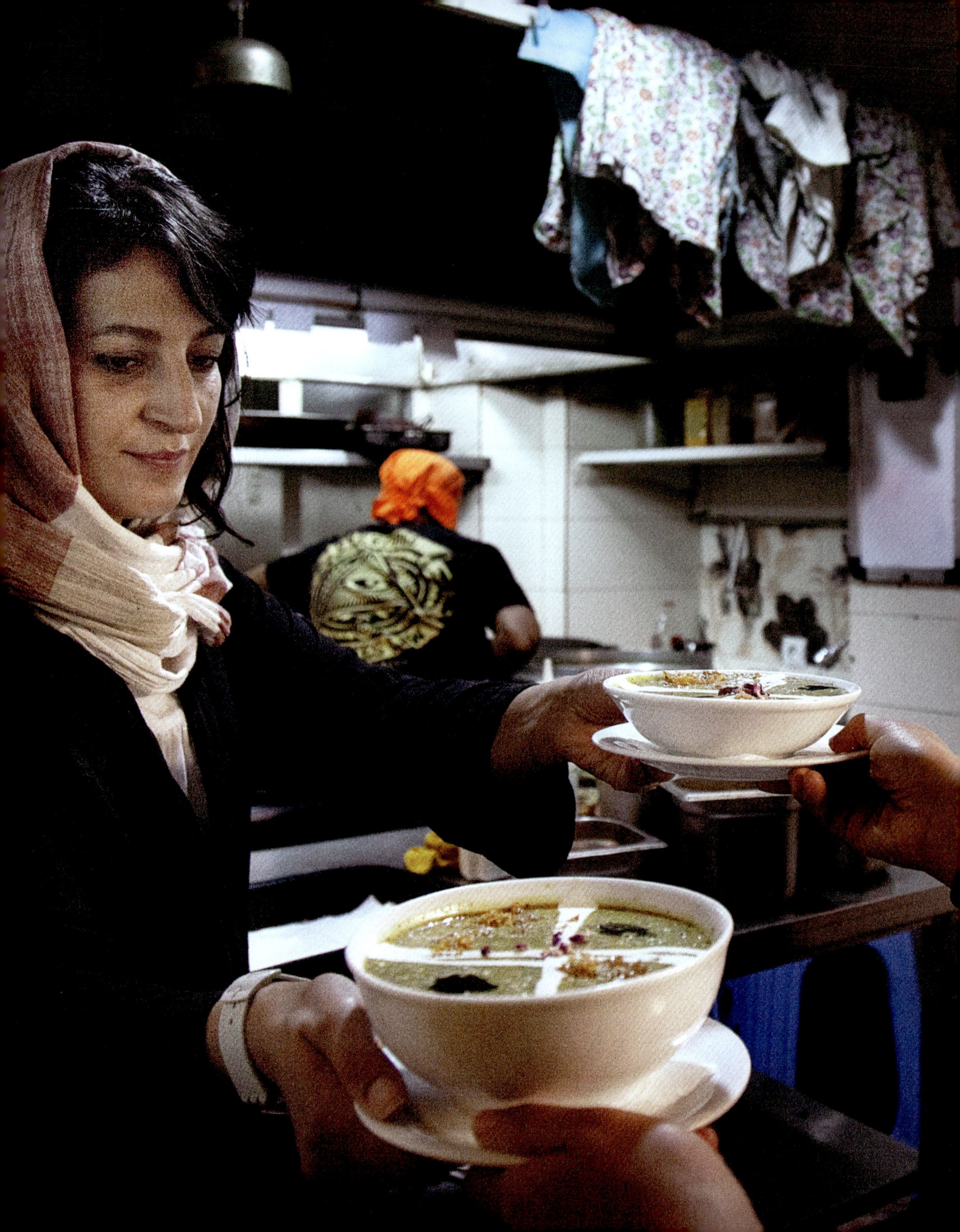

“Unfortunately, housework is still considered women’s work, even if we pursue a profession.”

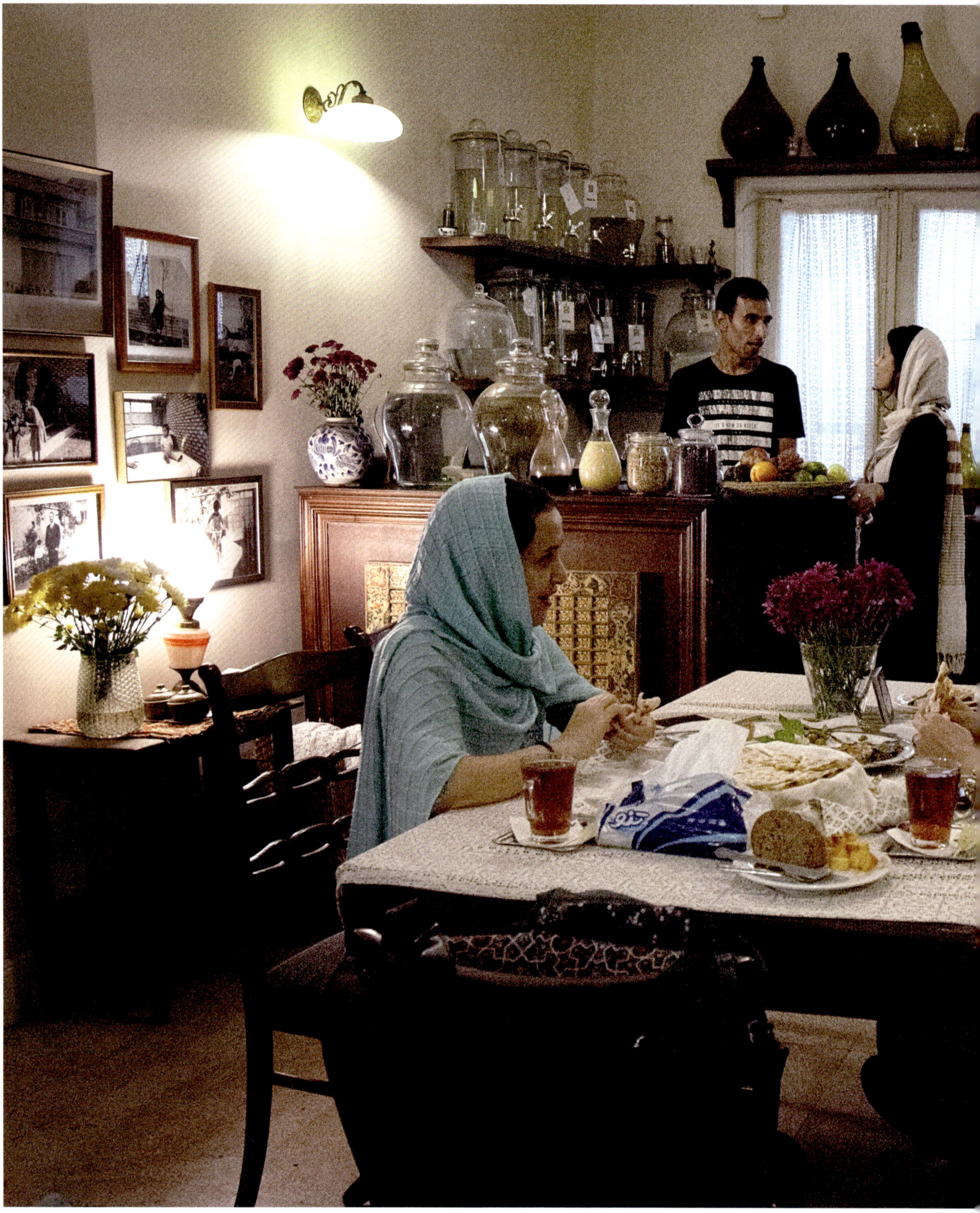

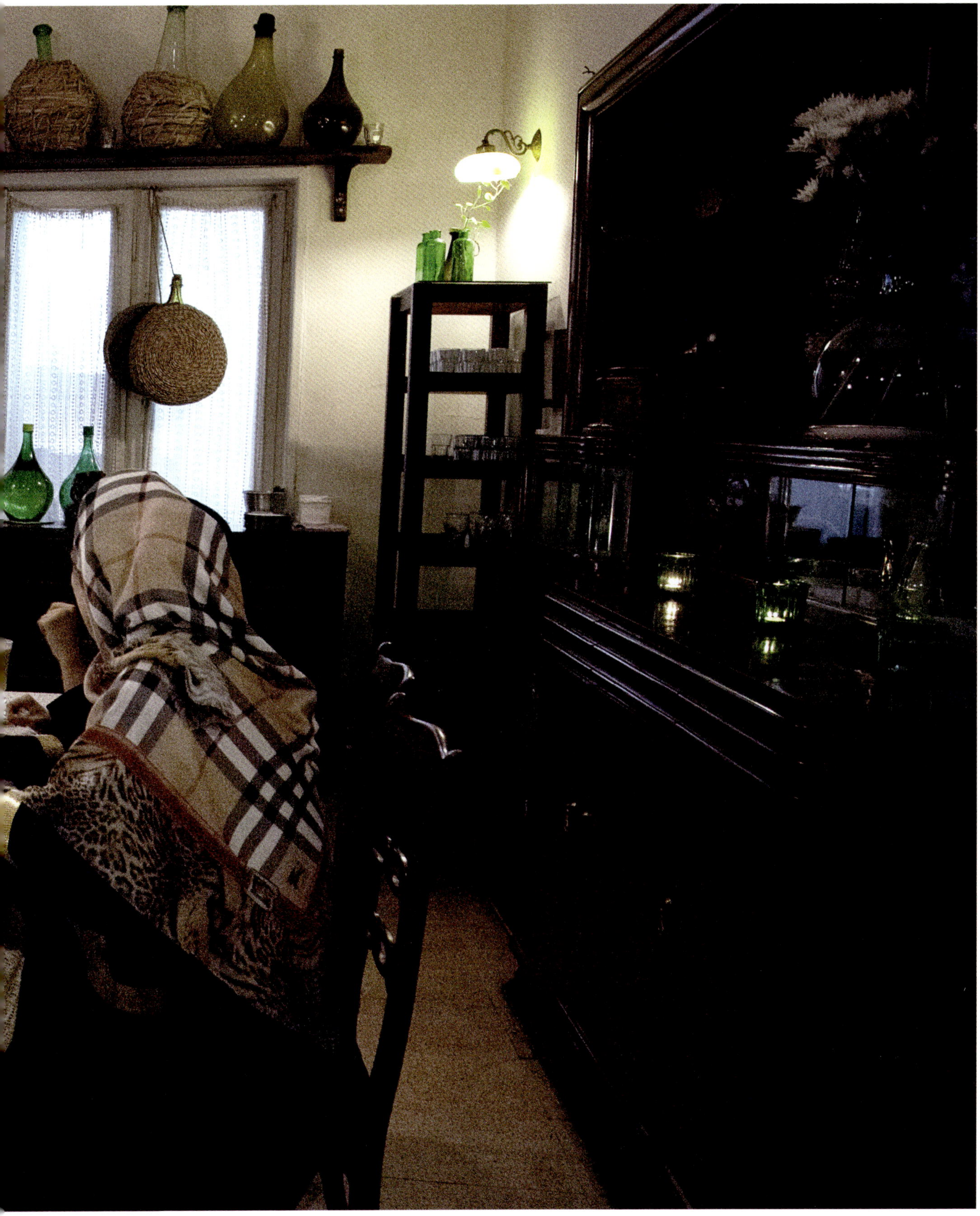

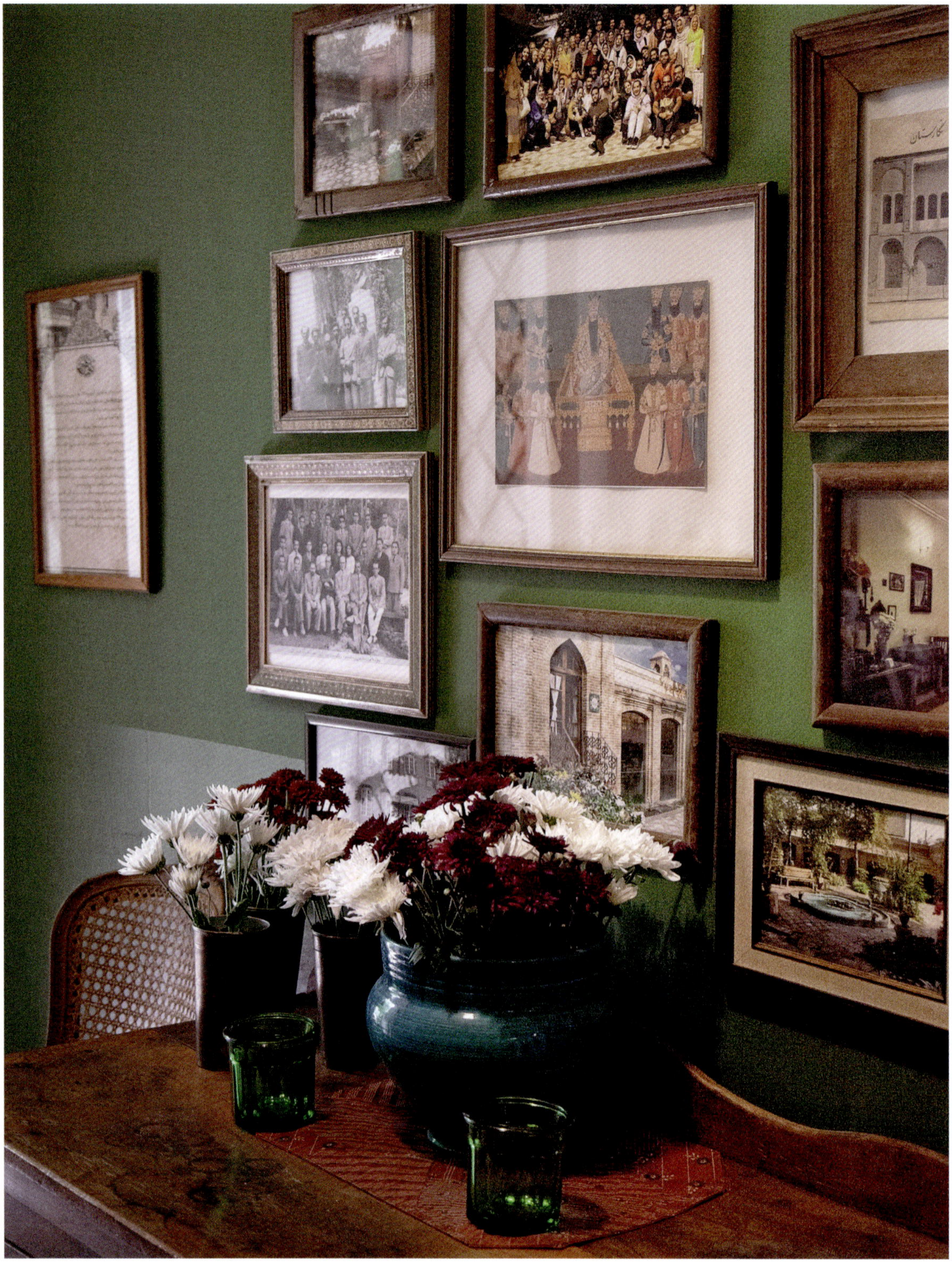

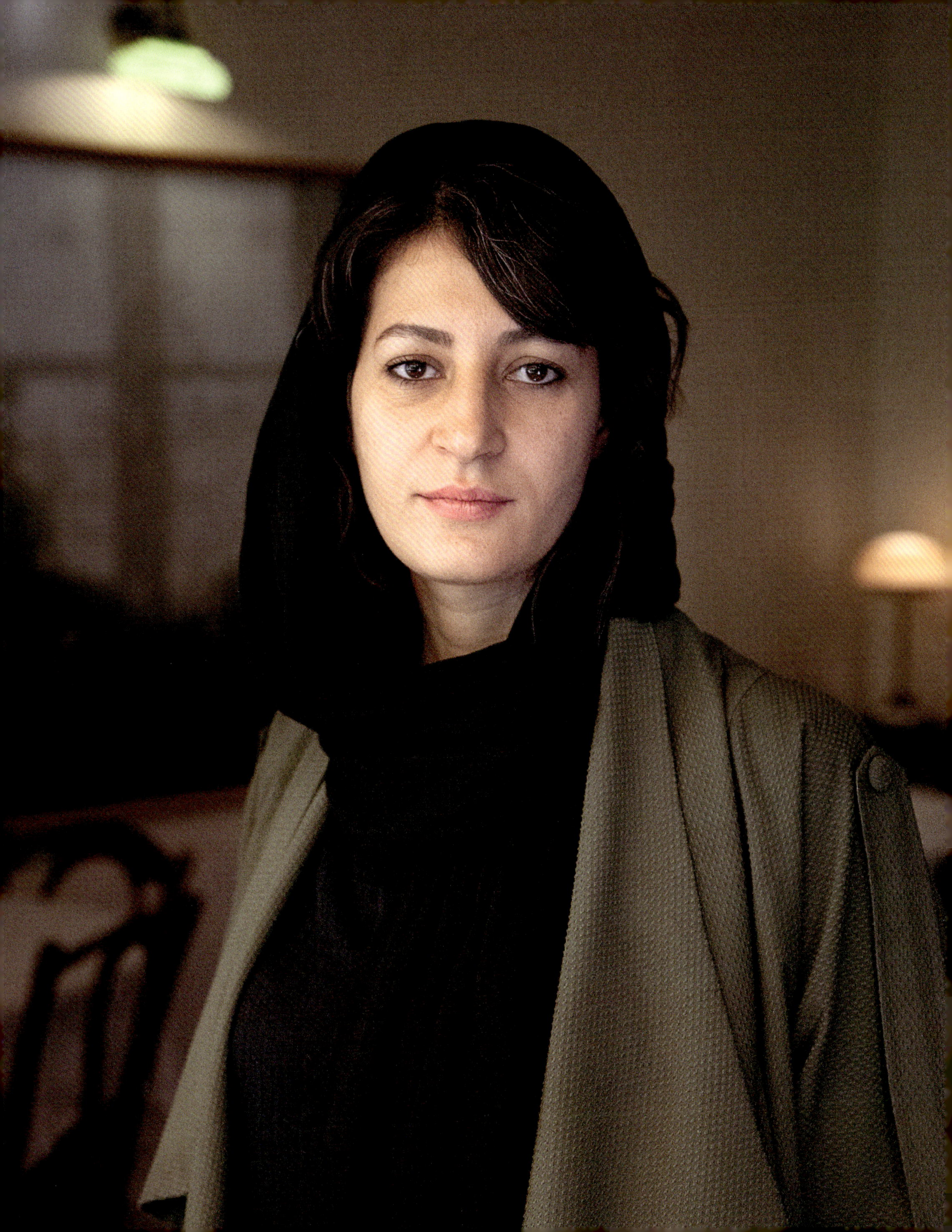

Mercedeh Sadeghi

Mercedeh is a teacher and the director of one of the most prestigious art schools in northern Tehran. She discontinued her studies in chemical engineering at Sharif University of Technology in Tehran, the highest ranked technological university in Iran, due to her passion for art. She retook the entrance examination for the field of cinema and eventually successfully completed her studies in this area. She divorced a few years ago and does not have any children. Mercedeh makes a considerable effort to provide her students with the best conditions to perform well in the annual national university entrance exams.

She believes that everyone, regardless of gender, should always strive to contribute to society—and she conveys this to her students: *"It is not important what profession we have but that we pursue a profession and are always present in society."* Hence, she places great emphasis on teaching her students to think and plan structurally, define goals, and work with focus to achieve them.

The forty-seven-year-old emphasizes: *"Three things are essential to me in an educational system: providing students with equal opportunities to learn, teaching them how to learn, and, at the same time, not neglecting the artistic-creative subjects."* Mercedeh believes that, in the future, creative thinking will be crucial, and less emphasis will be placed on rote memorization. A good, forward-thinking education can help children navigate the world of tomorrow, with subjects fostering creativity playing a crucial role. *"Our educational system should be constantly under critical observation. Things that are correct today may be outdated tomorrow."*

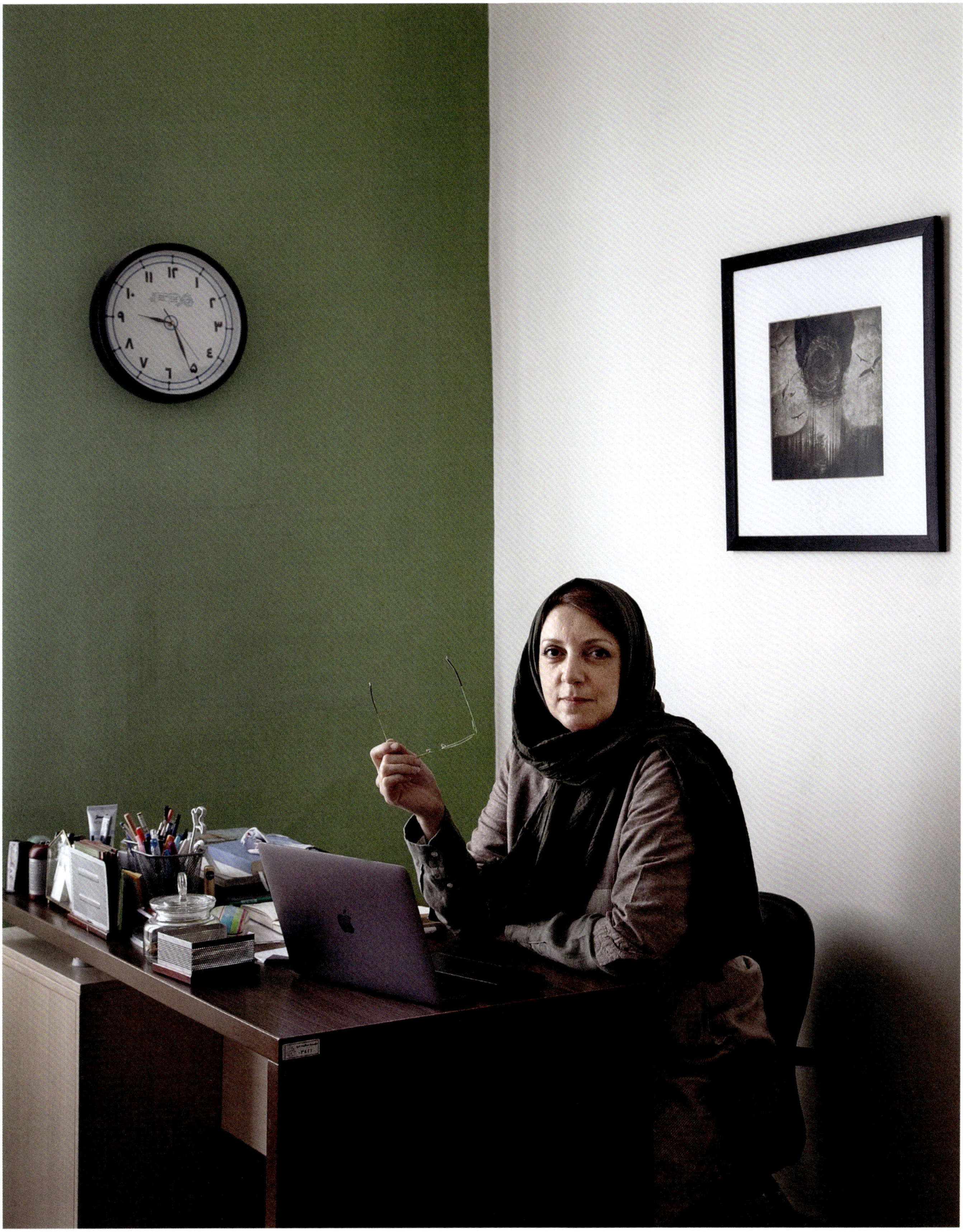

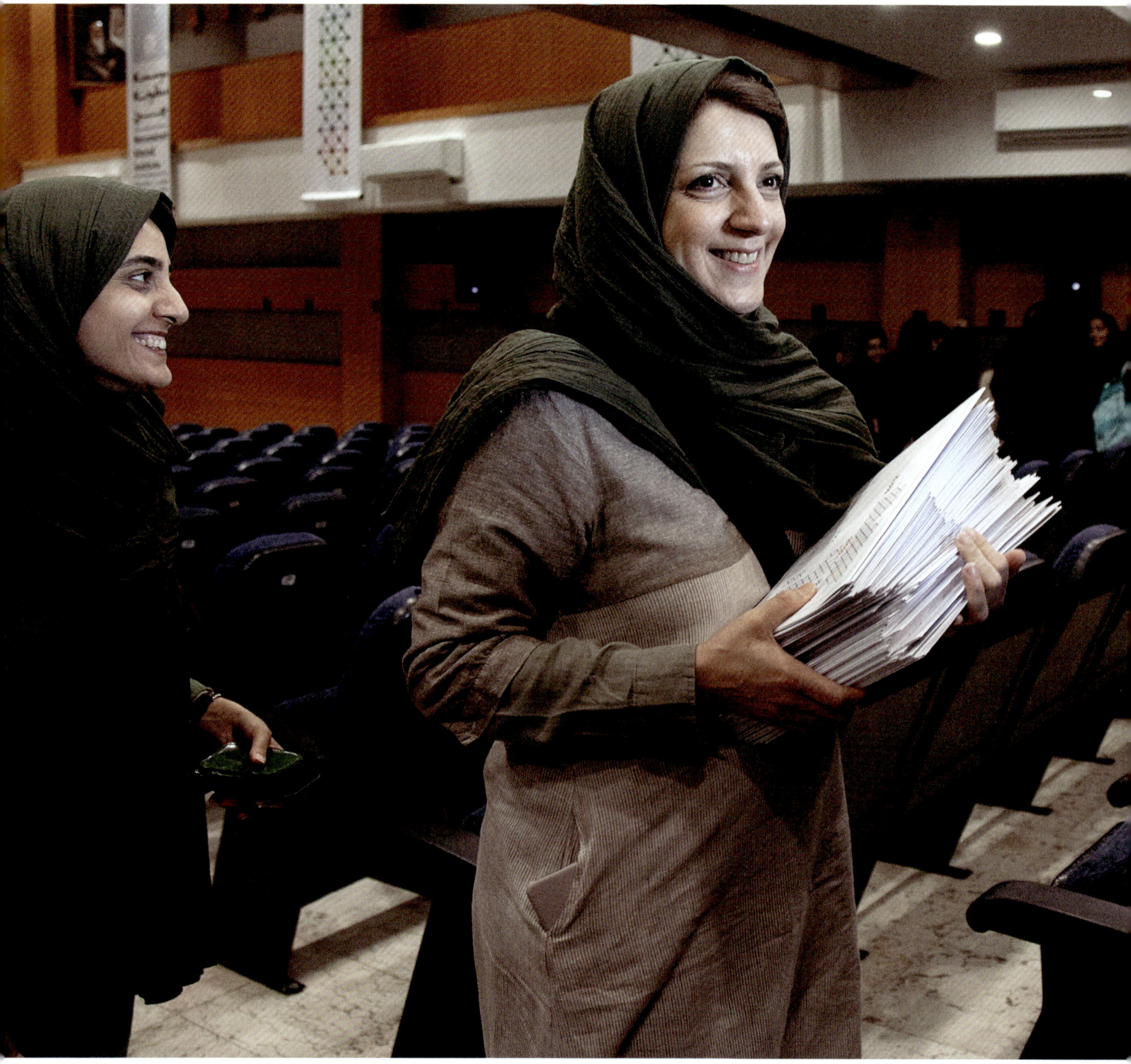

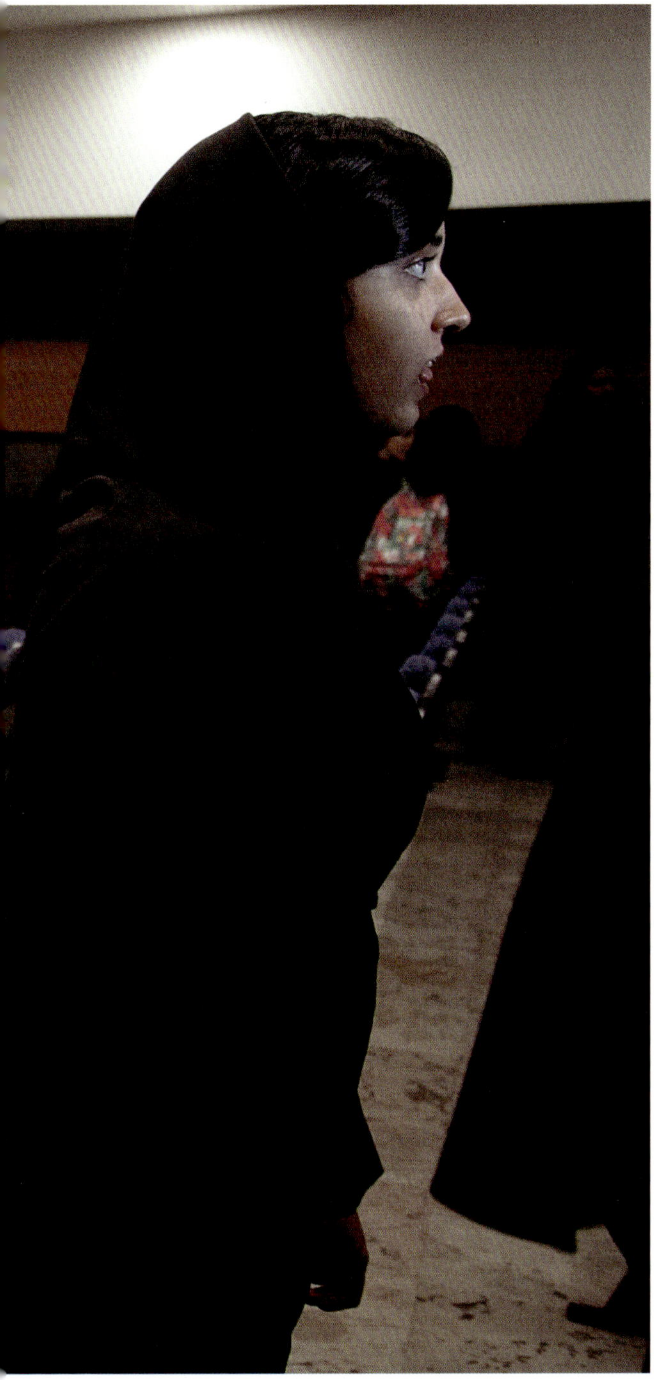

Every year, on September 21, the official beginning of autumn, the first day of school commences in Iran. Schools in Iran are segregated by gender. In the Manzoumeh Kherad School, before the students enter the classrooms, a welcome ceremony takes place in the school's auditorium, starting with a recitation from the Quran—mandatory for events in state institutions. This is followed by a welcoming speech from the director and some female teachers, and a concluding musical performance, planned and carried out by the school's female students.

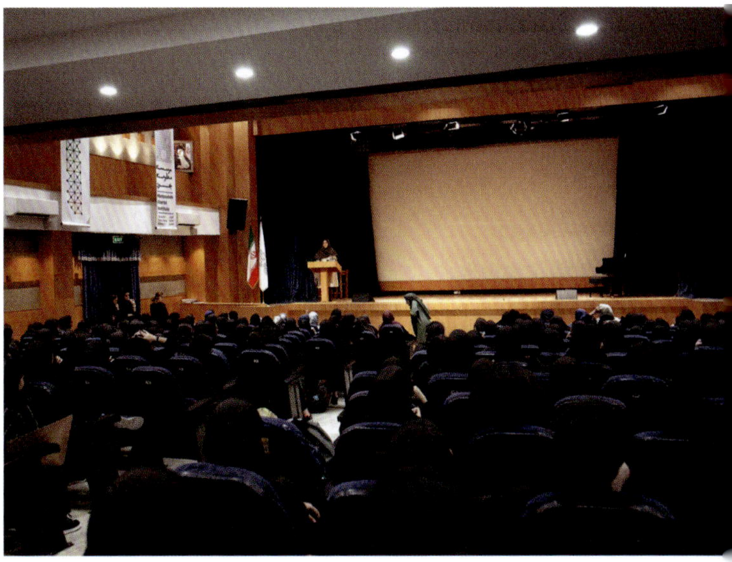

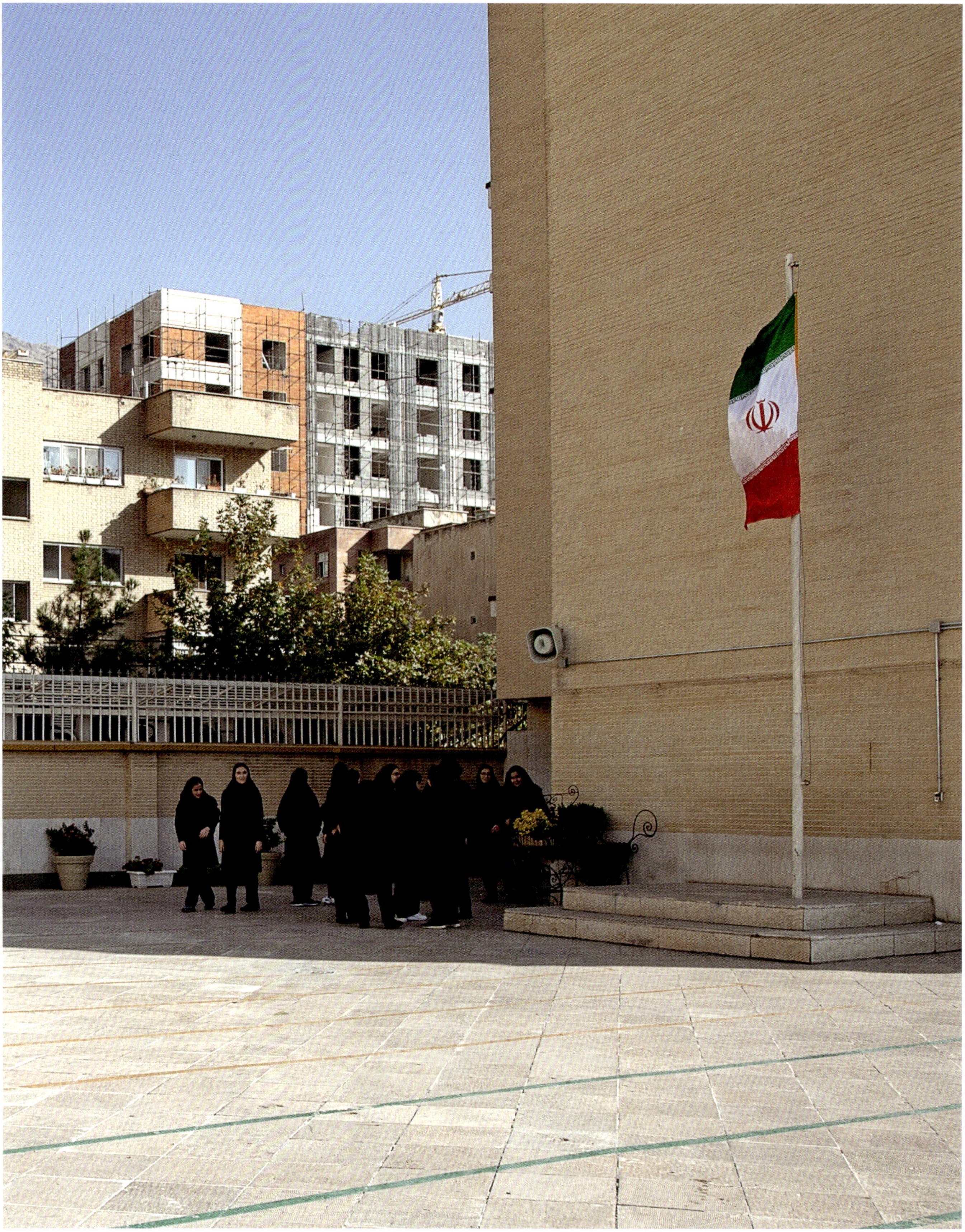

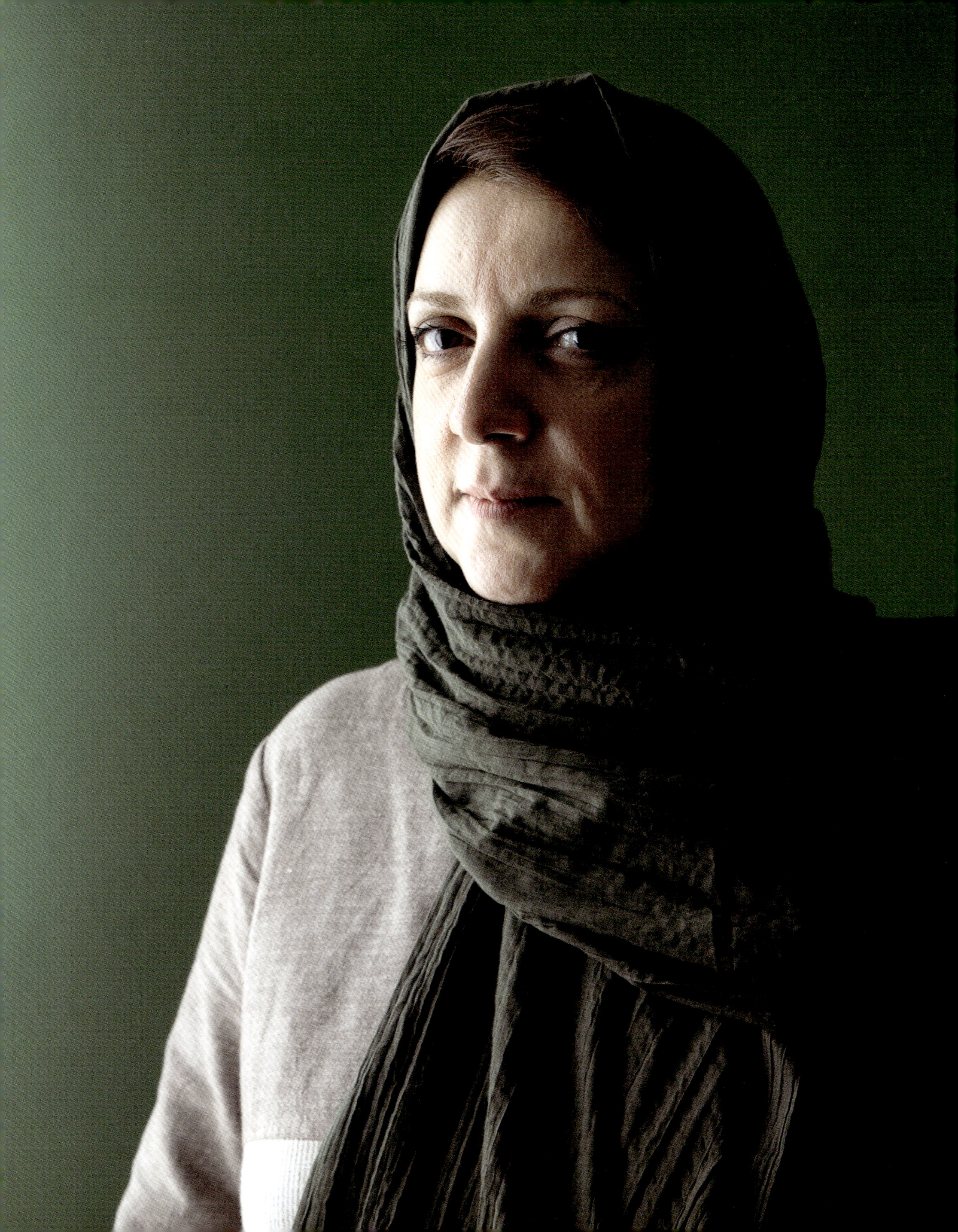

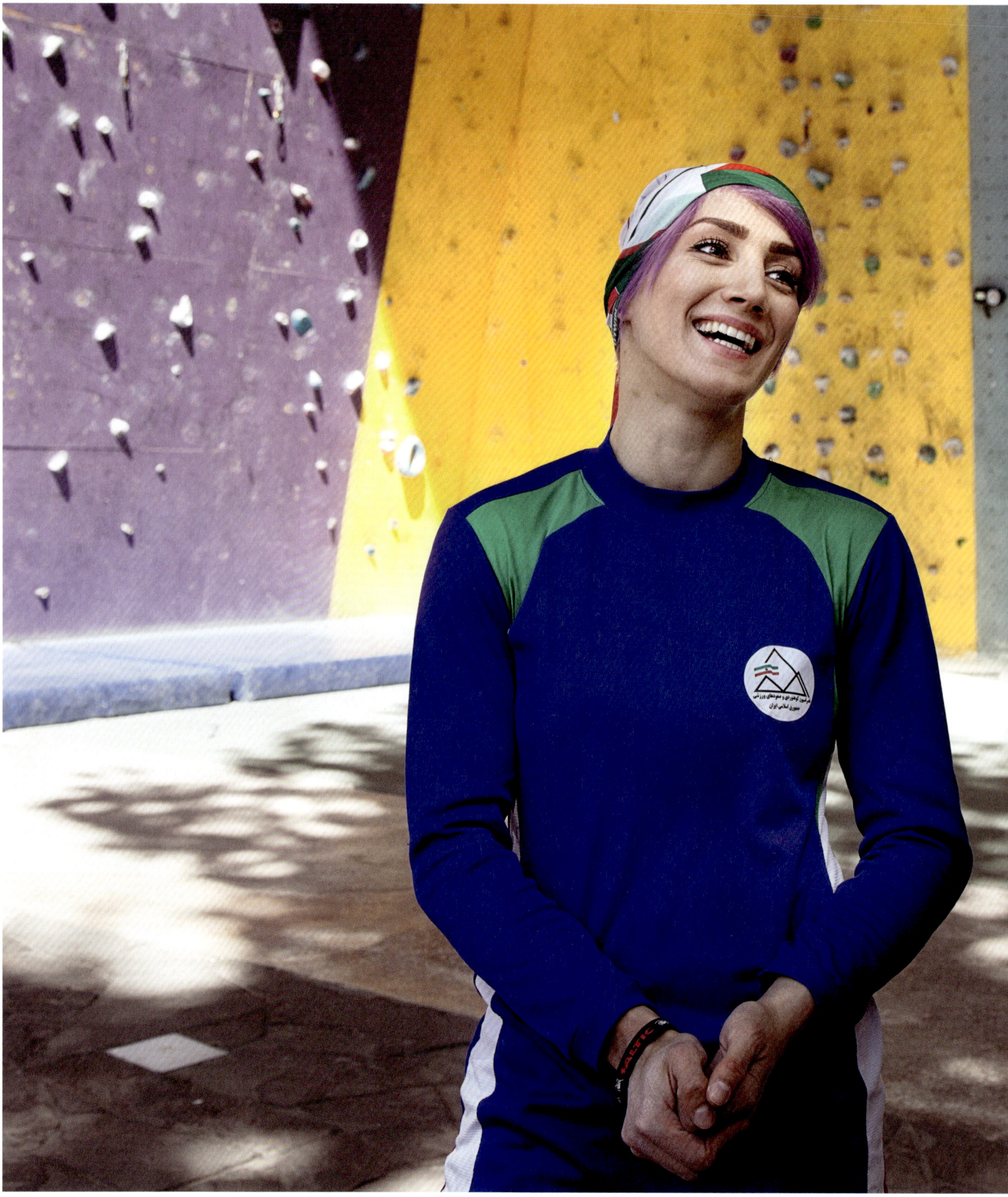

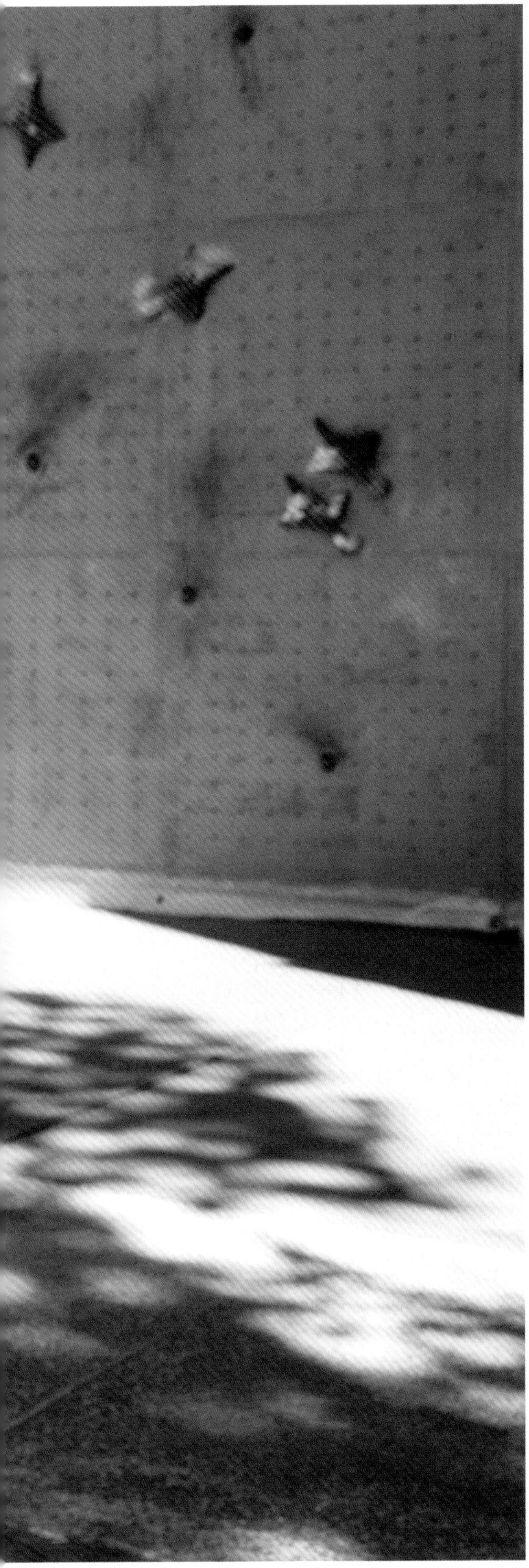

Farnaz Esmaeilzadeh

Farnaz is the fastest climber in Iran and is also known as Spiderwoman. Her parents were mountaineers and have climbed Iran's highest peak, Damavand, over twenty times. Climbing was ingrained in her from an early age, and she started sport climbing at the age of thirteen, continuing to pursue it to this day. *"My family always encouraged my brother and me to engage in sports. When I was seven, my parents asked the organizers of a bicycle race if I could participate, even though it was only for boys. I ended up winning that race."* In Iran, women's sports competitions are not televised, and also stringent regulations prohibit the presence of male spectators in women's sports halls. The absence of television coverage deprives these female athletes of the opportunity to showcase their talents on a broader scale, hindering the promotion and growth of women's sports in the country. The thirty-two-year-old remembers how challenging it was when she started climbing. The training facility she and her friends used was a windowless bunker, and in winter, it was so cold that they had to light a fire just to continue training.

Even today, her training conditions are suboptimal, as Farnaz has never had a professional coach. She learned her techniques from books and video documentaries. Currently working as a climbing instructor in Zanjan, Farnaz places great importance on acquiring new methods and techniques so that she can pass them on to her students. She was the first Iranian woman who, after all the struggles, managed to obtain permission to take part in the World Cup as a self-sponsored participant. Farnaz believes in the unique determination of young Iranian women who navigate their paths despite various restrictions in society: *"Women in Iran want to be noticed, and I firmly believe that we can achieve this."*

"Climbing gives me a sense of vitality. I feel physically and mentally strong and become more self-confident." Farnaz has been a member of the national team for sixteen years. In competitions, she has to wear a head-scarf, and her jersey is long-sleeved. She emphasizes: *"The biggest obstacles on the path to championship are the lack of appropriate training conditions, such as a standardized climbing wall. Additionally, there's a constant struggle for sufficient financial support, which has often forced me to cancel or miss international competitions, causing great sorrow as I prepare intensively for each of them. It's not uncommon for us to receive no support, and unnecessary obstacles are placed in our way."* She mentions that she has financed almost all of her national and international competitions out of her own pocket. *"Despite all the restrictions and obstacles, I have forged my own path."*
Her efforts and determination have been rewarded with numerous national championships in speed climbing, as well as international success as the first Iranian female climber (gold and silver medals at the Asia Championships) and an impressive 6th place in the global rankings.

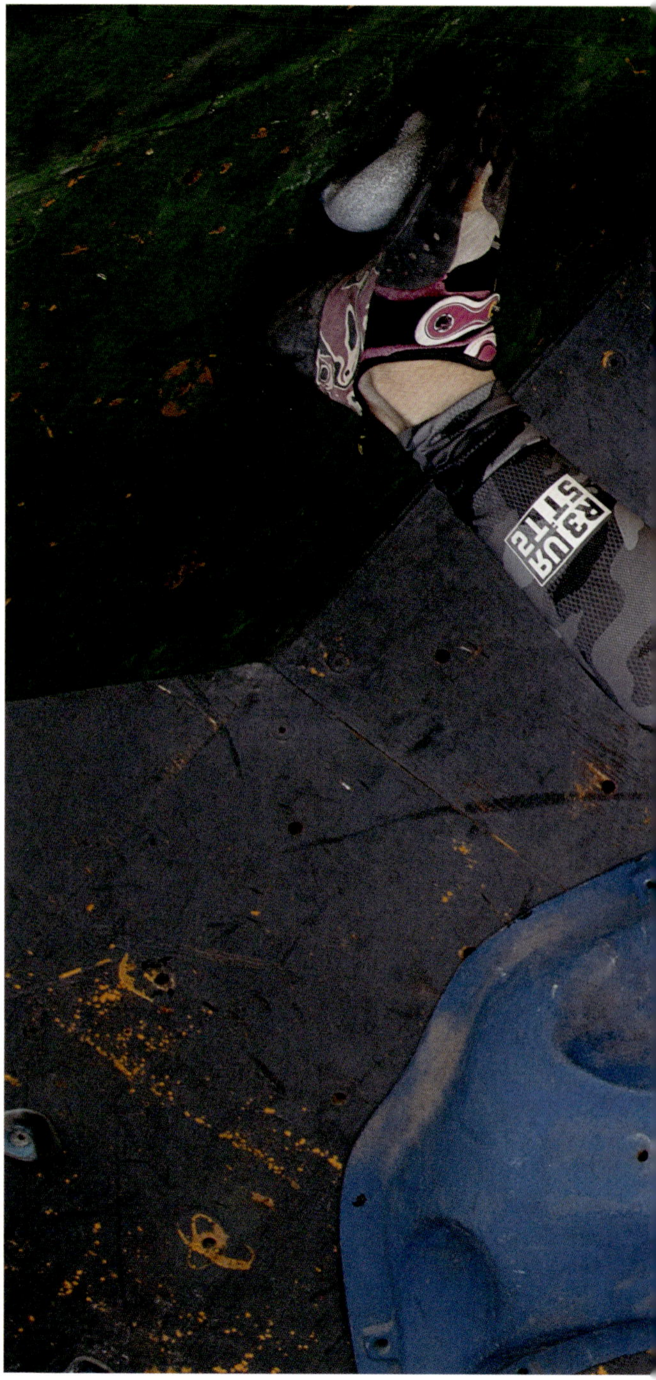

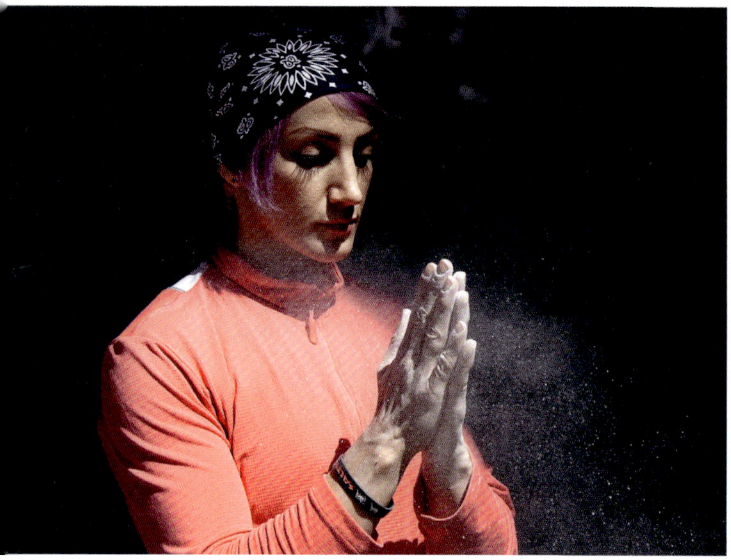

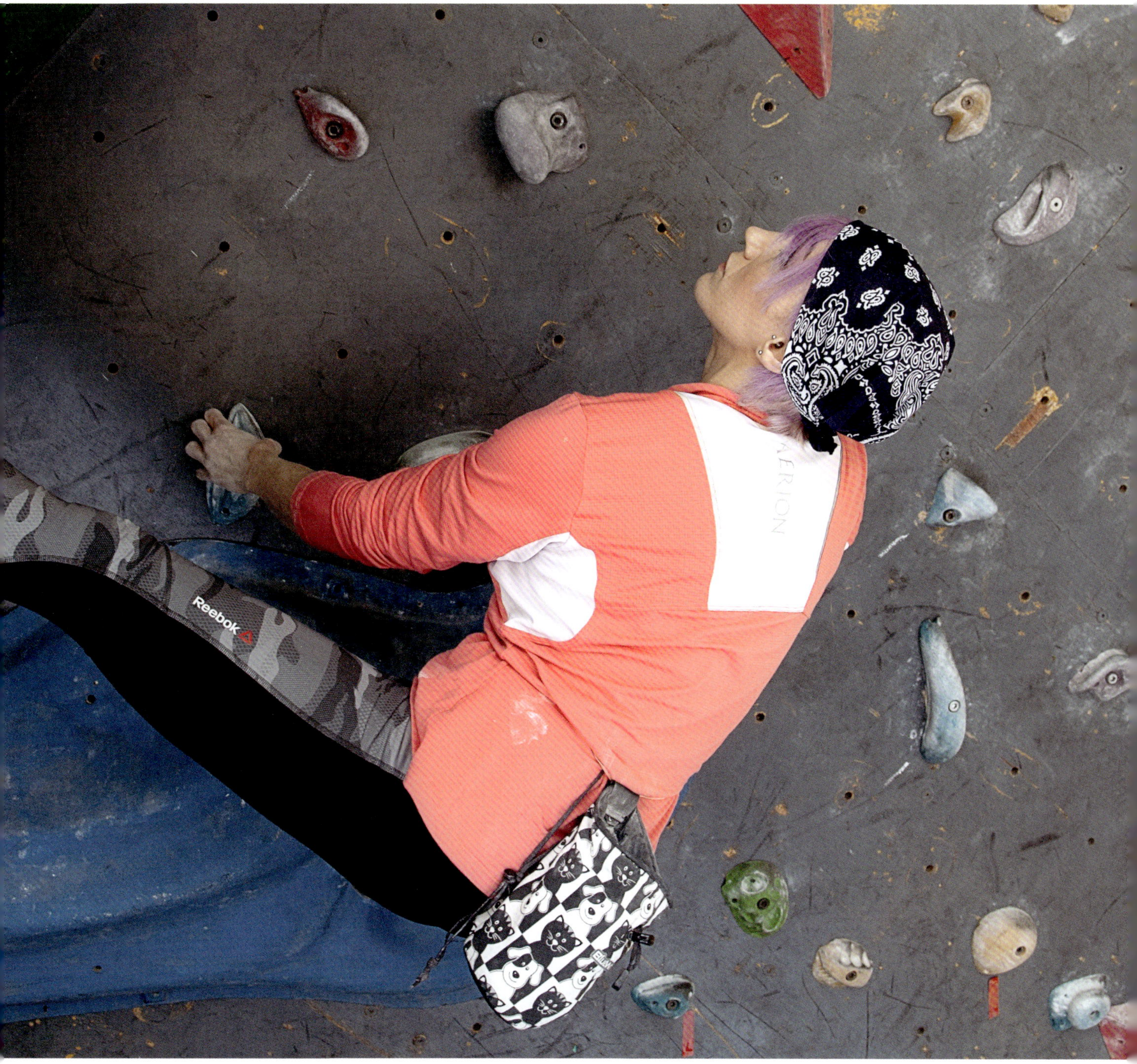
Reebok

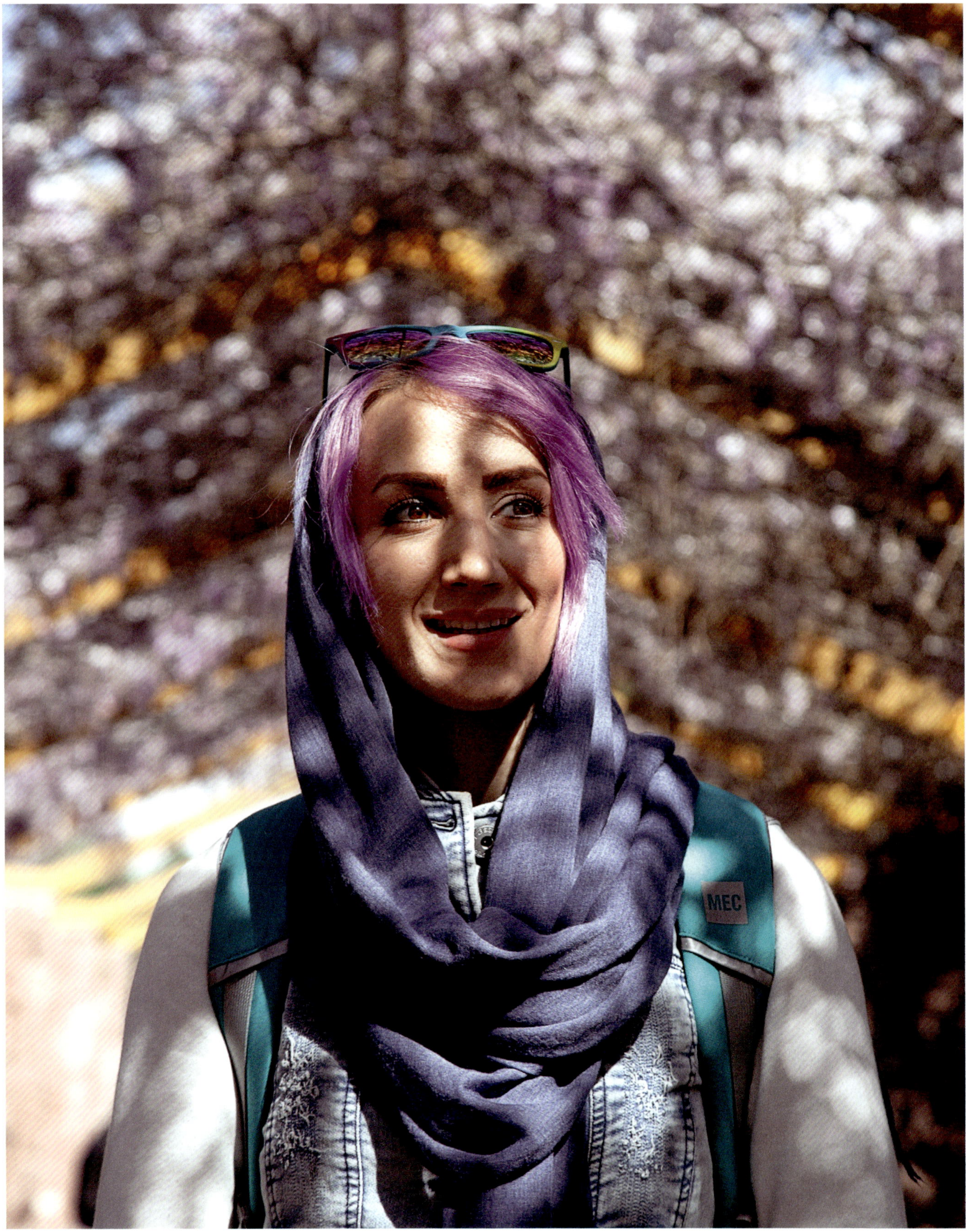
MEC

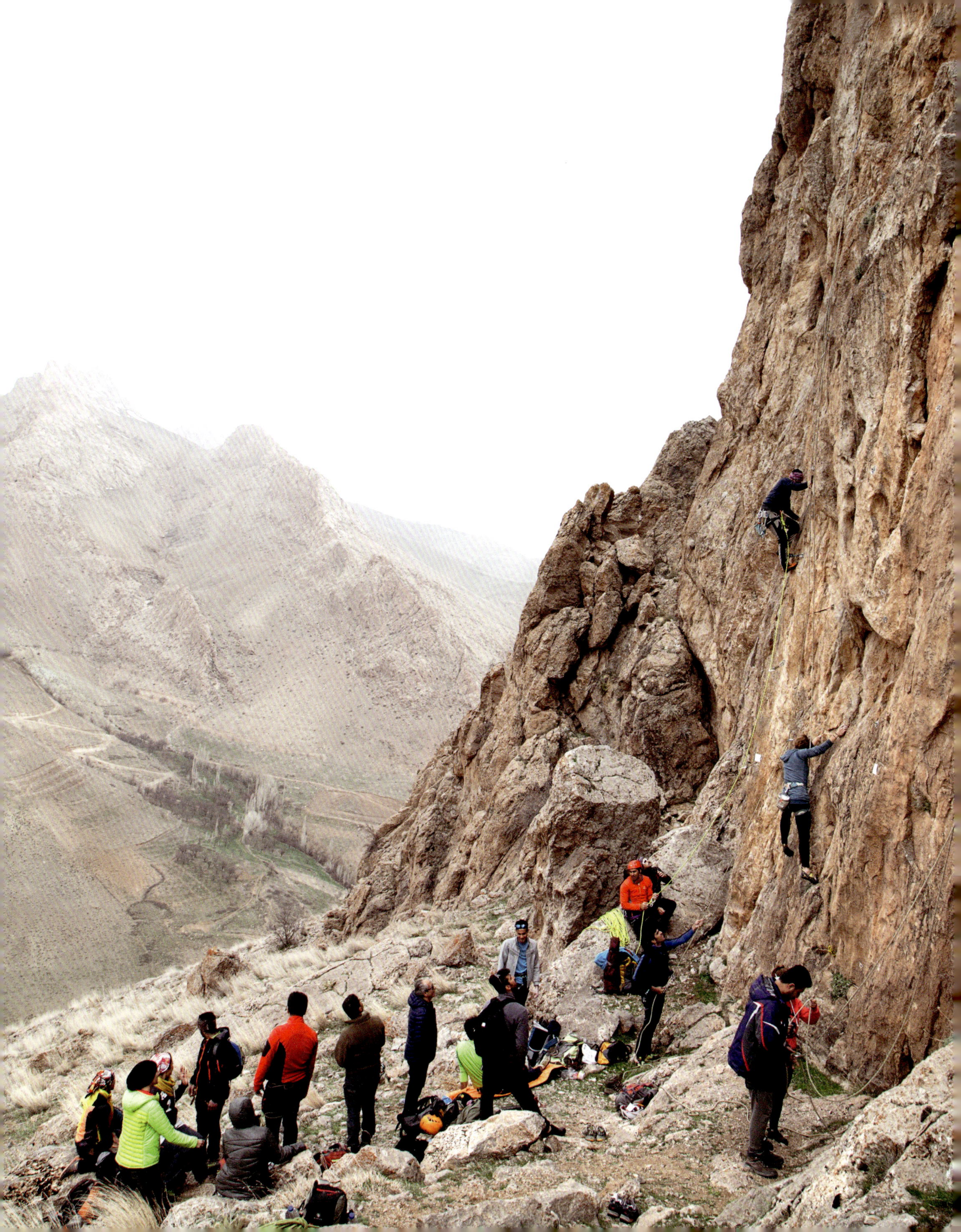

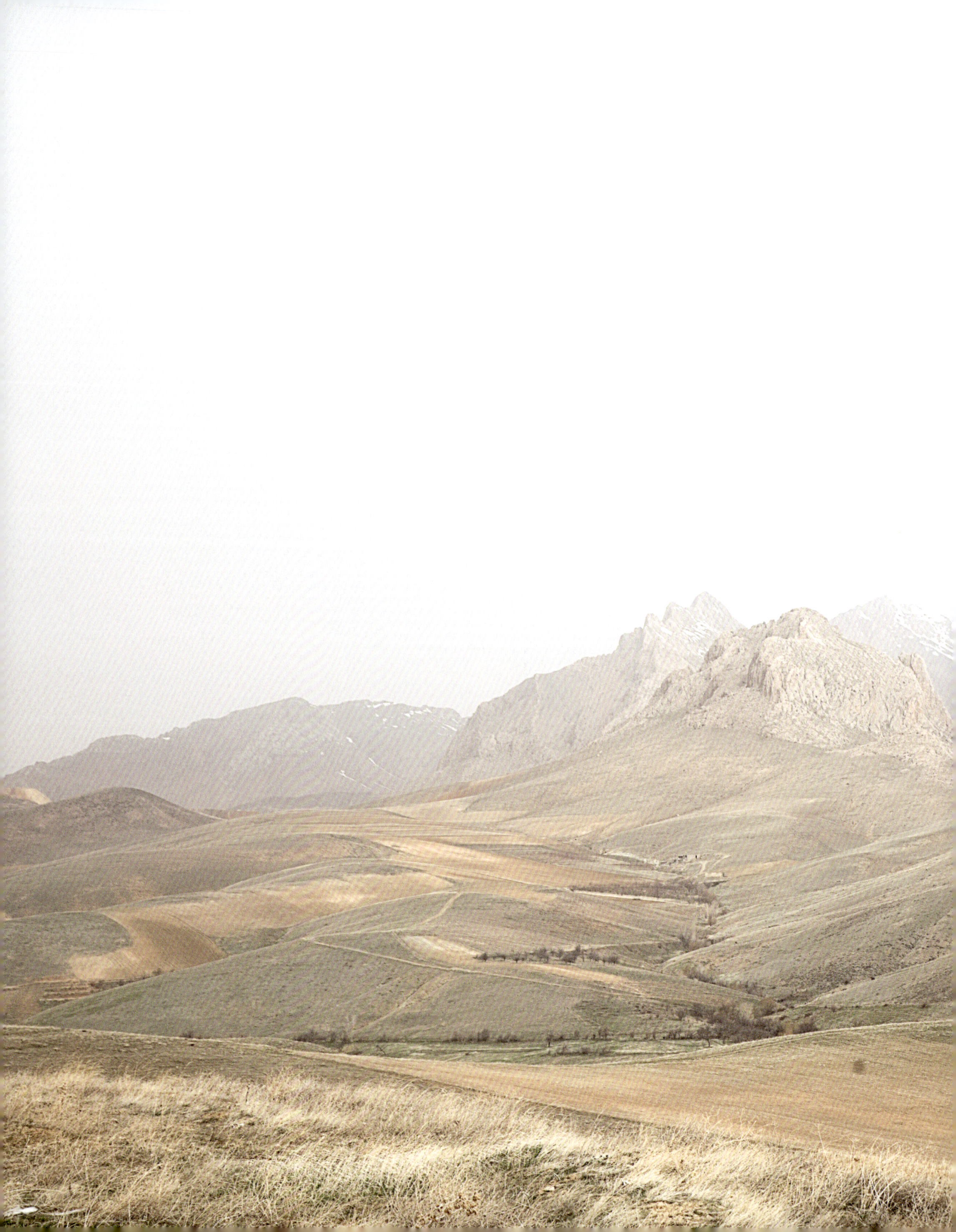

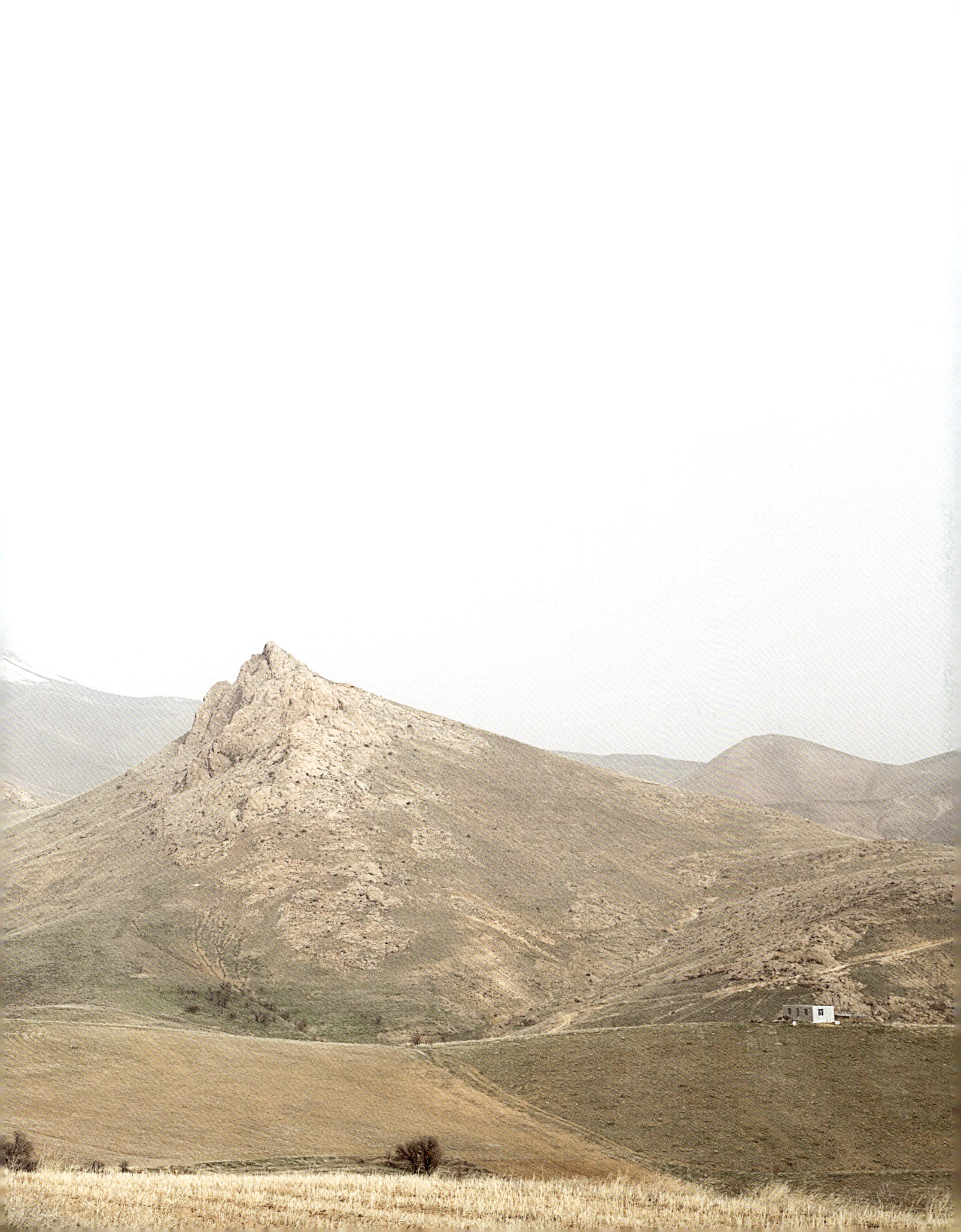

Special Thanks

In significant projects, one is always reliant on the help and experience of others. This work, which means a lot to me and has been a joy to complete, would not have been finished today without many people having played a part. First and foremost, I would like to thank my protagonists, who allowed and trusted me to tell their stories, supported me in my endeavor, and even encouraged me to continue this project after the publication of the book, to let more women have their say.

I am also grateful for the active support of my professors, family, and friends. Your patience, your moral support, and your experiences have significantly contributed to the success of this volume.

Special thanks are due to those who have made an outstanding contribution to my work. While I have learned a lot from numerous professors over the past few years, I would also like to take this opportunity to express my deepest gratitude to Prof. Jörg Winde, who also supervised me on this project.

The project phase in Iran would not have been so successful without the support of my parents, Mahin Montazami and Mahmoud Khosravi, who accompanied me on several trips in Iran and provided backing.

A heartfelt thank-you goes to Nasslie Bratzadeh, my sister-in-law, for her time spent proofreading and for the enriching conversations. Last but not least, I express my sincere thanks to my husband Jaser Bratzadeh for his unconditional support and loving presence.

Moreover, I would like to thank the many other people who have accompanied me on this project in various ways: PD Dr. Katja Föllmer, Prof. Dr. Pamela Scorzin, Prof. Kai Jünemann, Prof. Dirk Gebhardt, Jennifer Brade, Tania Kibermanis, Mahboubeh Karamli, Katayoun Ghods Rad, and Sara Saveh Shemshaki.

About the Author

Samaneh Khosravi, born in 1984 in Iran, relocated to Germany in 2008. She pursued studies in photography, earning Bachelor and Master of Arts degrees from the Dortmund University of Applied Sciences and Arts.

As a photographer and visual researcher, Khosravi has dedicated over a decade to examining the self- and external perception of women residing in Iran. Throughout this period, she has delved into diverse facets of this subject, capturing and documenting them from various perspectives through the medium of photography. Since early 2022, Khosravi has been conducting further research in this regard, with a special focus on Generation Z as part of her doctoral studies at the University of Göttingen and the Dortmund University of Applied Sciences and Arts. To support this research, she secured funding and has also been employed as a research associate since February 2022.

Her first book *Among Women*, about Iranian women and their views on beauty ideals, was published in 2015. And her photography projects have been featured in prominent publications. Today Samaneh Khosravi lives and works in Bochum.

Colophon

Editor
Samaneh Khosravi

Texts
Samaneh Khosravi

Design
Samaneh Khosravi
Jennifer Brade

Copyediting
Dawn Michelle d'Atri

Project management, Kerber Verlag
Lydia Fuchs

Production, Kerber Verlag
Jens Bartneck

Kerber Verlag
Detmolder Straße 60
33604 Bielefeld
Germany
+49 521 950 08 10
+49 521 950 08 88 (F)
info@kerberverlag.com
kerberverlag.com

Kerber publications are distributed worldwide
ACC Art Books
Sandy Lane
Old Martlesham
Woodbridge, IP12 4SD
UK
+44 1394 38 99 50
+44 1394 38 99 99 (F)
accartbooks.com
uksales@accartbooks.com

Artbook | D.A.P.
75 Broad Street, Suite 630
New York, NY 10004
USA
+1 (212) 627-1999
+1 (212) 627-9484 (F)
artbook.com
orders@dapinc.com

AVA Verlagsauslieferung AG
Centralweg 16
8910 Affoltern am Albis
Switzerland
+41 44 762 42 50
+41 44 762 42 10 (F)
avainfo@ava.ch

Zeitfracht Medien GmbH
Distribution, Germany
+49 711 7860 2254
bestellung@zeitfracht.de

The Deutsche Nationalbibliothek lists this publication in the Deutsche Nationalbibliografie: dnb.de.

info@samaneh.de
www.samaneh.de

ISBN 978-3-7356-0965-6

www.kerberverlag.com

Printed in Germany

Supported by
Stiftung Kulturwerk - VG Bild-Kunst

Bild Kunst
KULTURWERK